THE
PENTATEUCH

L. THOMAS HOLDCROFT

WESTERN Book
COMPANY
1618 FRANKLIN ST. • OAKLAND, CALIF. 94612

TABLE OF CONTENTS

ACKNOWLEDGMENTS

All photographs used in this book were taken personally by Professor Martin H. Heicksen, and it is through his courtesy that they appear.

Cover design by Rev. Everett A. Wilson. The drawing depicts a typical Egyptian bronze figure dating from the seventh century B.C. and considered to represent the bull-god, Apis. The stylized horns encase the traditional Egyptian circular sun-disc. It is possible that Aaron made the golden calf in this form.

Tabernacle furniture drawings by Dan Green and Ralph Gray.

Data concerning modern Judaic customs courtesy Rev. Morris Zutrau.

MAPS AND ILLUSTRATIONS

Figure:

Photographic Illustrations

A dolmen in the Transjordan dolmen field east of Damieth (Bib. <u>Adam</u>). There are literally thousands of dolmens throughout Palestine, as well as in other parts of the Near East. They were constructed by very ancient peoples who inhabited Palestine many centuries prior to Abraham. Dolmens were evidently used as burial chambers, and the room made by their massive stone slabs, providing at least a five foot ceiling, accommodated the body in a sitting position. The whole was covered with soil, but in most cases this covering has long ago eroded away.

ONE: The Book of Genesis -- Part 1

The fifty chapters that constitute the book of Genesis serve as a comprehensive introduction to the whole Bible. The facts of Genesis, set forth with neither apology nor argument, embrace virtually every major stream of truth that the Bible develops. As the first segment of the revelation of God, this book is vastly greater in scope than all others. Gabelein once described Genesis as: "the root out of which the tree of God's revelation has grown." Similarly, Bullinger declared: "Genesis is the seed-plot of the whole Bible, it is essential to the true understanding of its every part . . . [it] is at one the warp and woof of Holy Writ."

Although the book of Genesis is a basic link in the development of of Judaism, its appeal is as universal as the human race. Melanchthon, the scholarly associate of Martin Luther, said of this book, "The whole book of Genesis excels in sweetness all other books and histories . . . There is no more beautiful and lovable little book." Nowhere else in all of literature is there an account of the creation of the world and the beginning of human institutions and culture in any wise remotely comparable to the stories of the book of Genesis. It is evident that no unaided human mind could have produced anything so strikingly superb.

Background of the Book

Genesis was originally just one part of the Hebrew work known as the Law. When a Greek translation of this document was made (the Septuagint at Alexandria in 280 B.C.), the book of the Law was divided, and Genesis became the first part. The word "Genesis" is from the Greek word meaning "origin," and it was applied to the book as a whole by the Septuagint translators because they found this word used in each of the ten headings that divide the book (e.g. 2:4; 5:1; 6:9 etc.).

Authorship of the Book

Conservative Bible scholars agree almost universally that Moses is the author of the Pentateuch, and consequently, of the book of Genesis. The Bible itself, tradition and history all accord in ascribing the authorship to Moses. [1]

Purpose of Genesis

Genesis was written to reveal to man the fact that he was divinely created, that he suffered a fall , and that God proceeded to provide redemption. To this latter end, God is seen to choose the people of Israel as His human messengers who were to proclaim redemption's plan. The book provides a complete genealogy from Adam through to the sons of Jacob, and in the lives of these people His hand and His working are everywhere demonstrated.

The focus upon the history of Israel, and the seeming minimization of the general history of the world, is specifically in the divine plan. Considerable space and detail characterize the account of the patriarchs of Israel, because God's choice had made them to be channels for His highest purposes for the human race. The book of Genesis was never intended to be history for history's sake; it is an unfolding of the launching of a pattern of events whereby there might one day be possible the atonement of Calvary, and as a result, the forgiveness of every believer's sins.

ANALYSIS AND EXPOSITION

I. THE CREATION (Chs. 1, 2)

1. In the Beginning (1:1)

The first sentence of the Bible introduces the reader to God, and with neither apology nor explanation describes the creative efforts of the divine Being. In the light of such a beginning one must accept the fact of God's Person and Being if anything else in Scripture is to be rightly intelligible. Someone has remarked: "If I can believe the first verse of the Bible, I can believe the whole book." The lesson is conveyed that even as God is first in

---

[1] For an additional discussion of the authorship of the Pentateuch see Appendix One.

1

in revelation and creation, so He ought to be first in one's individual life.

The word for God used in this verse is Elohim, which, though plural in form, is followed by the singular verbal form bara (created). While this plural form gives no suggestion of a plurality of gods, it does hint at the fact of the divine trinity which is a Scriptural revelation that was granted much later. The form of the word Elohim is often described as a "plural of excellence." The fact that the verb is singular helps to make clear the unique nature of this form.

This verse limits itself to a simple statement that "In the beginning God created . . ."; it neither explains the nature of God nor argues for the fact of His existence. The plain sense of the statement explicitly supports some form of "fiat creationism" although no details or elaboration are given, for that is not its purpose. That which is especially set forth is the divine Creator-relationship which God holds toward His universe. Clearly, deism, and such antitheistic theories as atheism, naturalistic materialism, and pantheism are excluded. Any scientific theory that attempts to account for the universe apart from God, such as conventional naturalistic evolution, is likewise excluded. Nevertheless, it is obvious that this verse is not fundamentally concerned with the method of creation.

The problems of the reconciliation of scientific theory with the Bible record remain an active issue. Probably the most common contemporary approach is to consider Biblical truth and scientific truth as two separate streams which are both to be developed and tested on their own merits as more or less distinct disciplines. There is a tendency to leave to the realm of science all of the precise theorizing and technical detail that are necessary to explain the mechanisms and schedules of creation. The Bible thereby is spared involvement in petty disputes and identification with untenable theories that sooner or later will be discredited. To give primary emphasis to the fact of the Creator-relationship serves to elevate the Bible to its highest spiritual level.

This is not to say that the Bible scholar is indifferent to scientific theories; he regards them with high interest even though he does not base his faith upon them. The relationship of the Genesis creation record to scientific account has been variously interpreted:

The Gap Theory: A whole host of scholars, particularly those of the earlier decades of the twentieth century, favored this view. It holds that the original creation was at some time in the dateless past and that whatever may be needed to explain the geologic eras took place between Genesis 1:1 and Genesis 1:2. Pember may be cited as a typical spokesman of this theory:

> We see, then, that God created the heavens and the earth perfect and beautiful in their beginning, and that at some subsequent period, how remote we cannot tell, the earth passed into a state of utter desolation, and was void of all life . . . The very light of the sun had withdrawn; all the moisture of its atmosphere had sunk upon its surface; . . . [and] the ruined planet, covered above its very mountain tops with the black floods of destruction, was rolling through space in a horror of great darkness.[2]

The conventional arguments that have been offered in support of the Gap Theory (also known as the Hiatus Theory or the Restitution Theory) will be found in Appendix Two.

The Age-Day Theory: According to this theory (also called the "Day-Age" theory, "Geologic Day" theory, "Divine Day" theory, and "Concordism") the days of the first chapter of Genesis were lengthy periods of time equivalent to geologic eras. They were days only in a figurative sense (e.g. "In the day that the Pharoahs ruled Egypt . . ." may mean an era that is centuries in duration). By this interpretation some sincere Bible scholars have sought to reconcile Scripture with the conventional so-called "onion-coat" theory of geology. Most conservatives, however, feel that the Age-Day theory creates more problems than it solves, and thus they reject it. There is serious question if this theory in any genuine sense accords with the known facts of geologic

---

[2]G. H. Pember, Earth's Earliest Ages. New York: Fleming Revell Co., n.d., p.33.

science.[3]

The Flood Theory of Geology: This theory accounts for all of the phenomena reported by the geologist by means of an elaboration of the effects attributed to the great flood in the time of Noah. Thus, the creation story would be received literally, and all scientific explanations and descriptions that were not compatible would be assigned to the time and occasion associated with the Great Deluge. Such a concept seems, however, to transcend excessively the clear statements of Scripture, and thus it is not widely received. Its chief expression is found in the works of George McCready Price.[4]

The Ideal Time Theory: This outlook, especially developed by Philip H. Gosse in 1857, is a somewhat sophisticated claim that God created this universe at a given point in the past and in that creation it represents just as much ideal time as may be necessary for geological explanations. Thus, at the moment of creation, the universe may have represented in ideal time, millions of years; but in real time it began at time zero just a few thousand years ago. God created the earth with the various fossil remains that ideally represent vast eras, but in real time it was all done in a moment. The short title for Gosse's work was Omphalos which means "navel" and the serious contention of Gosse was that just as Adam was created instantly as a normal adult but with a navel as if he had undergone a normal pre-natal and natal development, so all phenomena in the universe, though created instantly at the stage in which it was found in Adam's time, nevertheless were given all the appearances of a prolonged development.

A likely reaction to the theory of Gosse would object to its failure to offer any real intellectual satisfaction, while at the same time admitting that it really offers no refutation. From the human viewpoint the theory disappoints common sense, for it opposes all conventional observations and experiences of mankind otherwise. It certainly could be the answer, but few scholars are so easily satisfied in their intellectual questings.

---

[3]For a further discussion of the Age-Day theory see page 5.

[4]For a further discussion of the Flood Theory of Geology see Appendix Three.

2. The Creative Week (1:2 - 2:3)

To those who separate 1:1 from the rest of Genesis the term "creative week" may be somewhat inaccurate, but it has the advantage of being convenient. All agree that it was during this week that God transformed a thing of chaos into a beautiful and populated earth. In verse two, in the statement "the Spirit of God moved upon the face of the waters," the personal divine influence is seen entering into a relationship with that which was helpless, lifeless chaos. The use of the verb "moved" (stirred or trembled) reveals that the Holy Spirit is a person and not a mere influence. The Holy Spirit, in the words of Mackintosh, "sat brooding over the scene of His future operations." The presence of the Spirit indicates expectancy of life, for from the beginning, the Holy Spirit has been the divine channel of life.

The First Day (1:3-5): God's words in verse 3, "Let there be light" suggest spontaneity and immediacy of action. These are the words of a creative God bringing light into existence by divine fiat. Thus, there would seem more probability to the idea that this light was a sort of phosphorescent, electronic, or cosmic radiance, than merely the natural light of the sun diffused by the pall of the fog. However, inasmuch as the cycle of days and nights began at that time, if it is assumed that the earth was rotating, then the light must have been at a fixed point just as solar light is in relation to this earth. The fact that God promptly named aspects of His creation: "Day . . . Night" (1:5) would imply to the ancients the fact of His sovereignty. To give a name is considered to be the exercise of sovereign right.

The Second Day (1:6-8): The word "firmament" means "expanse" or that which is hammered or pressed into shape; and it here refers to the extensive realm of the earth's atmosphere which supports water as cloud, fog, and invisible vapor. The reality of this realm is emphasized by the fact that the term is used nine times in this chapter, but Hebrew scholars point out that its identity is much more nebulous than any conventional "dome of heaven" concept. No special shape or form is here assigned to the firmament; it is portrayed simply as a vast realm extending upward from the earth's surface.

The work of the second day divided water into its two forms: liquid and vapor, and placed the latter in suspension in the firmament. It is said that the firmament in its cargo of clouds, fog, and invisible vapor, is capable of holding in suspension several times the amount of water in all the world's oceans. Whereas water in the oceans may be bitter and salty, that of the firmament has undergone evaporation and is of the highest degree of purity.

Only this day's work was not recognized by God as "good." Apart from the possibility that the omission is a mere literary variant and of no significance, three proposed explanations may apply: 1) the firmament provided a sphere for the activities of Satan "the prince of the power of the air" (Eph. 2:2), or 2) the separation of the waters released hordes of unclean spirits that had been trapped in the desolation and chaos of the ruined earth, or 3) this particular work of creation was not completed until the third day.

The Third Day (1:9-13): On this day the seas were put into their beds and the continents were formed. An accomplishment so vast, if explained in terms of human reasoning, would seem to require at the least a geologic era. Scripture confines the work to a single day. Since there is enough water on the face of the earth to cover its entire surface to a depth of two miles, this result was accomplished by raising some land portions and lowering others. On today's earth, the surface is 70.8% water and 29.2% land.

If the Gap Theory of creation is accepted, it would be held that this land that was brought forth already contained the fossilized remains of a past creation. The similarity of existing life forms to certain fossils is explained by the fact that the divine mind simply repeated the pattern of past creations. Likewise, in order to produce the plants it might be held that the Lord merely caused the germination and immediate growth of seeds remaining in the land. On the other hand, it would be admitted that the Lord readily could have brought something new into being. Scripture depicts God as saying simply: "let the earth bring forth . . ." If previously existing seeds did produce the plants on this day, there would be an interesting typical association with the fact of a third day resurrection.

The Fourth Day (1:14-19): The sun, moon, and stars are here called literally "light-bearers"

rather than "lights." Inasmuch as light had been brought into being on the first day, it is plausible to consider that the heavenly bodies were actually appointed as channels for the transmission of that which had been previously created. This day's work was not likely a matter of actually creating the sun, moon and stars, but rather at this time setting them in relation to earth as light-bearers. It is reported in Job 38:6, 7 that the morning stars were witnesses to the laying of the foundations of the earth.

That the sun is thus a light-bearer, appointed by God to give light to the earth, makes naive the concepts that would lead to sun worship. It has been observed that the fact that God did not at this time name the heavenly bodies may have been intentional in order to discourage worship of them. Scripture mainly emphasizes the role of the sun and moon in relation to day and night, but also points out (v. 14) that the heavenly bodies establish the seasons and years in relation to earth. The phases of the moon set apart our months (the word "month" derives from "moon"), and the solstices of the sun establish seasons and years.

The Fifth Day (1:20-23): God made fish and fowl on the same day, not apparently because they have much in common, but because they tend to be more simple life forms than the land animals. The word "create" is used in verse 21 for the first time since verse 1. Apparently the genera of fish and fowl were distinctly new orders requiring a specific creative act of God for their production. The expression "great whales" could be rendered "sea monsters." There seems to be no explanation why, apart from man, whales or sea monsters are the only distinct species mentioned in this chapter, however Von Rad comments concerning them: "mythical beings who live at the extreme limits of the created realms known to man, removed completely from human understanding and human use." [5]

The Sixth Day (1:24-31): At this point the scene shifts from the sea to the earth as God commands the earth to bring forth living creatures. Evidently this day's activity included not only mammals and reptiles, but even insects and

[5]Gerhard Von Rad, Genesis: A Commentary. Philadelphia: The Westminister Press, 1961, p. 54.

worms. The language of Scripture sets forth three classes of land animals: 1) beasts of prey and game animals, 2) domestic large animals (called "cattle"), 3) all other small animals and reptiles. The repeated expression "after his kind" contradicts the doctrine of evolution with its mutations and variants. Even though man did not immediately use the animals for food, they were necessary for his existence in the simple agricultural existence of early man.

As the crowning glory of His creation, God created man (Heb. 'adām) in His own image (v. 27). The triple use of the verb "create" in this verse, in view of only two previous uses of the word in the creation story, specifically indicates man's intended status as being distinct and above that of the beasts. God commissioned man to maintain his dominion upon the earth. Man's qualification to exercise this dominion was his creation in God's likeness; thereby he was endowed with intelligence, a will, and a moral nature. As created by God, Adam and Eve were the only two perfect specimens of our race, apart from the incarnate Christ. Although sin somewhat confounded the divine likeness, man retained the capacity for regeneration that the damage of the fall might be repaired.

Both Adam and Eve were created on the sixth day, although added details about Eve's creation do not occur in Scripture until later. In general, God's method of creating man is not described -- the report is theological, not scientific. The rule of the earth was given not to Adam only, but to Adam and Eve jointly, for the idea of mankind finds its full meaning in man and woman jointly and not in man alone. This first human pair received the blessing of God that through them the earth might be replenished, possessed, and subdued. The power of reproduction granted to mankind was specifically made separate from the image of God, and it constituted a distinctive blessing upon mankind. God's final approval of the entire created universe is recorded in verse 31.

The Seventh Day (2:1-2): On the seventh day, God rested from creating. It is evident that God rested, not because He was tired, but because His creative work was finished (cf. Jno. 5:17). It has been conjectured that God desired to contemplate His creative work, and perhaps also the destiny that He knew was to befall mankind. God's resting during this period would not interrupt His continuing to uphold and govern His created universe.

The fact that God rested serves as an object lesson to mankind likewise to observe a day of rest each week. However, on this occasion, God did not command man to follow His example for He was concerned only with benefitting man and not with imposing upon him. For the first time in Scripture the term "sanctified" is used, and in this instance applying to the seventh day, the word has its usual meaning of "separation." In general, the Church understands that in New Testament times God's "sanctified" day changed from the seventh day to the first. Mackintosh distinguishes the two days thus: "The seventh day stands connected with earth and earthly rest; the first day of the week on the contrary introduces us to heaven and heavenly rest."[6]

It is significant to note that the ancient Babylonians are known to have observed certain special days that they called "shabatum." Their observance of this day both agrees with and differs from the Sabbath of God. In general the Babylonian concept of deity and his relation with mankind was naive and grossly polytheistic. Part of their creation epic is a recital of the public glorification of the god, Marduk, and a listing of the fifty names whereby his deputy gods honored him.

Evidence That the Days of Genesis Were
Twenty-Four Hour Days

The conventional arguments that support the claim that the days of Genesis were twenty-four hour days and thereby seek to refute the Age-Day theory are as follows: 1) a geologic age does not have an evening and a morning as the days in Genesis, 2) the plants of the third day could not have survived a geologic era without the sun, 3) in Genesis 2:2 it is declared that God rested on the seventh day, and if this day were an age God would still be resting. As it is, He has effected the whole plan of salvation, 4) when the Hebrew word for day (yom) is accompanied by a definite number (first, second, etc.) as it is here, it always means a twenty-four hour day, and

---

[6]C. H. Mackintosh, Notes on the Book of Genesis. New York: Loizeaux Brothers, 1945, p. 22.

5) the divisions of time in Genesis 1:14 (days, seasons, and years) are used only in connection with twenty-four hour days and not geologic eras.

Although the Age-Day theory is said to have been held by Josephus and several Church Fathers, its modern following is rather limited. For the most part, the reconciliations that the theory makes possible are so inadequate and vague that the scholar accepting them soon proceeds to depart completely from a commitment to the Biblical account. It is understandable that there would be certain similarities between any two systems of explanation that necessarily proceed from the simple to the complex. However, any careful study inevitably discovers glaring discrepancies between the conventional step-by-step explanations of organic evolution and secular geology, and the successive steps of the Bible story. These discrepancies seem to invalidate soundly the whole reconciliatory concept.

The Typology of the Creation Story

The creation (interpreted according to the Gap Theory) may be seen as typical of the restoration of a sinner and the making of a saint. Successively, the steps are:

THE EARTH	MANKIND
Came perfect from the hand of God	Created in the image of God
Perfect earth made chaotic	Man fell, nature depraved
Spirit of God brooded	Divine conviction upon unconverted
Light sent forth	Spiritual life at regeneration
Plants spring from earth	Convert rises to walk in newness of life
Heavenly bodies unveiled	Heavenly citizenship revealed
Man in image of God	Christian conformed to image of Christ

The Date of the Events of the Creative Week

The margin of many Bibles dates the creation of man in 4,004 B.C. This date was calculated by a Christian scholar, Archbishop James Ussher of Ireland, in 1654, and thus it is not a part of the Bible text proper. It was first placed in the margin of the Authorized Version in 1701. To arrive at his conclusions, Ussher necessarily assumed that all Bible genealogies were complete and without omissions or gaps and he derived what is known as the "short chronology." There is evidence that Bible genealogies may often omit certain generations, and scholars who have allowed for these arrive at an earlier date for the creation of man.

It would appear to be best for the Bible student to avoid dogmatic conclusions concerning the date of the creation of man. As cautious an evangelical scholar as Griffith Thomas has written:

. . . The chronology is probably not complete, as there are ten generations before the Flood and ten afterward, indicating a summary only. The Jews often shortened their genealogies (see Matt. 1), so long as the connection was clearly maintained. The antiquity of the world and of the human race is not a Biblical problem, and no computation is found based on any figure prior to the time of Abraham.[7]

At the present time, in no field of human study is there any real certainty of dates prior to 3,000 B.C. Even the conclusions of Carbon 14 dating are questioned by some, although there does seem sound scientific basis for such procedures. Thus far, Carbon 14 dating has not found evidence of human civilization much prior to 7,000 B.C., although what are purported to be human bones are said to date back some 41,000 years.

3. The Generations of the Heavens and the Earth (2:4-7)

The word "generations" in verse 4 introduces the first of the natural divisions

_____

[7]William H. Griffith Thomas, Through the Pentateuch Chapter by Chapter. Grand Rapids: Wm. B. Eerdmans, 1957, p. 35.

of the book. This heading including the word "generations" (in Hebrew the word is toledot) is used in similar or identical form eleven times in Genesis. In this chapter the sequel to man's creation is presented, including the story of the establishment of Eden and the producing of Eve from the rib of Adam. These events were specifically part of the activity of the creative week.

The method in verses 5 and 6 whereby the earth was watered seems to indicate that atmospheric or meteorologic conditions on earth were then different from those today. However, the significance of the word "mist" is uncertain. Some interpretations have rendered it "overflowing river" or "spring." Some scholars feel that it represents an obscure, almost poetic reference to rain. It is held by many that the flood of Noah's day caused a radical change in the earth's atmosphere, and physical climate. If such changes actually did occur, they might invalidate the accuracy of Carbon 14 dating, as hinted above.

In verse 7, man is described as consisting of a physical body and a life principle, and the combination of the two resulting in his being a soul. Man's body was composed of the "dust of the ground" and thus might be nourished and renewed from simple plants and life forms which derive their constituent elements from the soil. The "breath of life" (literally: "lives") seems equivalent to what is termed elsewhere "spirit," and it is that which energizes the body and makes it alive. The term "soul" is what man is in general; the combination of a spirit making alive a body results in man's being a soul. In this usage, soul is equivalent to "person" or "personality."

Man differs from the animals not merely in possessing body, soul and spirit, for Scripture attributes these constituents to animals also. Neither is man's capacity to reason, unique, for a chimpanzee is able to reason as well as a two-year old child. Man's one outstanding distinguishing mark is his moral consciousness. By his capacity to distinguish right from wrong, man is set apart from all other created creatures of earth.

Critical scholarship usually declares that 2:4 to 4:26 is an attempt by a new author to describe the events of creation. It is pointed out that in verse 4, for the first time, the name of deity is changed from "Elohim" to "Jehovah Elohim" (from "God" to "Lord God" in the Authorized Version). It is claimed that the change of name indicates a change of author, and that Genesis is the product of an Elohist and a Jehovist writer, plus one or more redactors (editors). These views are the basis for the "Documentary Hypothesis" which is discussed in the appendix.

An evangelical would allege that the name "Jehovah" is the unique, distinguishing name for the Hebrew-Christian God. The name name "Elohim" may apply more generally, even to the imagined deities of heathendom. The designation "Jehovah-Elohim" in 2:4 simply sets forth a degree of the insight of Moses into the richness of the divine person. The name Jehovah occurs in other forms, including the commonly used "Yahweh." This uncertainty concerning the correct form of the name for deity is the result of the special reverence of the Jews toward it. The four consonants YHVH (known as the tetragrammaton) comprising the name were never pronounced, and in course of time the mode of pronunciation (the spelling) was forgotten.

The supposed "first account of creation" (1:1 to 2:3) is actually a statement of the universal and cosmos-wide implications of God's creative work, whereas the restatement (2:4 to 4:26) describes creation from the viewpoint of Adam. Until man appeared on the scene there was no occasion to speak of deity as Lord or Jehovah. The name "Jehovah" especially emphasizes the concept of deity as the covenant-keeping and Saviour God. Moses' introduction of this name into the record at this point lays the groundwork for his later account of God's efforts to redeem man. "Jehovah-Elohim" indicates that the creator-God is both truly a Saviour and a covenant-keeping God. Some scholars think that 1:1 to 2:3 constitutes a report of a vision given to Moses; whereas 2:4 to 4:26 is a selection from the annals of the nation.

4. The Garden of Eden. Eve Created (2:8-25)

The Garden of Eden constituted the most beautiful surroundings that man has ever known upon this earth; the Bible description seems more heavenly than earthly. It is agreed that not until the time of the new Jeru-

salem will man again know such a beauty spot.
The name "eden" means "pleasantness" or
"delight." The term "garden" as used in the
Bible, describes a tended and cultivated area
that today would usually be described as a
park. The bdellium of 2:12 is a resinous
substance of a reddish-brown color which is
used as a base for perfumes and medicines.
In being planted "eastward in Eden," the garden apparently was a smaller area within the
larger region that as a whole was named Eden.

In relation to modern geography the
exact location of Eden cannot be determined
because there is no known place that fits the
geographical description of Genesis. However, since the Euphrates and Hiddekel (i.e.
the Tigris) rivers are known, it is assumed
that the Garden was somewhere in the Middle
East, and probably not far from the site later
occupied by the city of Babylon. Although
certain ancient inscriptions call the Plain of
Mesopotamia "Edin," such a change of spelling constitutes a word quite different from
"Eden." It is usually held that the flood of
Noah, or some other change in the earth's
surface, was responsible for obliterating the
rivers Pison and Gihon. The "land of Ethiopia" (2:13) or "land of Cush" as it might be
rendered, is considered a territory in the
region of Babylon rather than the modern day
Ethiopia in North Africa.

The trees in the Garden derived their
names from their relations to man and not
from their own nature. However, they were
actual trees and the care of them made man
responsible to develop both his physical and
intellectual powers. There is no information
concerning the fruit borne by the tree of the
knowledge of good and evil, and except to
satisfy curiosity, such information is irrele-
vant. In commanding man to abstain from the
fruit of this tree, God gave but one command;
He avoided confounding man with a multitude
of regulations. In thus commanding, God
exercised His right to prohibit, and determined
that man's exclusive means to disobey Him
came through partaking of the fruit. Thus the
promised knowledge of good and evil came to
man as a consequence of his behavior in relation to God, and not because of any inherent
quality of the fruit.

The animals brought before Adam did
not satisfy his longing for a help-mate. How-

ever, he gave evidence of mature mental development in his insight into the nature of the
creatures and his use of vocabulary to name
them. When the woman was brought to him,
he recognized her as a very part of himself
and he gave her a name which was simply the
feminine counterpart of his own (man-ess). It
has been noted that in bringing Eve to Adam on
this occasion, God played the part of the father of the bride. Concerning the chronology
of events at this time, Keil and Delitzsch
comment:

The time when this took place must
have been the sixth day . . . there is no
difficulty in this since it would not have
required much time to bring the animals
to Adam to see what he would call them,
as the animals of paradise are all we have
to think of; and the deep sleep into which
God caused man to fall, till he had formed
the woman from his rib, need not have
continued long. [8]

In the days when people believed that
any method to ease pain was contrary to the
laws of God, Dr. J. Y. Simpson successfully
defended the use of chloroform by referring
to the deep sleep which God caused in Adam
when his rib[9] was removed. To the creator
there was no particular need for a portion of
Adam's body from which to construct Eve, but
it would appear that the Lord merely chose
this procedure as an object lesson. Adam
learned that the woman was a very part of
himself, and that she came from his side to be
a helpmate. It has often been said concerning
the relation between Adam and the woman that
the woman was: "Not made out of his head to
rule over him, nor out of his feet to be tram-
pled on by him, but out of his side to be equal
with him, under his arm to be protected, and
near his heart to be loved."

---

[8] C. F. Keil and F. Delitzsch, Biblical
Commentary on the Old Testament (Vol. I, The
Pentateuch) Edinburgh: T. & T. Clark, 1878,
p. 87.

[9] In Harmony of Science and the Bible,
C. Theodore Schwarze declares that it was
not Adam's rib but a portion of his side that
was used by God. The author points out that
the original word tsela appears 35 times in the
Bible, but that only in Genesis is it rendered
"rib." The usual rendering is "a curved
side."

The formation of woman, and her relationship to Adam, may be set forth as a type of the relationship between Christ and His Church.

ADAM AND EVE	CHRIST AND THE CHURCH
Adam fell into a deep sleep	Christ died on the cross
Very substance of Adam's body became his bride	The Church, while it is the body of Christ is also His bride
Adam and Eve brought into happy union	Christ and His Church to be united at rapture
Human pair shared government of the earth	Church is to rule and reign with Christ
Eve essential to Adam as his helpmate	Christ has committed to the Church His work on earth
Only one bride for Adam	Church is the special love of Christ
Woman partook of man's nature and called by his name	Church partakes of the nature and name of Christ. (i.e. Christians)

II. THE FALL OF MAN (Ch. 3)

It is here in the third chapter of Genesis that the record sets forth an exceedingly vital event in human history. Griffith Thomas once commented: "This chapter is the pivot on which the whole Bible turns." The events here described became the occasion when man rebelled against God, and voluntarily assumed for himself a depraved and carnal nature that thereafter led him to be described by God as "dead in trespasses and sins" (Eph. 2:1). Graham describes events at this time: "By accepting . . . [Satan's] word and [Satan's] system in preference to God's Word and God's order, they handed over the deed of trust to Satan and enthroned him as the legal ruler.

They transferred their allegiance from the Father of lights to the father of lies."[10]

1. Steps in the Fall of Man (3:1-6)

The entrance of the serpent into Eden brought discord and evil into what had been harmonious and good. That the serpent was a representative, or the actual embodiment of Satan, is evident from the context, although in Genesis he is not specifically named as such. He proceeded to deal with Eve, either because he felt that she might be an easier victim, or because it was necessary that he beguile her personally that she might not later plead her husband's headship. Eve registered no surprise when the serpent spoke to her, perhaps because animals in Eden before the Fall had the power of what is now exclusively human speech. Actually, of course, it was Satan who spoke through the serpent. (cf. ". . . that old serpent . . ." [Rev. 12:9, 20:2])

The serpent approached Eve by feigning ignorance and asking a seemingly sincere question. Such an approach continues to this day to be standard with the skeptic. Men shut their eyes to the Bible, plead ignorance of the voice and will of God, and ask: "Hath God said?" Eve ought to have followed the admonition of Scripture: "Resist the devil, and he will flee from you" (Jas. 4:7), just as Jesus did many centuries later, (Mt. 4:10). Instead, she foolishly acted, either in ignorance or petulance, and quoted God as saying: ". . . neither shall ye touch it, lest ye die" (v. 3). In these words, Eve both added to and took away from the Word of God.

It is interesting to note that in the early 1930's, near Ninevah, archaeologists found two seals that have been called the "Temptation Seals." These have been dated at about 3000 B.C. On each of the seals there is depicted a man, a woman, and a serpent. In the one, the woman is represented as picking fruit, and the serpent is standing upright behind her. If conventional dating systems are correct, these seals would establish the fact of the temptation story as a recognized historical event fully fif-

---

[10]James R. Graham, A Philosophy of Scripture: A connected Commentary on the Book of Genesis. Butler: The Higley Press, 1955, p. 81.

teen centuries before the time that Moses penned the Genesis record.

The serpent gladly accorded with the attitude of Eve's heart, and he proceeded flatly to contradict God's Word and make God a liar. With such preparation, it was only a matter of moments before the human pair stood, guilty and disobedient before God. They had participated in a course of moral education, and had scored a dismal failure. Adam, apparently, partook of the fruit not because he was deceived, but because he chose to share the fate of his wife (cf. 1 Tim. 2:14). Eve's downfall was typical of the course of many who depart from God:

EVE	BACKSLIDER
Looked: Saw tree good	Sees world and its attractions
Lusted: Desired to make one wise	Begins to long after world
Accepted: Took the fruit thereof	Fails to see harm in the world
Partook: Did eat	Partakes of pleasures of world
Shared: Gave to her husband	Usually others influenced when Christians sin

2. The Results of the Fall of Man (3:7-24)

An immediate result of the partaking of the fruit was the opening of the eyes of Adam and Eve so that they knew that they were naked. Inevitably, shame stands as the corollary of sin. One theory suggests that man previously had been clothed by the radiance of his spirit, but now he was spiritually dead and man thus had lost the glory of his spirit's covering. In all likelihood, however, man at this juncture acquired the discerning conscience that made him aware of a situation that he had not previously realized. Even the fig leaf covering did not satisfy, and Adam and Eve hid from the presence of the Lord. Disobedience to God may always be expected to lead to estrangement from Him.

Adam sought to escape divine judgment by blaming Eve (3:12) and Eve in turn, sought to fix the blame upon the serpent (3:13). God disregarded their excuses, and proceeded to pronounce a curse upon the animal creation, woman and man, and even the ground beneath their feet. The serpent was reduced to wriggling in the dust, Adam and Eve to sorrow, pain, toil, and physical death, and the whole earth and its vegetable kingdom were reduced to corruption and decadence. Some have seen a connection between the thorns that were visited upon the cursed earth with the choice of thorns to crown the Redeemer.

It is a remarkable fact that in the pronouncement to the serpent in 3:15, God uttered a promise of redemption which is the first prophecy of the Bible. These words have been called the "protevangelium" or "first gospel." As it were, God said, "Satan and mankind shall be enemies, but there shall be One born of woman who shall permanently defeat Satan (bruise [or crush] thy head) but who, in so doing, shall suffer temporary injury (bruise his heel)." Perhaps the virgin birth is intimated by the expression "seed of the woman." Biologically a woman produces ova and not sperm (seed). It was an indication of the mercy of God that He announced deliverance for man even before He had imposed sentence upon him.

God replaced the fig leaves with coats of skins, and thereby caused the death of innocent animals. Thus man learned that his covering before God must be by means of an atoning sacrifice, and that the good works of self-effort are inadequate. Just as God supplied the victim for the covering of Adam and Eve, so at Calvary, He provided the Victim whose atoning blood is yet sufficient for the penitent sinner. Christianity begins with the fact of man's being divinely clothed; religion expends all its energies vainly seeking to clothe man.

God sent forth Adam and Eve from the Garden as an act of mercy. Had they remained and partaken of the tree of life, they would have entered into eternal life as sinners, and thereby be subject to misery without respite. On the basis of the syntax of the original Hebrew at this point (3:22, 23), Keil and Delitzsch comment:

It follows that man had not yet eaten of

the tree of life.   Had he continued in fellowship with God, by obedience to the command of God, he might have eaten it, for
he was created for eternal life.   But after
he had fallen through sin into the power of
death, the fruit which produced immortal-
ity could only do him harm.[11]

In this instance,   and throughout Scripture,
God makes clear the fact that eternal life was
not a gift at creation; man could possess it
only by in some way appropriating it as a gift
from God.

With their clothing of animal skins,
and through the exercise of faith, Adam and
Eve outside of the Garden were nearer to God
than they had been as fallen sinners within
the Garden.   Man found it necessary now to
labor for his physical needs, but for fallen
man, honest labor actually contributes to the
sense of well-being and restricts the opportunity to commit evil.   To a limited degree, man
had worked in Eden (2:15), but his labor from
this time forth was to be marked by comparative futility and unproductiveness.   It is
Pember's suggestion that the gates of the
Garden served as a site to which man might
come to worship God and offer sacrifices.
Perhaps there is some relation between the
guardian cherubim and the winged bulls
(called colossi) which traditionally were
erected to guard entrances of Babylonian-
Assyrian royal buildings.   The cherubim,
standing in judgment at the Garden entrance
in Adam's time, contrast with those cherubim of Moses' day who in mercy overspread
the ark of the covenant, which was the place of
meeting between God and man.

III. THE EARLIEST CIVILIZATION (Chs. 4, 5)

1. The Line of Cain (4:1-24)

The first event in the new life outside
of Eden was the birth of Cain.   Eve remembered the promise of a deliverer, and in her
simplicity, thought that he had come.   Accordingly, the name Cain means "possession" and
in thus naming her son, Eve implied that she
thought that he was the possession that the
Lord had promised.   Literally she declared:
"I have gotten a man, the Lord [or Jehovah]."

The word "from" is not in the text. By the
time her second son was born[12] Eve was dis-
illusioned, however, and she gave him the
name Abel which means "vapor" or "vanity"
and implies uncertainty and weakness.

Cain is a type of the self-righteous individual who serves in his own strength. He
ignored the provision of shed blood, and offered instead the bloodless offering which was,
as it were, the work of his hands. It is evident that God rejected Cain, both because of
what he offered, and also because of the manner in which he offered it.   God truly com-
mends good works, but the approach to Him
must be by faith, and not by some special kind
of human effort.   The New Testament reports: "By faith Abel offered unto God a more
excellent sacrifice than Cain, by which he obtained witness that he was righteous, God test-
ifying of his gifts" (Heb. 11:4).   Comments
Mackintosh: "Cain offered to Jehovah the fruit
of a cursed earth, and that, moreover, without
any blood to remove the curse. He presented
an unbloody sacrifice, simply because he had
no faith.[13]   Although the Bible does not state
the divine procedure acknowledging the acceptable offering, it is commonly thought that God
received Abel's offering by consuming it with
fire.

In spite of God's message (vv. 6, 7), Cain
maintained his jealous anger against Abel. A
possible paraphrase of verse 7 may read: "If
you act properly you will be accepted [by God],
and if you do not, sin lies in wait for you, so
that you cannot go forth without meeting it. Sin
thirsts for your blood, but you should master
your own evil spirit and thus defeat sin." Since
the word "sin" may also be rendered "sin-offering" there are those who feel that this verse
teaches not that "sin thirsts for your blood,"
but rather "a sin-offering is readily available."
The suggestion is that even as God spoke, a
sacrificial animal was outside of the door of
the very place in which Cain was. Cain's murder of Abel has been described as "the man who
tried to be justified by works destroying the man
who was justified by faith in the blood that was
shed."   The murder of one's brother is called

___

[11]Keil and Delitzsch, op. cit. p. 107

___

[12]Some Hebrew scholars hold the interesting theory that the original Hebrew gives
evidence that Cain and Abel were twins.

[13]Mackintosh, op. cit. p. 62

fratricide.

Jude comments: "Woe unto them! for they have gone in the way of Cain, . . ." (v. 11). The "way of Cain" seems to include" 1) worship according to the inclinations of the natural man, 2) assault of those who do worship rightly, 3) refusal to repent, 4) rejection of God from an influence upon one's life, and 5) devoting oneself to the comforts of this world. In its basic identity, the "way of Cain" is the way of fleshly carnality. It begins with a refusal to confess sin, and to be reconciled to God according to the divine plan. As in Cain's case, it may proceed even to the point of staining the earth with innocent blood. Cain had invested all his energies in behalf of the soil, and now that soil was cursed by God to deny him its fruit (4:12).

Cain lied about his brother's whereabouts, and then superciliously retorted, "Am I my brother's keeper?" His response to the Lord's pronouncement of judgment was only to protest its severity. Thus it was the mercy and longsuffering of God that spared Cain to go forth as a fugitive and vagabond and gave him a mark to signify God's protection upon him. The mark of Cain was apparently some temporary physical feature, or a characteristic of personality (such as ferocity) that assured that men should not harm him. Scholars have suggested that the mark upon Cain was necessary because by this time it was possible for the earth's population to have been several thousand. On the one hand, the fact of Cain's mark would be a warning to all who saw him of the outcome of sin; on the other, it may have served as a token of the divine pledge whereby God in His mercy agreed to protect even the sinner, Cain. It is noted that the name "Cain" means "smith," and that anciently in some societies smiths were exempt from family vendettas. Thus, they were especially marked by their vocation.

Cain took his wife with him in his wanderings, and in course of time their first son, Enoch, was born. The "land of Nod" means "land of wandering," and it may refer to a way of living rather than to an actual place. Cain's wife would no doubt be his sister, since Eve was "the mother of all living" (3:20), and since in Abram's time men thought it permissible to marry a half-sister. Although today, incest is considered criminal and is forbidden by both human and divine law, in the youth of the race, when there were fewer inborn infirmities to augment by intermarriage, such practices were evidently not objectionable. Since lifespans were so great in this era, Cain's marriage and the birth of his first son may have been decades, or even a century or more, after the murder of Abel.

The descendants of Cain developed worldly arts and sciences that they might neutralize the curse, and make life as comfortable and attractive as possible. They lacked the believer's hope whereby they considered themselves pilgrims and sojourners in this world. Their civilization included many of the arts that are supposed to be reserved for an advanced culture, and their development was impressive, even by modern standards. It should be borne in mind that the period under consideration extended more than 1,600 years. A comparative span of time would extend backward from today to the era when the Roman Empire was at its height.

Cain's first son, after whom he named the city Enoch, was, of course, a different individual from Enoch the seventh from Adam of the line of Seth. The line of Cain included Lamech who was the world's first recorded bigamist. His boastful poem to his wives (v. 23) constitutes a confession of homicide, and it has been called "The Song of the Sword." It is the first poetry quoted in the Bible. In this poem Lamech implied that anyone who sought to harm him would suffer seventyfold vengeance. Because God at this time had reserved vengeance for Himself, Lamech's defiance reached the very domain of God. Included in the line of Cain was Jabal who may have been both a trader of cattle and a herdsman, Jubal who instituted music, and probably other fine arts, and Tubalcain who probably was something of a mechanical inventor.

2. The Line of Seth (Ch. 4:25-5:32)

In naming her third son "Seth" which means "appointed" it is possible that Eve's hopes once more were raised, and she believed that this child was to be God's appointed deliverer. Evidently in the time of Seth's son, Enos, some new measure of spiritual insight was gained. The expression "then began men to call upon the name of the Lord" seems to describe the beginning of worship, possibly public, by godly men. For the first time, men appear to have come to know deity not merely as the omnipotent creator (God or Elohim), but as the redeemer and covenant keeper (Lord or Jehovah).

The genealogies are in the Bible for the believer's profit, and they deserve careful scrutiny. It has been said: "The genealogies of the primeval age are memorials, which bear testimony quite as much to the faithfulness of God in fulfilling His promise, as to the faith and patience of the fathers themselves." The genealogy of this Bible chapter extends all the way from the time of Adam to the time of Noah, a period of at least sixteen centuries. Most scholars agree that the Old Testament genealogies do not necessarily include each generation in precise detail. In some instances it is possible that a relationship indicated in Scripture as father and son, may actually be grandfather and grandson. The word "beget" may legitimately be translated "became the ancestor of."

Enoch was the seventh in the line of Seth; while Lamech (the one of 4:18-24) was seventh in the line of Cain. In Enoch culminates righteousness, but in Lamech culminates sinfulness. Comments Mackintosh of Enoch, "The sons of Cain might spend their energies in the vain attempt to improve a cursed world, but Enoch found a better world, and lived in the power of it."[14] A portion of the teaching of Enoch is preserved in Jude 14, 15. His translation before the Flood is a type of the translation of the Church before the Great Tribulation. Enoch shares with Elijah the honor of being one of the two Old Testament figures who left this world without dying. It is of interest to note that the polytheistic Babylonian myths relate that the seventh king was carried off to the gods and shared in their secrets.

Enoch was the father of Methuselah, the grandfather of Lamech, and the great-grandfather of Noah. Although Enoch lived only one-third as many years as Methuselah, he left a favorable memory. Methuselah lived 969 years to become the oldest man who lived, and he did not die until the very year of the Flood. Some have seen significance in Methuselah's name which means: "after he has gone it shall be sent." It is held that Methuselah's longevity

was an instance of the mercy of God, for He had promised that as long as Methuselah lived, no universal judgment would be sent upon man. The Bible narrative introduces Noah at age 500 and names his three sons, Shem, Ham and Japheth. It is understood that in the case of Noah, and throughout the genealogies, the first year-number given is the year the man named became for the first time the father of a son.

During the antediluvian era, man's life-span vastly exceeded anything that has since been known. It has been suggested that early man lived long because the effects of sin and disease had not yet begun to take their toll upon him. Also, the climate in the pre-Flood era may have been more desirable, and man may have been more prudent in his diet. Man's extended lifespan was a means used by God to assure the rapid populating of the newly created world. In contrast to the plausibility of Scripture, even in these matters, the Sumerian king lists indicate life spans in excess of 43,000 years. The Sumerian historians seem to have been carried away in their zeal to convey the longevity of early man.

IV. THE FLOOD (Chs. 6-9)

1. The Days of Noah (Ch. 6)

It should be recognized that even though the story of Noah occurs near to the beginning of our Bible, the event did not actually take place until man had been on earth for at least sixteen centuries. In the intervening years, man had developed a materialistic, ungodly civilization that had so presumed upon the patience of God that He judged these human subjects no longer worthy to live. Rewinkel estimates that the world's population at the time of Noah's flood was about equal to that of today-- thus about three billion; while Whitcomb and Morris note that an "extremely conservative" figure would be one billion. The Lord Jesus spoke of the days of Noah as paralleling those of the time of His return, and described both periods as times of low moral standards (Mt. 24:37-39). St. Peter also referred to the Flood and considered it the confirmation of the doctrine of end time judgment inasmuch as it clearly reveals that God does not forever withhold intervention. The "days of Noah" are analysed by Pember to have had the following characteristics: 1) a tendency to deism, 2) an unnatural prominence of women and a disregard

---

[14]Mackintosh, op. cit., p. 81

of the laws of marriage, 3) progress in mechanical arts, 4) alliances of nominal believers with unbelievers, 5) rejection of the preaching of the faithful, and 6) the appearance on earth of beings from the Satanic realm.[15]

The intermarriage of the daughters of men and the sons of God (vv. 1, 2) clearly is an example of the breakdown of barriers in Noah's day, but the identity of these sons of God is a matter of dispute. Some students think they were the godly Sethites; others think they were angelic beings in human form. The first outlook places less strain upon the imagination and it accords with what is seen to happen in the case of some believers today. The expression "sons of God" is sometimes used in the Old Testament to refer to believers. (cf. Hos. 1:10; Deut. 32:5; Psa. 73:15). It is argued that the intermarriage of believers and unbelievers occurred otherwise quite frequently in Bible times and it inevitably resulted in God's disapproval. The Flood represented God's judgment upon men, and resulted in their destruction; it was not the kind of cataclysm that would affect angels. The women of the Cainite line are designated as the daughters of men because they had deliberately set out to make themselves attractive to eligible men. They were practising beguilements, and in some glaring way artificially enhancing themselves.

On the other hand, there are those who feel that the Scriptural language is too pointed and specific to be talking merely of the marriage of believers and unbelievers. The theory that the sons of God were angels is supported by the following: 1) In the book of Job the expression "sons of God" certainly refers to angels (Job 1:6, 2:1, 38:7). 2) The presence of giants on the earth may thus be accounted for (Gen. 6:4). In the original, the word "Nephilim" is used to describe these beings, and this word may be translated "fallen ones." 3) Angels may assume bodies with the appearance and form of normal humans (cf. Lot's visitors, Gen. 19:1, 5). In Mt. 22:30 our Lord was merely explaining that angels do not reproduce themselves in the manner of humans. What a fallen angel might do if he chose is not under consideration. 5) The women of the line of Seth would be as much the "daughters of men" as the women of the Cainite line. 6) This theory may be linked with Jude

6 and 7, and it anciently has had the endorsement of historians such as Philo and Josephus, and the apocryphal book of Enoch.

Together with a description of the gross wickedness of this era, Scripture presents a poignant insight into the grieving heart of the Creator-God. From His words in 6:3, it is concluded that there may come a time when a man is so confirmed in sin that the conviction and restraint of the Holy Spirit ceases to avail, and the Spirit simply withdraws. The 120 years mentioned would refer to the period from the announcement until the Flood, or to the life-span which at that time the Lord allowed to man. If the former, then the announcement must have been 20 years before the events of 5:32 (cf. 7:11).

God repented (6:6), not in the sense that He changed His mind, but in the sense that man came to be in a new relation to Him. Those creatures that He had sought to protect and care for, He now planned to destroy. They no longer were of the caliber and nature that He was able to look upon them with favor. Man's change from innocence to wickedness brought about an entirely new relationship between God and man, so that man became the object of God's opposition instead of His protection. The use of the language of human experience in order to describe God, so that the immutable God is said to repent, is termed "anthropomorphism." God casts Himself in the role of man so that He may clearly be distinguished from a mere abstract idea or principle.

Noah only, of all men on the earth, found grace in the eyes of the Lord because of his faith. He is described as "a just man and perfect," not because He embodied absolute perfection, but because he lived and believed in a manner that was pleasing to God. Noah is the last man of the Old Testament of whom it is said he "walked with God." Concerning Abraham it is said only that he walked "before God." The New Testament emphasizes Noah's faith. "By faith Noah, . . . prepared an ark to the saving of his house; . . . and became heir of the righteousness which is by faith" (Heb. 11:7). Noah's stand must have taken considerable faith. He: 1) built a great boat on dry land, 2) predicted a phenomenon (rain) that had never yet occurred and 3) preached 120 years and failed to win a single convert. Peter wrote, [God] spared not the old world, but saved Noah the eighth per-

---

[15]Pember, op. cit., pp. 225, 226.

son, a preacher of righteousness . . ." (2 Pet. 2:5).

The gopher wood from which Noah made his ark is believed to have been cypress wood which to this day grows abundantly in the Tigris-Euphrates Valley. The pitch that covered the ark was similar to asphalt or tar and it would serve as the caulking of the vessel. The data on the window of the ark is too vague for an exact picture; however the idea is conveyed that there was provision for ventilation and light. Since the ark was merely meant to float upon water, it had no means of propulsion or steering, nor was it likely to have a shaped hull, prow, or stern as a boat. Inasmuch as the length of a cubit varied from time to time, no one can with certainty make any comparisons of the size of the ark. However, if the cubit was eighteen inches (the least it could have been), the ark would have had about a 20,000 ton displacement which is a good size, even by modern standards. Since it was a mere empty box its space would have been devoted exclusively to cargo space, and the total area of the three decks would be equivalent to that of twenty regulation basketball courts. Historically, the first ship ever built that may have been larger was the Eturia in 1884.

On the basis of the foregoing measurements, which would have provided a capacity of nearly 1.5 million square feet, one scholar has calculated that the ark could provide: 10 square feet of floor space for each animal, 24 square inches of floor space for each insect and reptile, and 216 square inches of floor space for each bird. These area allotments provide for: 1,700 species of animals, 100,000 species of insects, 987 species of reptiles, and 10,087 species of birds. Since the ceilings in the ark were 14 feet high, there would be ample room for food storage above the cages of the smaller creatures. There are actually only a few species of large animals, and the average size of all animals is about that of a house cat. It has traditionally been claimed that during their long cruise many of the animals would have hibernated.

2. The Entrance Into the Ark (Ch. 7)

In Noah's six hundredth year, just seven days before the Flood began, God called Noah, his family, and the animals into the ark. The composite account of the entrance into the ark and the beginning of the Flood may be reconciled in the following schedule: 1) the animals enter the ark, 2) seven days elapse, 3) Noah and his family enter the ark, 4) God shuts the door, and 5) the rain begins. It is usually thought that the extra clean beasts that Noah took along were to serve as sacrifices when Noah worshipped after the Flood. The fact that God shut the door of the ark (7:16) would signify to Noah's godless contemporaries that the day of mercy had passed. In a similar manner, at a particular time of God's appointment, the Gospel age likewise will some day come to an end.

The rain not only descended from the sky, but "all the fountains of the great deep [were] broken up" (7:11). This statement may mean that there were violent discharges of water from subterranean caverns, or that the great oceans were hurled from their beds and swept around the earth in a series of huge tidal waves. It may be concluded that 7:20 implies that the water covered even the highest mountain[16] by fifteen cubits (at least twenty-two and one-half feet). This depth was presumably the maximum to which the ark sank in the water, since it was one-half the height of the vessel. The result of the Flood upon the creatures of earth is stated in verse 22, "All in whose nostrils was the breath of life, of all that was in the dry land, died." The fate of the fish is not reported, but in the turbulent waters, the flying wreckage, and the mingling of fresh and salt water, many must have perished. Apparently sufficient survived to propagate the species.

Although Bible believers do not doubt the fact of the Flood, the actual nature of the physical events that occurred is a matter of speculation. A discussion of the better known theories of the Flood is found in the appendix.

3. The Abating of the Flood (8:1-20)

After 40 days and nights the rain ceased, and after 150 days the ark was grounded upon Mount Ararat. In another two and one-half months the tops of the mountains were seen, and 40 days later Noah sent forth the dove and

[16]Mt. Everest in the Himalayas rises 29,141 feet above sea level.

raven. This latter, a carrion-eating bird, evidently found provision and it stayed away, but the dove returned. A week later the dove was again sent forth, and this time it returned with an olive leaf. When it was once more sent forth the following week, it did not return. Noah had thus used the birds to obtain necessary information concerning the exposed areas. His procedure was not unlike that of other ancient sailors who are said to have used birds both as message carriers and as a means of determining direction. It is noted that the rate at which the waters receded became increasingly rapid: Whitcomb and Norris estimate it at about fifteen feet per day.

Noah waited until the twenty-seventh day of the second month of his six hundred and first year before he ventured forth. Thus, he was in the ark one year and ten days, or counting both the day of the entrance and the day of departure, one year and eleven days. A year would have been 360 days. At that time, he and his family, and all living creatures left the ark. Noah's first act upon emerging was to build an altar and offer sacrifices to God. This eagerness to worship demonstrated the rightness of Noah's heart attitude. Comments Von Rad: "The first human work that the liberated earth, which is again restored to man, sees is an altar for God the Lord." The Lord was pleased with this worship, and Scripture declares that He "smelled a sweet savour."

In the secular Sumerian (Babylonian) "Gilgamesh Epic" the story of the Flood is corroborated. In this account, Gilgamesh was a great hero who visited the God Utnapishtim and asked him to tell the story of his attainment of deity. Utnapishtim's answer is an account of the great deluge. He depicts himself as the mortal to whom the plans of the flood were revealed, who thereby survived in a ship, and who in the subsequent sacrificial worship following his emergence from the ship was transformed into his present identity with the gods. The Gilgamesh Epic first came to the attention of scholars in 1853 with the finding of a series of clay tablets in Ninevah. These included both the story of creation, and also the story of the Flood from the standpoint of Chaldean paganism. Other more recent fragments containing the Epic have been found at Ashur, Kish, and Uruk, and notably at Nippur. The Nippur fragment is preserved in the museum of the University of Pennsylvania, and it includes an account of both

creation and the Flood, written in three columns on two sides of the tablet. In each instance, the Babylonian Epic is grossly polytheistic, but otherwise it is remarkably similar to the Bible story.

The ark, the vessel of refuge, is a type of Christ:

THE ARK	CHRIST
Provided according to the plan of God	God's plan of the ages involves the Saviorship of Christ
Men were invited to come into the ark.	"Come unto me, all ye that labor . . . and I will give you rest." (Mt. 11:28)
Entrance was through a single door	"I am the door: by me if any man enter in, he shall be saved." (Jno. 10:9)
Ark a refuge from divine judgment	Through Christ men escape the wrath to come
The ark bore the storms of judgment	God's outpoured wrath exhausted itself upon Jesus Christ
Place of absolute security	Christ saves to the uttermost

4. The Noahic Covenant (8:21-9:29)

The promises of God to Noah in 8:21 to 9:17 constitute what has been called the "Noahic Covenant." Herein, God is transformed from manifesting His punishing anger to revealing His mercy, and the story of the Flood that begins with the wrath of God ends with a gracious statement of His goodness and grace. The provisions of this Covenant included: 1) the future maintenance of the regular sequence of seasons, 2) man's supremacy over animal life, 3) the provision of the flesh of animals for food provided that the blood had been drained, and 4) man's authority over his fellows so that he might now administer judgment upon a murderer (cf. God had protected Cain from his fellow man). The Noahic Covenant was between Jehovah and every living creature

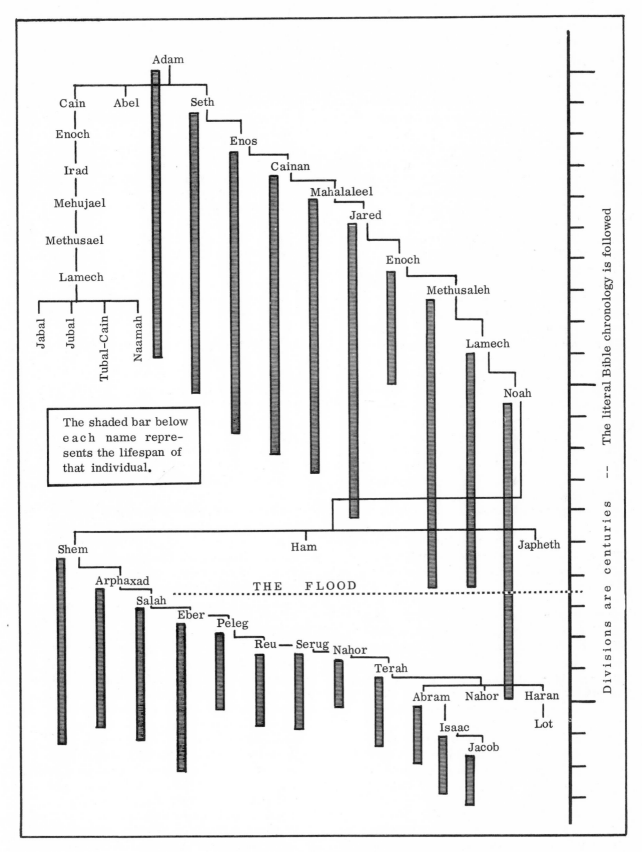

Figure 1 -- Genealogies and Lifespans in the Book of Genesis

upon earth, including the lower creation. While man was given the rule of earth and its creatures, he was to acknowledge his status below God. Von Rad comments: "Even when man slaughters and kills, he is to know that he is touching something, which, because it is life, is in a special manner God's property; and as a sign of this he is to keep his hands off the blood."[17] The Covenant set forth the foundations of civil authority with the provision for a governmental code and penal regulation. The era introduced by the Covenant has been designated "Human Government" and it has continued in effect to this present day.

The seal or token of the Noahic Covenant was the rainbow. This lovely sign in the sky became God's seal of a faithful pledge so that man might enjoy a visible token to remind him of God's faithfulness. Inasmuch as the "warbow" and the "rainbow" are interchangeable terms in the original, the portrayal of the rainbow implies that God has put away His weapon of war against mankind. Scripture intimates, but does not dogmatically assert, that at this time the rainbow was a new phenomenon and thus it may have been an outcome of the atmospheric changes associated with the Flood. The alternative would be that the rainbow as familar but that now God gave it a particular significance. Mackintosh says: "The whole creation rests as to its exemption from a second deluge, on the eternal stability of God's covenant, of which the bow is a token."[18]

Inasmuch as Scripture portrays Noah as a man of faith and righteousness, commentators usually excuse him for his drunkenness. It is thought that either fermentation was a new process that was the outcome of the atmospheric changes accompanying the Flood, or that Noah had not previously been responsible for preparing his own beverages and he did not know the properties of the fruit of the vine. Because of Ham's disrespectful attitude on this occasion, his posterity (represented by Canaan), suffered Noah's curse. The descendants of Canaan became the black races who for long centuries furnished the world's supply of slaves, and who suffered persistent hardship and bitterness. Events on this occasion teach the obligation of

---

[17]Von Rad, op. cit. p. 128

[18]Mackintosh, op. cit. p. 110

filial piety, and make plain the fact that this obligation extends to positive action and not merely to negative restraint.

It was pledged that the line of Japheth, the father of the gentiles, should be enlarged, and that the line of Shem, the father of the Semites, (in today's usage, one who speaks one of the Semitic languages) should be blessed. Today, and throughout all history, the great gentile powers have dominated and controlled the world. The statement, "Japheth. . . shall dwell in the tents of Shem," may imply that the gentiles are to occupy the room of the Semites and it may be linked to the grafted branches of the vine (Rom. 11:15-25). In the light of these pronouncements of divine dealings on the basis of racial background, it is gratifying to know that God will deal in kindliness and blessing toward any individual or any racial group provided he manifests simple faith and sincerity.

V. THE NATIONS AND THEIR DISPERSION (Chs. 10, 11)

1. The Table of Nations (Ch. 10)

On the basis of the Biblical record, it is evident that the families of the sons of Noah represent all of the racial groups upon the earth. This chapter lists a total of seventy individual founders of nations or racial groups, and divides them into the three primary classifications of: Shem, Ham, and Japheth. While much is unknown concerning the classification of nations, ethnologists generally agree that mankind divides into three basic groups. This chapter primarily favors the line of Shem, and after reporting the genealogies of subordinate groups, it develops the relationships of Shem's line in detail. Most evangelical scholars are willing to concede that in all probability the expression "sons of" need not always refer to individual people, but may mean a tribal or national group. Thus, in the Bible, the "sons of Ishmael" is another way of saying "the Arabs." Although some have held that the Genesis table of nations depicts geographic relations rather than racial affinities, it may be concluded that the Table is that which it proposes to be, but that inevitably geographical relations are involved. It is a human custom that people of one family are likely to settle within a specific community.

As indicated by the map, the Japhetic or Aryan race settled principally in Europe.

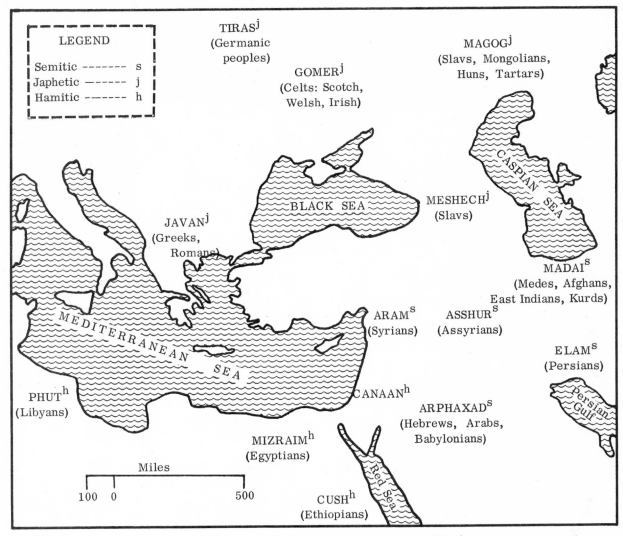

LEGEND

Semitic ------- s
Japhetic ------ j
Hamitic ------ h

TIRAS[j]
(Germanic peoples)

GOMER[j]
(Celts: Scotch, Welsh, Irish)

MAGOG[j]
(Slavs, Mongolians, Huns, Tartars)

BLACK SEA

MESHECH[j]
(Slavs)

CASPIAN SEA

JAVAN[j]
(Greeks, Romans)

MADAI[s]
(Medes, Afghans, East Indians, Kurds)

ARAM[s]
(Syrians)

ASSHUR[s]
(Assyrians)

ELAM[s]
(Persians)

MEDITERRANEAN SEA

Persian Gulf

PHUT[h]
(Libyans)

CANAAN[h]

ARPHAXAD[s]
(Hebrews, Arabs, Babylonians)

MIZRAIM[h]
(Egyptians)

Red Sea

Miles

100   0   500

CUSH[h]
(Ethiopians)

Figure 2 -- The Settlement of the Sons of Noah

From his European home, Japheth has been "enlarged" so as to extend throughout the western hemisphere. The descendants of Ham located chiefly in Africa, and they are distinguished by their physical hardiness and endurance. The Shemites, or Semites, made Asia their home, and they have been particularly characterized by their indifference to material things and their exercise of religious devotion. The distinctive physical traits and color of each of the three major types of mankind can probably best be accounted for as an outcome of direct divine intervention on the occasion of the confounding of the languages at Babel. Neither environment nor food are sufficient to account for the specific racial traits that have been established in the human genetic stream. It is certainly possible to hold that genetic type directed the choice of environment rather than vice versa.

Nimrod is described as a "mighty hunter before the Lord" (v. 9); however, it is generally agreed that this passage ought to read "a mighty rebel before the Lord." It is frequently suggested that Nimrod was an organizer and leader who established a strong political power throughout the Middle East. In identifying Nimrod, Price writes: "The most plausible identification is with Gilgamesh in the Babylonian legend where he is called two-thirds god, one-third man."[19] The legend might be considered a form of popular tribute to the prowess and influence of Nimrod. Although the wife of Nimrod is not mentioned at this time, she also is thought to have figured prominently in history.

_____

[19]Ira M. Price, The Monuments and the Old Testament. Philadelphia: Judson Press, 1925, p. 138

Traditionally she is named Simiramus. According to an ancient legend, after Nimrod's death this woman bore a son whom she claimed was supernaturally conceived. The child, named Tammuz, was declared to be a reincarnation of the dead Nimrod. Thus began the cult of Tammuz which was a snare for Israel in Ezekiel's time, and which some scholars hold to be the basis of the mother-child doctrine that occurs persistently in many pagan religions, and that accounts for Mariolotry in Christianity.

A statement in 10:25 that describes a division of the earth in the day of Eber has been variously interpreted. Scholars have suggested that it may refer to the dividing of the nations due to the confusion of languages at Babylon. On the other hand, it may refer to the establishment of some sort of boundary, or perhaps a canal, that was of considerable significance to early man. It may have been a vast and cataclysmic earthquake that resulted in upheavals of land to form our present continents. The latter suggestion, however, is usually doubted, for it seems to be too vast a phenomenon for such a casual reference. It is noted that it was this Eber (a name which probably means "immigrant") who gave his name to the children of Israel so that they later were often called Hebrews.

2. The Tower of Babel (Ch. 11)

Although God had not sanctioned community or city dwelling, it was convenient and appealing to early man. The land of Shinar is held to have been the fruitful plain region between the Tigris and Euphrates rivers. Man chose to settle there and to undertake the building of a tower "lest . . . [he] be scattered abroad upon the face of the whole earth" (11:4). Although Nimrod is not mentioned in connection with the tower of Babel, since it was located at his headquarters, there is a good deal of probability that he was the guiding influence in its construction. The project was motivated by human pride and self-will, and this fact is plainly evident from the many first person pronouns in verses three and four.

Since there was no natural stone in lower Babylon, buildings customarily were built of brick. However, in the case of the tower, kiln-dried rather than the usual sun-dried brick was used. It is likely that the

brick would be finished in a surface of brightly colored glazing. The "slime" would be a mineral pitch similar to asphalt. The exact purpose of the tower is not too clear, but it would appear that it was built as a community dwelling place to guard against further scattering. Other possible uses of the tower include: a refuge in case of another flood, a memorial to that generation, a center of worship, a fortress, or an astronomical observatory.

The Tower of Babel was patterned after the Babylonian ziggurats. The name "ziggurat" means that which is raised up as a mountain peak or a tower, and as the Babylonians constructed them, they were in the form of a pyramid. The ruins of more than two dozen have been found in the Middle East, with one of the oldest being at Uruk (the Erech of Gen. 10:10), and one of the largest at Ur of the Chaldees. A ruined base of a ziggurat located near Babylon is called Birs Nimrod, and it may actually be the remains of the Biblical tower. In most cases, the ziggurats were of a simple type of brick (usually sun-dried), with a mortar of bitumen, but decorated, glazed kiln-dried brick was also used. They rose to a great height in a series of terraces, and on the flat Babylonian Plain were conspicuous landmarks. The famous "Hanging Gardens of Babylon" constructed by King Nebuchadnezzar, actually consisted of a terraced ziggurat.

The building of the city and tower was not in obedience to God's command to till the ground. It would appear that man planned to be great without taking God into account although the rebellion is more implied than declared. Concerning the success of man's efforts, Newell comments: "Man's tower, instead of reaching to Heaven as he had fancied, was so minute that God had to come down to see it." God responded to man's rebellious efforts by imposing a penalty that exactly fitted the offence. Men who had sought to remain together were scattered abroad "upon the face of all the earth" (11:8a). Even though today there are considered to be upwards of 3,000 languages spoken by mankind, it is generally agreed by philologists that all human language can be demonstrated to have a common origin. It is interesting to note that the name "babel" which was given to the tower, in Hebrew means "confusion." In Chaldean, a similar sounding name means "gate of god."

When men found that they could communicate only with the members of their own family, they proceeded to migrate abroad in family groups. Scripture indicates that not until the millennial time will all men speak a uniform language. (See Zech. 3:9). Probably the miraculous events on the day of Pentecost were a foretaste of this latter day. In the divine providence, this scattering of families became the first step in the plan of God to call apart a peculiar people. The genealogy of the family of Shem leads to the first mention of Abram, and serves to reveal the immediate parentage and family connections of this man who is to be the leading character of the narrative to follow. It should be noted that, according to the conventional literal shorter chronology, from the Flood until the birth of Abram was 292 years. The mention of Abram serves to divide historical time into the earlier primeval history and the subsequent era of actual sacred history.

VI. THE STORY OF ABRAHAM (Chs. 12:1 - 25:18)

1. The Call of Abram (Ch. 12)

The ninth descendant of Shem was Abram, who became the object of God's special call. Comments Blaikie: "The call of Abram was the most important event in the history of God's kingdom that had occurred since the Fall." The importance of this call was emphasized by God's personal appearance for the first time since the expulsion from Eden. In so appearing to Abram, God was as it were making His third start with humanity. The choice of Abram must be ascribed to the sovereignty of God, although it is evident that Abram had potential to become the great man of God that he became.

a. The Background of Abram

The father of Abram was Terah who traditionally is said to have been an idol-maker. Joshua declared: "Your fathers dwelt on the other side of the flood[20] in old time, even Terah, the father of Abraham, and the father of Nachor: and they served other gods" (Josh. 24:2). The formula for the offering of

the first fruits identified the family of Abram with Syria—thus "A Syrian ready to perish was my father . . ." (Deut. 26:5). It is considered that Abram was deeply attached to his father, and that, in fact, this filial concern delayed his response to the call of God. Scripture does not reveal by what process Abram emerged from idolatry and became a devout believer in Jehovah. That the transformation was genuine is reported by the writer of Hebrews who says: "By faith Abraham, when he was called to go into a place which he should after receive for an inheritance, obeyed; and he went out, not knowing whither he went" (Heb. 11:8).

b. Abram's Home in Ur

That Ur was a city with a well-developed civilization in the time of Abram's call has been impressibly demonstrated by archaeological investigations. That part of the Tigris-Euphrates valley in which Ur is located was known as Sumer (the northern part was called Akkad) and in the region many villages of the time of Abram and even earlier have been thoroughly excavated. Characteristics of their civilization from this extremely early era include: adobe houses (i.e. sun-dried brick), stones for grinding flour and ovens for baking bread and pastries, flint weapons and tools, an assortment of pottery vessels and jars with attractive ornamentation, beads and amulets for personal adornment, and artistic figurines perhaps intended to be goddesses. Characteristically, ancient nations manufactured miniature replicas of humans or animals, not for mere ornamentation, but for purposes of religious and cultic exercise. It is evident that in the time of the ancient city of Ur, the name "Abram" was not uncommon, for several Babylonian texts bearing this name have been assigned by archaeologists to this era.

Ur of the Chaldees was a city of about 150 acres with an estimated population of some 24,000. It included two-story houses, a city sewer system, and neatly laid out streets. The royal tombs of Ur, dated probably a little prior to Abram, have produced a collection of magnificent golden vessels that are the delight of archaeologists. Ur has been found to have been a city of literary culture, and findings have included tablets that were dictionaries, grammar books, mathematical tables, calculations in square and cube roots, cuneiform writing, and copybooks for learners.

---

[20]Presumably the "flood" was Joshua's name for the River Euphrates.

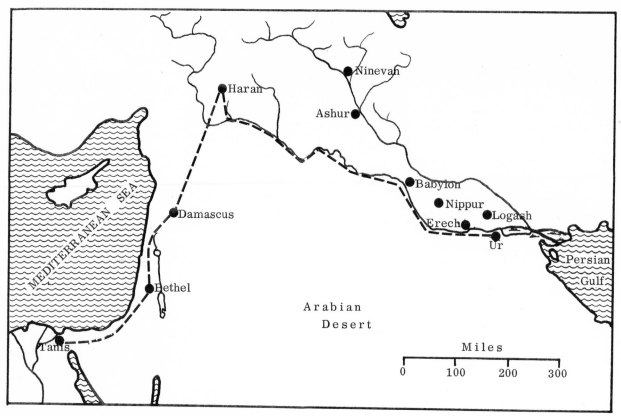

Figure 3 -- The Migration of Abram

In spite of the advanced civilization and many worthy insights, Ur remained basically idolatrous and polytheistic. The very name "Ur," in addition to referring to the city, was also the name of the moon-god. The pagan priests of Ur evidently were harshly oppressive and demanding of the people. Archaeologists report that Urukagina, a reforming ruler, found it necessary to issue a decree prohibiting the appropriation of fruit or wood by the priests from a poor woman. Also, the ruler ordered that burial fees should be cut to a fifth, and that no priests should assume private ownership of temple land. The worship temples that served the citizens of Ur were usually ziggurats built with various rooms and facilities. Excavations have shown that as well as worship activities, ziggurats also served to accommodate light industry such as weaving cloth, which probably was sold to augment temple income.

c. Abram's Departure to Haran

The departure of Abram from Ur is recorded (11:31) prior to an account of the reason for the departure (12:1-3). The Bible makes clear that the original call of God upon Abram came while he was still in Ur. "The God of glory appeared unto our father Abraham, when he was in Mesopotamia, before he dwelt in Charran [i.e. Haran]. . ."(Acts 7:2). God's promises to Abram at this time are known as the "Abrahamic Covenant" and twice again (18: 18; 22:18) God extended similar promises to Abram. Abram's migration was undoubtedly an act of faith in response to the leading and covenant of the Lord. In receiving the Covenant, Abram received a promise from God of divine blessing upon his descendants and upon all who blessed them. Those who cursed the descendants of Abram should be cursed, and his people should be a channel of blessing to all mankind. The land of Canaan was to be the guaranteed inheritance of the seed of Abram. The Abrahamic Covenant was renewed to Isaac (26:4) and also to Jacob (28:14).

Although Stephen's address in Acts 7:4 indicates that Abram did not settle in Canaan until after his father's death in Haran, the Genesis chronology would indicate that Terah lived another 60 years after Abram left Haran (cf. 11:26, 32, 12:4). This apparent discrepancy would be reconciled either by noting that by the time of Abram's departure, Terah was as good as dead insofar as any interest or influence that he had in Abram's spiritual purposes, or else by considering that Stephen had reference to a later historical incident when Abram actually settled in Palestine after his various wanderings. Terah figures in the story only as the father of Abram, and when the two separated, the fate of Terah ceased to have significance so far as the Bible account was concerned.

It is usually judged that Abram's years in Haran while he remained with his father were years deprived of Canaan's blessings. The name "Terah" means "delay", or as one scholar translates it "wait a bit." During his years of waiting, Abram endured his life in Haran. The name "Haran" means "parched." Although today Haran no longer exists as a city, Abram's residence there is recognized, and the people of the era, being Mohammedans, count him as a saint of Islam.

d. Abram in Canaan

As Abram arrived at Sichem (Shechem), the Lord appeared to him and once more confirmed the covenant. Abram promptly built the first altar to Jehovah ever erected in the holy land and there he took the first step in the lengthy process of cleansing the soil of Canaan that it might truly be the holy land of the people of God. Shechem, the site of Abram's first altar, was of no little importance in Israel's history. (cf. Josh. 24:1; Jud. 9:6; 1 Ki. 12:1). He next proceeded to a site between Bethel and Hai (or Ai) and there he built a second altar and temporarily established his headquarters. Throughout this era, Abram remains the man of the tent and the man of the altar.

Abram's faith was as yet by no means perfect. When famine befell the land, he unhesitatingly migrated to Egypt. Since Palestine was dependent upon rainfall for its water, whereas Egypt was sustained by the Nile, it is understandable that there would be food in Egypt when there was none in Canaan. In Egypt in order to avoid any threat upon his own life, Abram manifested cowardice and petty deceit, deliberately giving a false impression concerning the status of Sarah. Although Sarah was now 65 years of age, apparently her fair skin contrasted so distinctively with that of the dusky Egyptians, and the status of her supposed brother made her such a desirable acquisition,

that Pharoah proceeded to set her apart as his bride elect.

It is noted that during the time of Abram's prosperity resulting from the supposed contribution of his sister to Pharoah, his domestic animals included camels (12:16). Critics once denied that camels were domesticated at this early date, but the discovery of clay figures, carvings, and pieces of camel bones dated at least as early as the time of Abram, have proved that even then, they were a common domestic animal.

The Egyptian ruler discovered Abram's deceit as a result of God's intervention in sending plagues. Abram was expelled from Egypt without suffering physical harm, and in fact, apparently with all of the possessions that he had acquired. Unquestionably, however, Abram suffered a loss of status and testimony by his deceitfulness. Evidence that Abram's fears for himself were not groundless is set forth by the Egyptian papyrus "Story of the Two Brothers" which is an account of Pharoah's murdering a man in order to secure the man's wife in marriage. Abram's mistake was in considering that only by deceit could he enjoy divine protection.

2. Abram and Lot in Canaan (Ch. 13)

Abram returned once more to the original site of his home in Canaan and there he enjoyed a restoration to Jehovah. He proceeded to solve the problem of conflict between his herdsmen and Lot's by magnanimously offering to give to Lot whatever portion of the land he chose. He made his offer in spite of the fact that the first choice ought to have been his by divine right and by the fact of his natural seniority. Though Lot appears to have presumed upon Abram's generosity and to have taken the very finest of the land, the ultimate outcome was to Abram's advantage, for Lot's portion became the site of a destructive judgment of God. It would appear that Lot's mistake was to be concerned only for his material interest while he remained indifferent to his spiritual needs.

Although in modern times the valley of the Jordan, which was the portion chosen by Lot, has been an uninhabited desert, it is evident that its ancient character was just as the Bible describes it. Nelson Glueck has made

extensive investigations in this region, and on the basis of his findings, contends that anciently the valley was one of the richest parts of Palestine. He has found the sites of more than 70 ancient villages, and there is evidence that at one time the area was densely populated. However, the material prosperity in the Jordan Valley was in no wise matched by any manner of spiritual prosperity. Inasmuch as Lot "pitched his tents towards Sodom" he was taking the first step in indentifying himself with those who were "wicked and sinners before the Lord exceedingly."

After separation from Lot, Abram was granted a new visitation from God, and once more promised ownership of the land. In spite of the concessions made to Lot, it pleased God to reassure Abram of his ultimate heritage. On this occasion, God particularly stressed that Abram's descendants should some day comprise a great and populous nation. Abram proceeded to establish his residence at Hebron in Mamre, and there he built an altar that he might maintain divine worship. The city of Hebron was one of the oldest in the world, for according to Numbers 13:22 it was "built seven years before Zoan in Egypt."

3. Abraham's Army delivers Lot (Ch. 14)

The first war recorded in the Scripture took place in the land of Canaan when four kings from the Euphrates Valley attacked and overcame five kings of Southern Palestine. The cities of Sodom and Gomorrah with which Lot had become identified were among the victims of the invaders. Thus, after twelve years of oppression these cities undertook to obtain their freedom, but again they suffered defeat. These southern defenders evidently discovered that their asphalt or tar pits (slimepits) along the shore of the Dead Sea were more of a liability than a means of defence. The unhappy Lot, as a consequence of such events, suddenly found himself in captivity as a prisoner of war. The conclusion of the incident was Abram's mobili-

◄━━━━━━━━━━━━━━━━━━━━━

Remains of the East Gate of the ancient city of Shechem. Archaeologists trace the history of the city from as early as 7,000 B.C. The East Gate was the main entrance and it led directly to the great temple. Abram's altar to Jehovah on this site undoubtedly contrasted with the prevailing tokens of paganism.

zation of an "army" of 318 men and his speedy liberation of his nephew and defeat of the kings of the middle east.

Abram's interview with Melchizedek is an interesting event in this chapter. It is in connection with Melchizedek that the word "priest" is first mentioned in the Bible and this occasion is the first that mentions the paying of tithes. The name Melchizedek means "king of righteousness." In this account, Melchizedek appears as a normal human being serving in the post of priest and king. He is associated with Salem (which some identify with Jerusalem) and in giving to Abram bread and wine, he exchanged the traditional tokens of friendship and hospitality. However, in Hebrews 7:3 there is a rather startling description of Melchizedek that has led some commentators to conclude that he was actually Jesus Christ in an Old Testament theophany. More plausible, however, is the simple claim that "Without father, without mother, without descent . . ." merely means that his genealogy was lost. In declaring that Melchizedek was ". . . made like unto the Son of God," this Scripture depicts him as a type of Christ, rather than Christ Himself. Our Lord is Himself, not merely like Himself.

An attempt has been made to identify Amraphel (v. 1) with Hammurabi the great legislator who prepared the celebrated "Code of Hammurabi." Since Hammurabi lived about 1700 B.C., comparative chronologies would make an identification with Amraphel possible. On the other hand, scholars generally doubt that the Hammurabi of secular history ever fought a war in Palestine, and certainly there is no evidence of such an event. Further, as Von Rad notes, the identification of the two names is philologically untenable. The racial group called "Horites" in v. 6 have been revealed by archaeological finds to have been an important and powerful people in this area. They are either related to, or perhaps are identical with, the Hurrians and the kingdom of Mitanni.

4. Abram is Divinely Encouraged (Ch. 15)

At this juncture, possibly in response to Abram's personal discouragement, the Lord granted to him a special revelation. God described Himself as "thy shield, and thy exceeding great reward" and Abram addressed Him as "Adonai Elohim," that is "Lord God" or "Master God." In this visitation, God reaffirmed the promise of innumerable seed, and assured him that his lineage was to be by way of a natural born heir rather than through Eliezer, his servant. Although Abram later could not refrain from asking for confirmation of the Lord's covenant (v. 8) he was genuinely receptive of the divine message and Scripture says both here (v. 6) and in Rom. 4:3 that his belief was "counted unto him for righteousness." In this passage is the first Scriptural mention of the doctrine of justification, and the first use of the words: believe, impute and righteousness. It was upon this incident that St. Paul based his exposition found in Romans 4 of the doctrine of justification by faith. Abram was among the first of God's servants to acknowledge the truth: "The just shall live by faith." (cf. Hab. 2:4, Rom. 1:17; Gal. 3:11).

It is evident that Abram's concern that Eliezer, his steward, would become his heir if there were no natural born children is specifically in accord with the customs of the time. Finds of some thousands of clay tablets at the city of Nuzi, the capital city of the Horites during the second millennium B.C., have made clear that if there were no natural son, an adopted son would be given all of the status and rights normally reserved for the former. Adult adoption was commonly practised, so that in an instance such as Abram's, his adult steward might come to hold all of the legal rights and privileges of an actual son.

In order to confirm the covenant, and to reveal something of the future, God made use of certain sacrifices. The five creatures offered spoke in various ways of Christ: heifer-- fruitfulness and faithful work; she-goat--sacrifice for sins; ram--meek surrender; turtle dove--sorrow and love; pigeon--life of faith on earth. In Oriental symbolism, the pieces of the divided animals represented the covenanting parties and the act of passing between them implied the establishment of unity. The unity was made the more impressive by virtue of the bond of common blood. In this instance it was the smoking furnace and the burning lamp that passed between the pieces, and Abram was only a passive spectator. It has been suggested that these objects represented the first and second persons of the Godhead who were covenanting together to fulfill the divine promise to Abram. Thus, a covenant was being made between equals. This process of covenant by a

divided sacrifice is found also in Jeremiah 34:18, 19, and the effect there also is the expression of a sealing.

It is held by some that the smoking furnace and the burning lamp (or lamp of fire) speak respectively of Israel in their various periods of affliction, and God in His intervention and relief. Both directly, and by type, Abram was given some measure of insight into the tragic future of his people. The "horror of great darkness" (v. 12) that fell upon Abram was probably associated with his prophetic insight into the events of the future. The fowls of prey that attacked the carcasses would be symbols of the forces of evil that are always ready to prey upon the elements of sacrifice. It is pointed out that the covenant at this time specified "the river of Egypt" as a boundary of the promised land. Since Egypt itself was never part of God's covenant to Abram, the river of Egypt is thought not to be the Nile, which is the central life stream of the land and not truly a boundary, but rather the "brook of Egypt" (nahal Mitzraim) which later became a southern boundary of Palestine. (cf. 1 Ki. 8:65). The brook of Egypt is actually a gully or wadi that contains water only during the rainy season. Its Arab name is Wadi el 'Arish.

5. The Birth of Ishmael (Ch. 16)

When Sarai found herself to be 76 and without children, she proceeded to give to Abram as wife, Hagar, her Egyptian handmaid. Although Christian ethics would permit no such arrangement, in the society in which marriage was understood to be for the purpose of bearing children rather than for companionship, such a procedure was not uncommon. The law of that day permitted such an act, and custom sanctioned it, for the Code of Hammurabi approvingly describes such a case. Tablets attributed to Hurrian (i.e. Horite) scribes includes marriage contracts that prescribe that in the case of a childless marriage the wife was obliged to provide her husband with a handmaid who would bear children.

The pending birth of Ishmael occasioned considerable jealousy between Sarai and Hagar, and thus in the typical phrase of the time, Sarai appealed to Abram for legal protection: "My wrong be upon thee," or more literally: "My wrong is your responsibility." With Abram's permission, Sarai proceeded to make the lot of the handmaiden so intolerable that she fled from her mistress. In her flight she was met by the "angel of the Lord" (who is here mentioned for the first time in Scripture), and granted comfort and a cheering promise. It is evident that God was concerned for Hagar because He was concerned for all of Abram's household. The angel requested Hagar to return to her mistress and left the handmaid so impressed that she was moved to worship Jehovah (v. 13). God's promise to Hagar concerning the nature of her descendants has been literally fulfilled in the Bedouins. These people are to this day desert dwellers who despise any form of town life, and who live in a constant state of feud with neighboring tribes. Hagar returned to Sarai, but thereafter the family relationships between the two women remained somewhat strained.

At the time of Ishmael's birth, Abram was 86 years old. The name "Ishmael" means "asked of God." Although Abram had faith to ask, he appears not to have had faith to believe that by supernatural means God would fulfill his request. In the ultimate outcome, the birth of Ishmael hindered rather than helped the unfolding fulfillment of the promises of God.

6. The Renewal of the Covenant, Circumcision Instituted (Ch. 17)

The lack of faith, and the natural impetuousness associated with the birth of Ishmael, resulted in a thirteen year lapse in divine dealings with Abram. Abram was now 99 and Sarai was 89, so that in the natural all hope of their becoming parents was utterly gone. Because the birth of a promised son was to be a specific divine visitation, it would appear that God chose in the lives of Abram and Sarai to exhaust utterly all hope in human resources before He proceeded to display His power. As so frequently occurs, man's extremity became God's opportunity.

The divine appearance at this time was especially reassuring and encouraging. For the first time, God revealed Himself as the El-Shaddai ("Almighty God"- A.V.) which means literally "the breasted one" and under the analogy of the female breast implies that He is the Nourisher, Strength-Giver, and One who Satisfies. On this occasion the name Abram (exalted father) was changed to Abraham (father of multitudes), and the name Sarai (either "my princess" or "the contentious") was changed to Sarah (princess [of all the race]). Marcus Dods makes the point that the significance of these name changes was not to be found so much in their meanings, as in the fact that at this time Abraham and Sarah acquired names of religious or spiritual origin and association.

God herewith instituted circumcision as the seal of the covenant. There is some evidence that circumcision already existed as a custom, but on this occasion it was given new significance. Previously, in the establishment of the Abrahamic Covenant, Abraham had been merely a spectator, but now he was required to perform a tangible act that required his own blood to flow. The performance of the act of circumcision raised Abraham to the dignity of a covenanter with Almighty God. Notwithstanding, even for the Old Testament believer, circumcision involved more than merely a physical act. Had circumcision alone been sufficient, Ishmael would have qualified. It is evident that from the very outset, implicit in the physical act of circumcision was the accompanying inner cutting off of self and carnality. St. Paul rightly interpreted God's intention when he wrote " . . . he is a Jew, which is one inwardly; and circumcision is that of the heart, in the spirit, and not in the letter; . . ." (Rom. 2:29).

God once more assured Abraham that Sarah was to bear a son. Abraham's reaction to God's promise is reported in v. 17, Then Abraham fell upon his face and laughed . . ." Though the immediate context might indicate that this was the laughter of unbelief, Romans 4:18 and Isaiah 41:8 indicate that it was the laughter of anticipation. In simple sheer delight of heart and soul in contemplation of the wonder of a son to call his own, Abraham reacted with the sincerity and simplicity of everyday hearty laughter.

7. The Entertainment of Heavenly Beings (Ch. 18)

In reporting this event Scripture says, "And the Lord appeared unto . . . [Abraham] and, lo, three men stood by him: . . ." The fact that there were three suggests the trinity, though most commentators take the view that only one was deity and that the other two were angels. Deane says, " . . . we shall not err in seeing herein a Theophany, a manifestation of the Logos, a revelation of the Second Person of the Holy Trinity, who appeared, as He did after

His resurrection, with two attendant angels."[21]
Regardless of the exact identity of the visitors,
Abraham did his best to entertain them as lav-
ishly as he was able. It is evident that Abraham
exemplified the truth of the New Testament: "Be
not forgetful to entertain strangers, for thereby
some have entertained angels unawares" (Heb.
13:2). Traditionally, scholars have debated
whether heavenly beings would really eat physical food, but Scripture plainly says they did.
(18:8).

The first mission of the heavenly visitors was the confirmation to Abraham of the
certainty of the imminent birth of a son. Sarah
overheard the conversation, and in view of
what seemed to her the ludicrousness of the
situation, she was moved to inward laughter.
It is usually considered that whereas Abram
laughed in anticipation, Sarah laughed in skeptical unbelief. In response to Sarah, the Lord
uttered the classic promise, "Is any thing too
hard for the Lord?" (v.14).

The second mission of the visitors was
the announcement of the proposed destruction
of the sinfully degenerate cities of Sodom and
Gomorrah. God could no longer remain indifferent to such a flagrant disregard of His
righteous nature. It is interesting to note that
Scripture reports the divine soliloquy whether
or not to reveal the future to Abraham. (18:17-
19). The news of the impending destruction left
Abraham spiritually burdened and led to his
fervent intercession that they might be spared.
Abraham based his prayer upon the principle
"Shall not the judge of all the earth do right?
(v. 25). Our Lord's parable of the unjust
judge (Lk. 18:1) applied the principle of per-
sistence in prayer here demonstrated by Abraham. At the request of the patriarch, God
agreed to spare the cities for even ten righteous
people. A tragic outcome was that not even ten
could be found, and thus the destruction of the
cities proceeded on schedule. Abraham discovered that God ceases to give only when
suppliants cease to ask. Scripture expressly
notes that it was God's concern for His promise that led to the events of the next chapter:
". . . God remembered Abraham, and sent
Lot out of the midst . . ." (19:29).

---

[21]William J. Deane, Abraham, His
Life and Times. New York: Fleming H.
Revell Co., p. 104.

8. The Destruction of Sodom and Gomorrah (Ch. 19)

It is possible that Lot's heavenly visitors were the same who had been the Lord's
attendants when He visited Abraham. They came
to warn Lot to flee before the coming destruction
that was to befall the city. Lot was found seated
in the gate of Sodom thus indicating that he was
at the place of meeting of the town leaders. Customarily, ancient city gates provided stone
benches where people might gather to exchange
views, to trade and bargain, and to meet socially.
It was often the location for performing legal
transactions and was a convenient place from
which proclamations might be made. The fact
that Lot was found there is an indication of his
interest in the affairs of the city.

Abraham had only a tent, but Lot is
found to have had a house in the city of Sodom.
Scripture describes Lot's hospitality as providing only "bread," and thus it contrasts with
the meal prepared by Abraham, although "bread"
may be understood to be a general term implying a complete meal. Certainly the obnoxious
conduct of the perverted Sodomites who attempted to assault Lot's guests sadly marred
the visit. The characteristic sin of the people
of Sodom (homosexuality) is to this day frequently known as "sodomy" and the term is
widely used in English-language laws. Lot offered his daughters to his rapacious townspeople
because evidently he valued the virtue and wel-
fare of his guests above that of his own daughters. However, his intended heroic gesture
was rendered unnecessary by the miraculous
power of his heavenly guests. Such a rude and
violent "culture" undoubtedly called for heavy
doors on one's dwelling, and archaeology confirms that characteristically at Sodom this was
so.

In spite of the angels' warning, Lot and
his wife and two daughters so delayed their
flight that the angels found it necessary to lay
hands upon them and virtually drag them forth
from the city. They left behind the young men
described as "sons in law" who probably were
merely betrothed to the daughters, since the
latter were still living in their father's house.
Eventually Lot and his daughters made their way
to refuge in a cave, but Lot's wife was transformed into a mound of salt because she insisted
on looking back upon the burning city. Perhaps
her looking backward actually took her backward
too, and she was found too close to the place of

judgment. Our Lord used Lot's wife as an il-
lustration of one who allowed earthly interests
to hamper flight in time of judgment. (cf. "Remember Lot's wife" [Lk. 17:32]). It is probable that Lot's wife perished and was entombed
in a manner similar to that which was suffered
by the victims in the celebrated destruction of
Pompeii in 79 A.D.

The exact location of Sodom and Gomorrah is unknown, although it is conjectured that
the two cities were in the vicinity of the Dead
Sea. It has been suggested that since there were
five principal cities of the plain, and there happen to be five streams feeding the Dead Sea at
the southern end, it would be plausible to hold

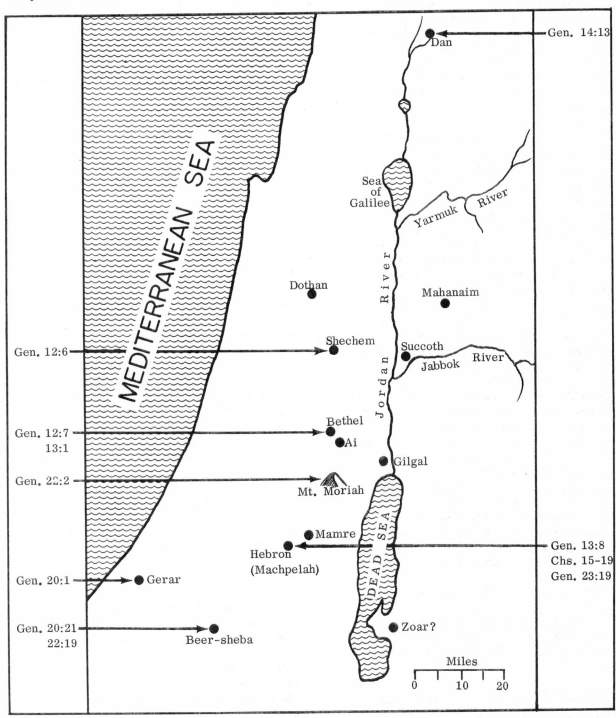

Figure 4 -- Scenes From the Life of Abraham

that each city would have been built on an individual stream. A popular theory suggests that these cities were located in the region that is now the southern part of the Dead Sea and that in their destruction they sank and were buried by the sea. Finegan says: "A careful survey of the literary, geographical and archaeological evidence points to the conclusion that the infamous "cities of the valley" . . . were in the area that is now submerged beneath the slowly rising waters of the southern part of the Dead Sea . . ."[22]   Other authorities are much less confident than Finegan in this matter, and its final determination awaits future insights.

The destruction of the cities by fire and brimstone (sulphur) from heaven remarkedly suggests a bombing raid in modern warfare. To this day the Plain of Sodom is strewn with tarry asphalt and sulphur. Even the stones in this region that might be used as building materials will burn once they are properly kindled. Lot and his daughters at first took refuge in the village of Zoar (which means "a trifle"), but apparently the threat of further destruction led them to proceed by themselves to the solitary heights of the mountain.

Lot's history ends in shame, for we find him committing incest with his two daughters. The children born of this relationship were Moab and Ben-ammi, whose descendants (the Moabites and Ammonites) frequently caused Israel to suffer in her later history. Though according to 2 Pet. 2:8, in his relationship with the people of Sodom, Lot "vexed his righteous soul from day to day with their unlawful deeds"; yet his persistent presence at the gate of Sodom led to his downfall. Mackintosh contrasts Lot at Sodom with Abraham, the pilgrim, and says, "The tent of the stranger of Mamre was in no danger, though Sodom were in flames." Grant says of Lot, "his death is unrecorded: he had died before."

9. Abraham and Sarah in Gerar (Ch. 20)

After he had resided fifteen years in Mamre, Abraham once more manifested a lapse of faith and departed from the land of

promise. This time he proceeded to Philistia. Someone has commented "Why Abraham should twice lapse by going to a foreign country would be a mystery if we did not know our own heart and history." In Philistia, Abraham once more denied his wife on the basis of the half-truth that she was his sister. History indicates that, in general, the Philistines did not colonize Palestine until much later than the era of Abraham. Thus, Egyptian monuments of the 12th century tell of the repulsion of Philistines from mainland Egypt in fierce sea battles and the settlement of the defeated nation in Palestine. In Abraham's time the chief home of the Philistines was the island of Crete in the Mediterranean; however there is no major problem in considering that at least some colonies were already in Palestine. They were evidently a numerous people and it is well possible that the island of Crete was already beginning to prove inadequate for their population.

It is remarkable that once again, God permitted Abraham to profit by his deceit. The divine moving on Abimelech's heart was such that he gave freely of his riches to Abraham. Upon Abraham's household was granted the first recorded manifestation of the power of divine healing. God described Abraham to Abimelech as a prophet, and thereby for the first time the term occurs in the Bible. The Lord implied that to Abimelech this man was the divine channel for the communication of truth. The name Abimelech is actually an official title which means "Father King" and it applied to several rulers of Philistia. It is noteworthy that this Abimelech was a man of integrity whose behaviour stands as impressively commendable.

10. The Birth of Isaac. The Jealousy of Ishmael (Ch. 21)

Abraham returned from Gerar and dwelt in Beer-sheba and it was probably there that his son was born. Abraham was then in his 100th year and Sarah was 90. The birth of a child, so uniquely apart from the normal course of nature, is typical of the birth of Jesus. Sarah who had previously laughed in unbelief, now laughed in joy and in satisfied delight. God appropriately commanded that the child be named "Isaac" (laughter). At last Abraham had a true heir and as Mackintosh comments, "it was not Ishmael changed, but it was Isaac born." It is probable that Isaac was the first child born who was ceremoniously circumcised on the eighth day.

The rivalry between Ishmael and Isaac came to a climax at the celebration marking Isaac's weaning. In Eastern fashion, Isaac would be from three to five years old at this time. While others celebrated, Ishmael cruelly mocked. The family feud was thus precipitated once more, and inevitably a separation was demanded so that the expulsion of Hagar and Ishmael became necessary. In the providence of God, Ishmael was spared to become the father of an abundant people and thus an important branch of the Arab tribes found its origin.

Though Hagar and Ishmael were given few provisions and seemingly were cruelly treated, such a procedure was not without warrant. As Henry Ward Beecher once commented, "To go forth into the wilderness in that day was not so hard a thing. She went forth from no house, from no luxuries, simply from a tent. She went forth from nothing to nothing." It is well possible that southern Palestine was a much more hospitable region in those times than it is today. Archaeologist Nelson Glueck has reported that the Negev, now a region of desolation and seering heat, was once the home of flourishing civilizations. He has found remains of elaborate systems of water conservation and irrigation and evidence of populated villages and towns. It is to be noted that by this time, Ishmael was no mere helpless child but probably was actually a boy in his early teens, and thus, able to assist his mother in providing family support.

In Gal. 4:24, St. Paul refers to the events of this chapter as an allegory (i.e. as a figurative account). Hagar represents the law: She was in bondage to her mistress just as all under the Law are in bondage, and she was cast out just as the Law has been displaced. Ishmael represents the flesh: He was born in the ordinary course of nature just as any spiritual life under the Law is mere good works, and he was opposed to Isaac as the flesh is opposed to the spirit. Sarah represents the covenant of grace: She was free and the one born of her was also free. Isaac represents the spiritual nature: He was born supernaturally just as the believer is born from above. He endured opposition from Ishmael just as "the flesh lusteth against the spirit." He was true heir even as believers are joint-heirs with Christ.

As they saw God's gracious dealings with Abraham, the Philistines prudently extended a covenant of friendship. Abraham gladly agreed to such a covenant, although he made it the opportunity to redeem for himself the well at Beersheba that he had dug. The name Beer-sheba means "well of the seven" or "well of the oath," and is so called because Abimelech pledged to Abraham the perpetual use of this well on the basis of a redemption payment of seven ewe lambs.

11. The Testing of Abraham (Ch. 22)

Though carnal believers may constantly be tempted by the world, Abraham had reached the stage in spiritual growth where he was tempted (actually "tested" or "proved") by God. Inasmuch as Abraham's contemporaries sacrificed their children to idols, there was a sense in which this test was to determine whether Abraham loved God as much as the heathen loved their idols. It was not really the sacrifice of Isaac that God wanted, but the surrender of Abraham's will. Comments Deane:

> Abraham longed impartially to see the day of Christ, i.e. the redemption He was to effect, the sacrifice He was to pay. And he saw it, he saw it in representation. Nowhere else in all his history could he behold with his eyes the doctrine of redemption . . . To instruct Abraham in this great doctrine, and to teach him the boundless extent of God's goodness toward men, God made him act this picture, and himself feel what it was to lose a beloved son.[23]

Abraham seems never to have wavered throughout the test, but he "rose up early in the morning" and hastened to effect the will of God. Abraham's words to his servant, "I and the lad will go yonder and worship and come again to you" indicate genuine faith. Hebrews 11:9 says, "Accounting that God was able to raise him [Isaac] up, even from the dead; from whence also he received him in a figure." Mackintosh has written, "Take away faith, and Abraham appears on Moriah as a murderer and a madman: take faith into account, and he appears as a devoted worshipper--a God-fearing justified man."[24]

---

[23]Deane, op. cit., p. 140

[24]Mackintosh, op. cit. p. 233

The Judean Wilderness in the region of the Dead Sea is dry, barren, and exceedingly rough in topography. Whereas this portion is west of the Dead Sea, it is not unlike the areas of Lot's residence and similar to the territory of Hagar's flight.

God provided the ram as a substitute for Isaac. As it were, Abraham had sacrificed his son, though he had not slain him. Abraham revealed that, even though he knew that Isaac was the fulfillment of God's promise, he was willing to forego the promise in the face of the challenge to offer him up to God. Undoubtedly his willingness to perform such a sacrifice was particularly the external act that made certain the fulfillment of the promise to him. It is noteworthy that at this time Isaac was a mature adult and his submission and cooperation were necessary if Abraham were to carry out his plan. In the following aspects it may be considered that Isaac was a type of Christ:

Isaac	Christ
Only true son	Only begotten Son
Allowed himself to be bound	Permitted all the atrocities of Calvary
Obedient and truly submissive	"Obedient unto death" Phil. 2:8
Had complete confidence in his father	"Father, into thy hands I commend my spirit" Lk. 23:46
Rose again from the altar	Resurrected from the dead

Abraham named the site of this incident "Jehovah-Jireh" which means "the Lord will provide." The same location, being Mount Moriah, later became the site of Solomon's Temple and the altar of sacrifice.

12. The Death of Sarah (Ch. 23)

Sarah's death occurred at Kirjath-arba in Hebron when she was 127 years of age. It is of interest to note that Sarah is the only woman whose age is reported in Scripture. Since Abraham lived to be 175, he survived his wife by some 38 years. The report that Abraham mourned and wept (v. 2), is the first such account in Scripture. So also is the mention of a burying place. (v. 20).

In order to lay to rest the body of Sarah, Abraham was obliged to secure possession of a suitable piece of land. By divine promise, he had been assigned the entire land of Palestine, and yet to this point, he possessed none of it. Thus, he undertook to purchase the cave of the field of Machpelah from Ephron the Hittite. Archaeologists report that the involved process of bargaining such as Scripture here describes was exactly typical of real estate transactions according to ancient Hittite law and custom. The 400 shekels that Abraham gave to Ephron the Hittite in the presence of the sons of Heth, is equivalent to about $260.00 although 6 to 8 shekels a year was the average salary of a working man. It is to be noted that the money was weighed (v.16), for evidently coinage was not yet established. At this time a shekel was a unit of weight rather than a coin of a specific value. Because Abraham insisted that Ephron receive the money, he was assured the undisputed, legal title to the property.

The cave of Machpelah, which was the sole portion of Palestine that Abraham possessed in his lifetime, became in succession a burial place of: Sarah, Abraham, Isaac, Rebekah, Jacob, and Leah. This cave is now covered by the Turkish Mosque, Haret el-Haram, and thus is a Mohammedan shrine.

13. The Bride for Isaac (Ch. 24)

According to the customs of the day, the project of securing a bride for Isaac was the basic responsibility of his father Abraham. Thus, in a dramatic and impressive manner, Abraham commissioned his servant (probably Eliezer) to represent him in securing a suitable candidate.

The procedure of requiring a servant to place his hand under his thigh signified that the oath was being established both for the contracting parties and also for their posterity. If the oath were broken, even though the covenanters may not be able to achieve compensation, their children were expected to do so. The custom was sometimes described as "swearing by posterity." The servant's journey was providentially guided, and in Nahor of Mesopotamia he met and promptly selected the beautiful Rebekah. Since Rebekah was actually the second cousin of Isaac, she easily qualified to be counted within the family line, and yet she was far enough removed that according to the customs of those times she was not disqualified by reason of consanguinity. After only a day's delay the maiden consented to go with the servant and become the bride of Isaac. In course of time the journey was completed; there was a sentimentally appealing meeting between Rebekah and Isaac "and she became his wife and he loved her."

Although the choice of a bride for Isaac is not a Biblical type, it has traditionally been interpreted as being rich in spiritual lessons. Abraham in this story represents God the Father who desires a bride for his son. Isaac represents the Lord Jesus Christ who is now in the heavenlies and will remain there until His bride (the Church) is brought unto Him. The servant illustrates the ministry of the Holy Spirit, who carefully selects and wins the bride and then carefully guides them through this world to bring them safely home. The Holy Spirit, just as the servant, ministers to exalt the Father who sent Him and the Son on whose behalf He has come. Rebekah represents the believer who loves without seeing, is given rich clothing, (cf. garments of His righteousness), and who goes willingly.

14. Abraham's Marriage to Keturah. His Death (Ch. 25:1-11)

Abraham's marriage to Keturah and the subsequent birth of six sons would seem to indicate that his youth was divinely renewed. It is possible that the rejuvenation associated with the birth of Isaac was a permanent gift to Abraham. Another possibility is that Abraham had married Keturah in his early life and only at this place is the fact reported. This latter view is strengthened by the fact that 1 Chron. 1:32 calls Keturah a concubine. Abraham's latter-day marriage to Keturah has been seen by some scholars of typology to represent God's end-time dealing with the Jews.

When Abraham was 175 years old, he died and was buried with Sarah in the cave of Machpelah. Thus ended the earthly pilgrimage of an outstanding saint of God and the only Old Testament believer designated by God as "my friend" (Isa. 41:8). The importance of the life of Abraham is indicated by the fact that its record extends through some 13 chapters of the book of Genesis. At the time of Abraham's death, Isaac was 75 and Jacob and Esau were youths of 15. The name Abraham is held sacred by the Arabian, the Persian, the Jew, the Christian, and the Mohammedan.

There is a sense in which Christian believers today look to Abraham as their spiritual father. "Know ye therefore that they which are of faith, the same are the children of Abraham" (Gal. 3:7). It is often believed that the "star-seed" of Abraham represents Christian believers; while the "sand-seed" represents the natural descendants who are God's covenant people. (cf. Gen. 13:16, 15:5, 22:17). St. Paul named Abraham as an example of a man of faith who practiced the way of faith. "Abraham believed God, and it was counted unto him for righteousness" (Rom. 4:3).

15. Ishmael, the Son of Abraham (Ch. 25:12-18)

The genealogy of Ishmael completes the story of Abraham and serves as a witness that the promises of God which were made to Ishmael (Gen. 16:10, 17:20) were wholly fulfilled. It is generally held that the Ishmaelites are the forebearers of today's desert Bedouin.

TWO: The Book of Genesis -- Part 2

The portion of the first twenty-five chapters of Genesis considered thus far set forth the stories of Adam, Noah and Abraham. The balance of this book further proceeds in reporting the narrowing of the divine choice leading to the story of Isaac, Jacob and Joseph.

I. THE STORY OF ISAAC (Chs. 25:19 - 27:46)

1. The Birth and Early History of Isaac's Sons (25:19-34)

Isaac and Rebekah had been married for twenty years before the birth of their sons, and had the Lord not answered their prayers, they might have continued childless. Although Esau and Jacob were twins, Esau was the first-born. The two infants differed markedly in appearance, and as they grew, it became apparent that their temperament and character too were vastly different. The name "Jacob," given the younger child, evidently was an ordinary name of that time, for it is mentioned in an inscription found in Upper Mesopotamia and dated approximately in the 18th century B.C.

Before the boys were born, God had promised Rebekah: "The elder shall serve the younger" (25:23). In Genesis we have the life of each of the sons portrayed: Jacob zealous for spiritual achievements and sincerely anxious to be faithful to God in spite of his natural tendencies otherwise; Esau so spiritually indifferent as to sell his birthright, marry Hittites, and plot his brother's death. Hence, in the next reference to Esau, Scripture states, ". . . I loved Jacob, and hated Esau" (Mal. 1:3). In Rom. 9:13, this passage is paraphrased: "Jacob have I loved, but Esau have I hated." On the basis of these Scriptures, those who do not care to commit themselves to an unqualified doctrine of election consider that at first the Lord's distinction between the brothers was merely a choice, and that it was only after Esau had lived his spiritually impoverished life that God adopted an attitude of hatred toward him.

The incident of the purchase of the birthright by Jacob with a serving of pottage (red bean soup) occurred at a time when the sons had become young men. The birthright in this particular case included: 1) the father's blessing, 2) a double portion of the father's property, 3) becoming the family head, 4) being the family priest, 5) being in the line of the Savior, 6) inheriting the title-deed of Canaan, and 7) being patriarch of a great nation. Esau's careless sale of the birthright for a few cents worth of food is typical of the behavior of those who forego spiritual blessings for the sake of a passing sensual gratification. Such incidents were not without their precedent in ancient times, for the Nuzi Tablets include the story of a man named Tupkitilla who gave over to his brothers his inheritance of an orchard in exchange for three sheep.

2. The Abrahamic Covenant Renewed. Isaac's Spiritual Lapse (Ch. 26)

It was in a time of seeming adversity that God appeared to Isaac and confirmed to him the Abrahamic Covenant. Famine had befallen the land, and Isaac was found in the land of the Philistines just as his father had been in an earlier era. God promised to bless and prosper Isaac, but He strictly enjoined him not to depart into Egypt. It is apparent that on this occasion, God did not oppose Isaac's residence in Philistia, even though in general, it would have seemed to have been God's plan that His chosen people remain separate and in their own land. In Philistia, Isaac followed the precedent of his father and likewise denied his wife. And just as certainly, Isaac's deceit was found out, although the forgiving Abimelech imposed no penalty. Instead, Isaac was given his freedom in the land with the explicit proclamation of Abimelech to assure his protection. Isaac enjoyed such phenomenal success as a farmer in Philistia that his wealth eventually incurred the jealousy of the native Philistines so that they requested his departure.

The well-digging episode illustrated Isaac's fundamental characteristics of meekness, patience, and forbearing endurance. In general, these qualities stood Isaac in good stead, although there may be some hint that they resulted in a

certain mediocrity in his character. Isaac's
recorded achievements are inferior to those
of either his father or his son, and in fact this
is the only chapter of the Bible entirely devoted
to him. In dealing with the Philistines in the
contest over the wells, he simply retreated
from Esek (the place of strife), and Sitnah (the
place of hatred), and took up his abode at Re-
hoboth (the place of room). In these actions,
Isaac stands as a type of the devout Christian
believer calmly adjusting to the enemies'
efforts to deprive him of those sources that
keep faith alive, and thereby pressing on to an
even more vital revelation of God. Thus, at
Beer-sheba following the well digging experiences, Isaac was granted a very special revelation of God. Isaac's act of renaming the site
of Beer-sheba (v. 33) with the same name that
it already had was common practice in ancient
societies, and it simply constituted a personal
recognition and identity with the particular
name of the site.

Esau's marriage to the Hittite maidens
was a further manifestation of this young man's
carelessness in spiritual matters. Characteristically, alien wives would persist in their
national pagan religions and inevitably influence
their husbands, and more especially their children, in the practice of paganism.

3. The Stolen Blessing (Ch. 27)

It is difficult to know why Jacob stooped
to petty deceit in order to obtain the blessing,
for he had previously gone to some trouble to
purchase it and make it legally his. However,
Isaac's dulled senses, both in the natural and
spiritually, invited just such a deception. God
apparently permitted the scheme to succeed because the outcome was His will. Inasmuch as
the four individuals involved were each acting
from a wrong spirit and in disregard of the
highest ethical standards, it is the more remarkable that the will of God was done. The
"savoury meat" that Isaac desired was simply
meat that had been seasoned or spiced.

The blessing upon Jacob was not
lengthy in extent (it is stated in vv. 28 and 29)
but it was vitally significant in establishing the
fact that Jacob was to be considered the elder
son and thereby he was to assume the blessings
of the first born of the chosen line. Those
things that Isaac promised to Jacob have been
summarized as follows: 1) Prosperity [v. 28],

2) Prestige [v. 29], 3) Patriarchal succession
[v. 29], and 4) Protection [v. 29]. Jacob framed
the blessing in poetic form. The procedure in
thus basing so important an issue upon a verbal
pronouncement conforms to practices of the day.
The Nuzi Tablets record an occasion in which a
father upon his death bed bestowed a certain
wife upon a younger son. When the older brother
contested the marriage, the report of the sick-
bed blessing was sustained in court and the
younger brother was awarded his bride.

In this Bible account, there does not
seem any legitimate justification for the actions
of Rebekah and Jacob. Even though Jacob had
legitimately purchased the blessing, and though
God's promise had made clear that Jacob was
to enjoy the blessings of primogeniture, the
principle still remained that there had been no
justification of fraudulent behavior as a means
of bringing about the will of God. Such procedures inevitably must result in suffering and
punishment. In the case of Jacob and Rebekah,
the devoted mother and son were immediately
separated, and for what proved to be the next
two decades Jacob was destined to remain in
Padan-Aram. As far as is known from Scripture Jacob and Rebekah never saw one another
again.

It is evident that Isaac had misjudged
the prospects of his death. One chronology
has determined that he would be 137 at this
time and that he lived an additional 43 years.
However, Isaac is not again mentioned in Scripture except on the occasion of his death (35:27-
29).

II. THE STORY OF JACOB (Chs. 28-36)

1. Jacob at Bethel (Ch. 28)

The flight from Esau gained a new incentive when Jacob was commissioned by his parents to find himself a wife in Padan-aram.
Jacob's journey was indeed a memorable one.
At Bethel he experienced his first recorded
divine revelation in the remarkable vision of
the ladder and the ascending and descending
angels. The Lord, who stood above the ladder,
confirmed to Jacob the promises made to Abraham and divinely assured him that he had been
granted the birthright and established as a
member of the chosen line. Apparently the
angels ascending and descending represent the
interrelationship between earth and heaven.

The New Testament describes angels as "ministering spirits, sent forth to minister for them who shall be heirs of salvation" (Heb. 1:14). They serve as messengers to link heaven and earth and bring closer together the activities of each sphere.

Though Jacob's ladder formed only a temporary bridge between earth and heaven (whereas Christ has forever bridged the gap for us), his vision was sufficient to move him to a new consecration. God's promises had been unconditional but Jacob, when he awakened, undertook to add his pledge to the fruitfulness of God. Jacob proceeded to erect a pillar (massebah) as a memorial of the occasion, and he used this pillar as an altar upon which he poured out oil and confirmed his dedication to God. In later times his pillar became associated with debauched pagan worship and such devices were condemned by God's prophets (cf. Hosea 10:2). Included in Jacob's covenant on this occasion was his promise to return to God one-tenth of all that he should be given. This proportion of a tithe (the word tithe means tenth) serves as a model for minimum Christian giving.

2. Jacob at Haran (Ch. 29)

Haran was a portion of the district of Padan-aram, which, in turn, constituted the northern part of Mesopotamia. Jacob's experiences in this place were no doubt permitted and directed of God in order that he might gain vital experience and maturity. The maiden, Rachel, must have been very young when Jacob met her, for in oriental society, it was customary for girls older than twelve to be kept in seclusion. Notwithstanding, her charms were such that Jacob promptly fell in love with her. So far as is known, it was not the custom in those times to require a husband to buy his wife, but apparently Laban's greediness was responsible for the particular bargain that was imposed upon Jacob. On the basis of practices revealed by the Nuzi Tablets in this era it is likely that the negotiations resulted in Laban's actually adopting Jacob as his son rather than counting him merely as a son-in-law. Such an arrangement would better explain some of the later events according to the customs of the time.

Jacob's seven years of service seemed "but a few days, for the love he had to . . .

Rachel" (v. 20). Someone has commented "No man could be a bad man who loved as Jacob loved Rachel." When Laban substituted brides, Jacob's protests were necessarily mild, for he was only reaping the same kind of deception he had practised upon his own father. He here discovered that others beside himself could drive hard bargains, and thus he meekly launched upon another seven years of service. This episode of the exchange of Jacob's bride has been called "The Hebrew Comedy of Errors."

This chapter records the birth to Jacob and Leah of four sons: Reuben, Simeon, Levi, and Judah. Thus, the first four of the twelve tribes of Israel came into being. The choice of Judah as the chosen tribe was obviously based upon some other principle than priority of birth. In each case the sons seem to have been named by their mother, and the name given was of significance in describing Leah's attitudes and hopes toward her husband at the time of their birth.

3. Jacob's Family and Flocks in Haran (Ch. 30)

The seven additional sons and one daughter reported in this chapter completed the number of Jacob's children born in Padan-aram. The birth of Joseph to Rachel was an especially noteworthy event. The incident involving the mandrakes (vvs. 14-16) would seem to reveal a popular superstition (which appears to be without foundation in fact) that this plant would promote the sex drive. The mandrake, which is also called the mandragora or May apple, is a plant with dark green leaves and a fruit like a small apple.

When the fourteen years of service for his wives was completed, Jacob made a new agreement with Laban whereby he was to work for wages consisting of livestock. At the outset, Jacob was to be given animals that were spotted, speckled, or ringstraked (marked with circular bands of color). Since eastern sheep are usually all white and goats are all black, Jacob stood to be at a disadvantage. However, the arrangement (and all those subsequently adopted) worked remarkably in Jacob's favor, and in spite of Laban's scheming, Jacob's possessions increased rapidly. Undoubtedly the real reason for Jacob's prosperity was the intervention and provision of God on his behalf. However, humanly speaking it is interesting to note that geneticists have determined that the

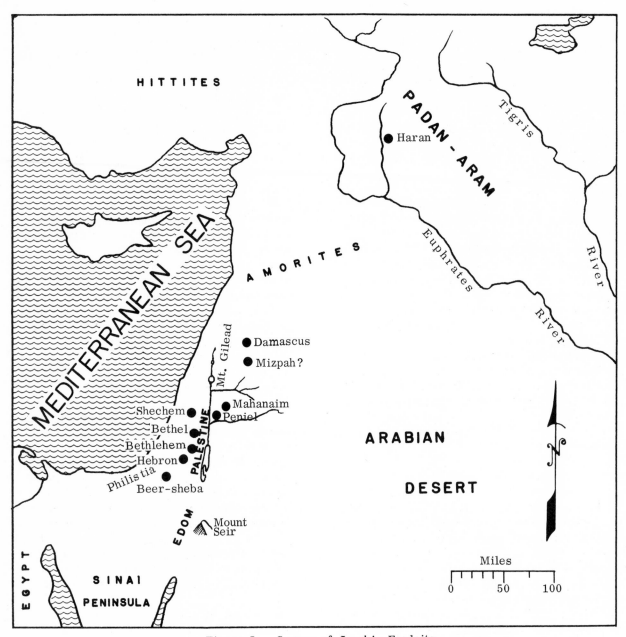

Figure 5 -- Scenes of Jacob's Exploits

spotting of goats is a recessive tendency that will be dominated by the tendency to solid color. Thus, goats of one color through many generations may carry the tendency to spot and when appropriately mated produce spotted off-spring apparently without reason.

It is generally agreed that in the natural course of events, Jacob's efforts to influence the markings of unborn cattle would be of no effect. Laban was too shrewd and experienced in animal husbandry to have risked his wealth on outcomes so readily influenced. Jacob's

efforts succeeded only because the Lord inter-vened and supernaturally directed the outcome. Says Calvin in commenting upon this incident, "He [God] purposed to connect His grace with the labor and diligence of Jacob." Of course, the selective breeding practised by Jacob in assuring that his stock were strong and healthy was quite in keeping with successful stock rais-ing in any age. The word "pilled" which occurs in this episode is an old form of "peeled." The fact that Scripture records Jacob's superstitious ventures in prenatal influence does not thereby sanction their truth or validity.

4. Jacob's Flight. The Farewell at Mizpah
   (Ch. 31)

Jacob was finally influenced to be willing to leave Padan-aram by: the obviously increasing jealousy of Laban and his sons, the command of God (the first recorded revelation to Jacob in his twenty years in Padan-aram [v. 13]), and the consent and approval of his wives. It was somewhat typical of Jacob's character that he should choose to leave secretly.

The images taken by Rachel were teraphim which were statuettes of the human form to which were attached some religious significance. Frequently they were used for divination (telling the future or revealing otherwise unavailable information). Manley cites Kenyon: "An ancient Hurrian tablet says that possession of a father-in-law's household gods gave a son-in-law title to be regarded as his legitimate heir, which explains the motive of Rachel's theft of the images."[1] However, it is not recorded in Scripture that Jacob ever attempted to make such use of these images, and, in fact, it is never clearly stated that he ever learned of Rachel's theft. In view of all of Rachel's virtues it seems strange that she had no misgivings about deceiving her father, but at least none are recorded and perhaps the fact that she was indeed her father's daughter is here emphasized.

Not until the third day did Laban become aware of the departure of his family. Thus, when he overtook the fugitives they had already arrived at Mt. Gilead, but owing to Rachel's subtlety, his pursuit and search yielded no incriminating evidence. God warned Laban to be kindly in his treatment of Jacob so that this meeting simply constituted a cordial farewell. Jacob and Laban erected a memorial cairn to mark the place of their separation, and they departed with the Mizpah blessing: "The Lord watch between thee and me when we are absent one from another." It is evident that this blessing was an agreement that neither party should molest the other and that they would maintain a peaceful separation. The procedure of eating together seated upon a heap of stones was an Oriental method of ratifying a covenant.

5. Jacob at Peniel (Ch. 32)

God's pleasure at Jacob's return to the land seems to be indicated by the fact that there were angels to welcome the pilgrim. The name "Mahanaim" means "double camp" and indicated that Jacob recognized that the camp of angels united with his own at that place.

Although twenty years had elapsed, and in spite of divine reassurance, the prospect of once more meeting Esau caused Jacob considerable uneasiness. He thus proceeded to arrange a strategy to minimize any possible damage that Esau might do. The report that Esau was on his way to meet him with 400 men was no consolation to Jacob. The gifts that he prepared for Esau included a total of 580 animals. Jacob hoped that these would lessen the supposed wrath of Esau, but if this measure failed, he hoped that the divided company would assure the survival of at least half of his family. Along with these external measures, Jacob prayed and humbly entreated God to deliver him from his brother.

In the face of the threat of this hour, Jacob manifested an intense spiritual piety. Sampey has commented: "At Peniel, when he thought of the near approach of the brother whom he had wronged, he was far more spiritual than when he deceived his blind old father. He betook himself to earnest prayer, confessing his unworthiness and pleading for protection for his family."[2] Evidently in the process of assuring himself that all his party had crossed safely, Jacob was separated from them by the Brook Jabbok. It was at this time that he was engaged by the "man" who wrestled with him. This "man" is often referred to as an angel, but Jacob said: "I have seen God face to face" (v. 30). In this most remarkable experience, Jacob came to an insight that he might understand his personal worthlessness. Mackintosh says, "To be left alone with God is the only true way of arriving at a just knowledge of ourselves and our ways." Jacob's weakness was to become his strength; when he saw himself as a weak human, then he was prepared to become a mighty prince. With his thigh disjointed and his strength gone, Jacob could only

---

[1] G. T. Manley, The New Bible Handbook. London: The Inter-Varsity Christian Fellowship, 1947, p. 80.

[2] James R. Sampey, The Heart of the Old Testament. (Nashville: Broadman Press, 1922), p. 38.

cling weakly to his adversary and cry for a blessing. Few men have undergone a more dramatic or forceful confirmation of the fact of their nothingness.

The heavenly being announced that Jacob's name should be changed to Israel. Jacob means "supplanter" or "deceiver," while Israel means "a prince with God" or "a wrestler with God." Jacob neither consistently was called Israel thereafter (e.g. Gen. 46:2), nor was he always a credit to the princely associations of the name; but he may be vindicated in that he appears henceforth to have "followed after" perfection, just as a New Testament Christian strives to do. According to Hosea 12:4, Jacob's wrestling on this occasion completed his striving for the birthright. It is usually considered that Peniel was a ford over Jabbok, and that Penuel was a mountain nearby, though both words mean "face of God." The "sinew that shrank" is considered by the orthodox Jews to have been the sciatic nerve, and to this day they carefully refrain from eating it.

6. Jacob Meets Esau (Ch. 33)

Jacob was indeed meekly humble when he met Esau. He begged forgiveness and requested Esau's friendship. These favors Esau graciously extended, and he seems no longer to have borne ill will against his brother. It may be implied from v. 10 "I have seen thy face, as though I had seen the face of God" that Esau now manifested in his face a reflection of the goodness of God. So thoroughly forgiving and undemanding was Esau that it was necessary for Jacob to urge him to receive the proffered gift. It would appear that Esau accepted Jacob's tokens of generosity only because to fail to do so might have indicated a continued strain of relationships. Esau's kindly attitude on this occasion was something of a rebuke to his brother for his many fears and suspicions.

The brothers separated when Esau left to journey to Mount Seir. Jacob promised to follow along behind and meet Esau at the Mount. The reasons for Jacob's failure to do so are not clear, but perhaps he simply gave up the idea as impractical rather than intentionally deceiving. His first stopping place was Succoth, but after a temporary stay he moved on to Shalem, a city of Shechem. There at Shechem, Jacob purchased a parcel of land (v. 19)

and thus he extended the land holdings in Palestine of the chosen family. The land that Jacob bought on this occasion later became his burial place.

It would seem that Jacob ought to have known that God's place for him was Bethel (cf. 31:13), and that to stop short at Shechem was to court failure. However, it is interesting to note that this place was the area he bequeathed to Joseph, and it was the site of Jacob's well which figures in the story of St. John, chapter four. The name of Jacob's altar, El-elohe-Israel, means "God (the mighty) is the God of Israel." However, the events of the forthcoming chapter raise a question concerning the measure of Jacob's genuine inner piety at this time. In Jacob's case, as in the case of all men, devotion is no substitute for obedience.

7. The Defilement of Dinah (Ch. 34)

The events described in this chapter brought sorrow and humiliation to Jacob and indirectly degraded the name of Jehovah. Although the Arabs traditionally bestowed the death penalty for seduction, the violent massacre of the Shechemites and the procedures of deception and utter disregard of honor would lack justification among any civilized people. Actually the sons of Jacob were aware that God had forbidden intermarriage in any circumstances. No superficial process such as circumcision could qualify the Shechemites to intermarry with the chosen people. Simeon and Levi as the full brothers of Dinah may have won the satisfaction of vindicating their sister's honor but in the process they compromised their father's testimony. Jacob for his part reproved his sons but feebly, probably because his conscience was not clear in the matter of his presence at Shechem. Personal shortcomings, inevitably disqualify the moral counselor.

8. Jacob at Bethel and Bethlehem (Ch. 35)

After the sordid events of the preceding chapter, Jacob once more became responsive to the voice of God and the call to Bethel. He and his family underwent a spiritual revival and they scrupulously put away all their pagan gods and heathen fetishes. It may be conjectured that the images that Rachel had stolen from Laban (31:19) were among the objects that were hidden. At Bethel, Jacob built an altar and promptly experienced a new visitation from God. The Lord confirmed the change of Jacob's name to Israel and once more renewed to him the Abrahamic Covenant. The death of Deborah, the maid of Rebekah, at this place gave the site an added solemn association. In addition to his altar, Jacob also set up a stone pillar and made the first drink offering that is mentioned in Scripture. It is probable that the stone pillar that he had erected 30 years previously was no longer standing.

Jacob and his family continued southward from Bethel, to Ephrath (Bethlehem) and there in giving birth to Benjamin Rachel died. Jacob mourned her death sincerely, though her passing was somewhat softened to him by the birth of Benjamin "son of my right hand." The tomb of Rachel near Bethlehem was evidently preserved for many centuries, however, the present structure was built by the Crusaders in the twelfth century.

The death of Isaac is here somewhat by way of anticipation. According to the Bible chronologies, when Isaac died, Jacob was 120 and Joseph was 29. Thus the latter youth had been in Egypt several years and was on the threshold of becoming a great man in Egypt. The reconciled brothers, Jacob and Esau, united in conducting the funeral and perform-

ing the interment of their father. Isaac was laid away in the family tomb of the cave of Machpelah at Hebron (see Ch. 23).

9. The Generations of Esau (Ch. 36)

The genealogy of Esau at this point completes the Scriptural story of his family and thus prepares for the development of the story of the promised line. Although the family of Esau later had some incidental dealings with Israel, they are for the most part, dropped from the Bible narrative. The land of Israel had been promised to the line of Jacob and not to the line of Esau, therefore, it was according to the divine program that Esau leave the land. Esau and his descendants took up their residence in the area previously known as Edom, Mt. Seir or Idumea. The original inhabitants had been the Horites, or as they are otherwise called, the Hurrians. The descendants of Esau were not particularly friendly toward Israel and at times they were openly hostile, however, during the reign of the Macabees (167-63 B.C.) they were forcibly absorbed by the nation of Israel. The Herods of the New Testament were Idumeans, including Herod the Great who sought the life of the infant Jesus, Herod Antipas who slew John the Baptist, and Herod Agrippa who slew James the brother of

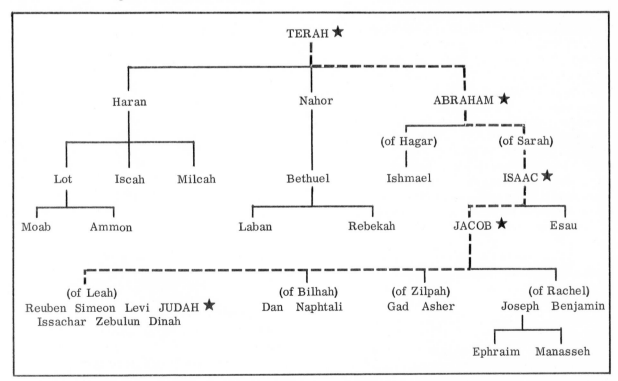

Figure 6 -- The Chosen Line in the Book of Genesis

John. (cf. Mt. 2:13, 14:3; Acts 12:1).

The three wives of Esau mentioned in vs. 2, 3 are given different names from those mentioned previously. (cf. 26:34, 28:9). It thus may be necessary to conclude that either Esau had more than three wives, or else that each of his wives was known by an alternate name. Certainly it is possible for a person to be known by more than one name or for different persons sometimes to be known by the same name. The term "duke" in this genealogy implies: "chieftain, leader, or tribal head" and it has no particular connection with the modern use of the title. Some scholars believe that the list of Edomite kings (vs. 31-39) implies that the royal office was won by election or popular appointment rather than established as a post obtained by hereditary succession.

III. THE STORY OF JOSEPH (Chs. 37-50)

1. Joseph with his Family. Sold into Egypt (Ch. 37)

Joseph, the first born son of Rachel, would have been a child of five or six at the time that the family left Mesopotamia and migrated to Palestine. Thus, Joseph was chiefly reared in the land of Palestine and this would be the home that he knew and understood. It is understandable that Jacob's favoritism extended to Joseph caused resentment in the brothers. And for his part, Joseph did not help the situation by his lack of tact in reporting his dreams. His brothers showed their jealousy and hostility by nicknaming him "the dreamer." This situation of tension and actual hatred in Jacob's family may be thought of as one of the inevitable outcomes of polygamy. Probably one reason why Joseph's dreams so grieved his brothers was because in their inner selves they recognized the plausibility of that which he dreamed. Ancient tomb paintings depict tribal leaders as wearing many colored coats and it may be assumed that there was more than sentimental significance in the coat that Jacob made for Joseph.

When the brothers acted to rid themselves of Joseph, the lad was spared immediate physical harm only because of the intervention of Reuben. He alone seems to have possessed a sense of fraternal responsibility and kindness of heart. The cistern into which Joseph was placed would be a well or a pit with a narrow opening. Without a ladder one would be unable to climb out. Since Joseph had followed his brothers to Dothan, they were many miles from home and there was ample time to contemplate the fate of the younger brother. The opportunity to sell him into slavery seemed to them to be a humane solution to their problem. The selling price, twenty pieces of silver, was equivalent to about $15.00 at today's values, and it later became the minimum price of a useful slave. (cf. Lev. 27:5). It would have provided exactly two pieces of silver for each of the brothers.

The merchant men who bought Joseph are referred to both as Ishmaelites and as Midianites. Since both the Ishmaelites and Midianites were descendants of Abraham, they were very much alike in habits and appearance. It is understood either name might serve to describe a particular caravan. The cargo that these merchants were carrying to Egypt consisted of ingredients that would be used in embalming. They were no doubt glad to add a slave to their cargo, for the young Joseph would have been a marketable commodity in Egypt. Papyri have indicated that at this time slaves from the region of Palestine were highly prized in Egypt and that the word "Canaanite" was synonymous with slave.

While the brothers had been so indifferent to their younger brother's fate that they sat and ate bread--probably the very bread Joseph had brought--while the young lad in the pit cried for help, Jacob, on the other hand, was deeply moved by the loss of his son. In spite of the efforts of his family "he refused to be comforted." He felt that the grief of his heart was sufficient to bring him to his grave (Heb. Sheol). The callous hearts of Joseph's brothers is even more glaring in their indifference to their father's unnecessary grief, than to Joseph's plight. It is significant to note that at one time or another each of the three patriarchs was called upon to give up a son and, as it were, receive him from the dead.

2. Judah and Tamar (Ch. 38)

This story does not have to do with Joseph and it is inserted in the Scriptural record as a parenthesis to report the genealogy of the chosen line. The outcome of the events reported in this chapter was the estab-

The mound or tell of Dothan as it appears today. It was at this place that Joseph was imprisoned by his brothers and sold into slavery, for Dothan was an inhabited city for some 4,500 years. The mound is now about 125 feet high, with the top 90 feet being artificial accumulation from successive civilizations. The top of the tell is 25 acres in extent. The name Dothan means "two wells."

lishment of the three great families of Judah: the Shelanites, the Pharzites, and the Zarhites. (cf. Num. 26:20). Pharez and Zarah were the twin sons of Judah by his daughter-in-law, Tamar, and Shelah was the son of his wife Shuah. Pharez became an ancestor of Joseph the husband of Mary (Mt. 1:3). Thus, in spite of the questionable circumstances of the birth of Pharez, he served as one more link in the unfolding events fulfilling the divine plan.

This chapter illustrates the custom of levirate marriage which prevailed as a bind-

ing obligation in ancient times. The custom provided that in the event of the death of a husband, the surviving brother must marry the widow of the deceased. Since marriages were commonly arranged by the parents it was Judah's responsibility to provide his surviving son, Shelah, to Tamar. His neglect of his obligation in this matter prompted Tamar to entice her own father-in-law in an effort to dramatize his indifference and neglect. Judah was deceived because Tamar appeared disguised and in the role of a devotee of the religion of Astarte in which ritual prostitution was considered an act of worship. Tamar's goal in her actions seems to have been that she would place Judah under obligation so that he would be forced to provide his younger son as her husband. That this episode should have resulted in the perpetuation of the chosen line is a testimony to the remarkable ways of God.

3. Joseph in Potiphar's House. In Prison
   (Ch. 39)

Although chronologies are uncertain, it may be inferred that in Joseph's time, Egypt was a prosperous, thriving nation. By means of the composite bow and the chariot of war, the Egyptians had extended their borders freely. They were at this time enjoying the fruits of extensive possessions and abundant slave labor. Thus, the people were free to develop their culture and to cultivate their leisure time.

In Potiphar's household, the success of all of Joseph's achievements soon won for the youthful servant the unrestrained admiration of his master. Hence Joseph was given the full management of all of Potiphar's domestic affairs and in him was placed implicit trust. He was not at all to blame for the designing intentions of Potiphar's wife, and in running away he did the only thing he could under the circumstances. Though he afterward found himself in prison, he had the satisfaction of knowing that he had maintained his virtue and that his conscience was clear towards God. It has been rightly said, "Joseph took care of his character and left his reputation in the hands of God," Joseph wisely recognized the principle: every sin against man is primarily a sin against God.

There is a possibility that Potiphar may have had some suspicion concerning the validity of his wife's accusations against Joseph. A typical outcome in such a case would have been the immediate execution of the slave, so that Joseph's fate was quite mild. It is of interest to note that ancient Egyptian records have produced the Story of the Two Brothers which is a narrative concerning the younger brother who is falsely accused by the older brother's wife. This story confirms the plausibility of the Bible account of Joseph. Scripture twice notes that even in prison the Lord was with Joseph and thus promotion and the commitment of authority soon resulted. In the divine providence the future administrator was being prepared for his task. In the life of Joseph, the seeming tragedy of a prison cell was after all simply a subterranean passage to the throne.

4. Joseph and the Butler and the Baker (Ch. 40)

The offices of butler and baker apparently were important in ancient Egypt, for figures of each are often found on Egyptian monuments. In an era and an environment of unrestrained court intrigue, a trusted butler and baker were vital to prevent the poisoning of the ruler. Evidently, the major responsibility of the butler was to be concerned with the king's beverages. A plausible tradition says that the reason that the butler and the baker of Joseph's time were confined to prison was because they had conspired against their master. If this is so, it is evident that Pharaoh judged that the baker was actually the responsible party in the plot and therefore, he released and restored the butler. From the standpoint of the Bible story, the significance of the fate of these men hinged on the fact that Joseph had opportunity to be the interpreter of dreams. Thus he qualified for his later associations with Pharaoh. The fact that the butler, in spite of his promises, forgot Joseph for the next two years, undoubtedly was a bitter disappointment to Joseph and yet it may have taught him that patience which it was necessary for him to learn. Furthermore, the restored butler being himself of uncertain tenure was likely in no position to plead on behalf of another supposed guilty party.

5. The Dream of Pharaoh. Joseph's Exaltation (Ch. 41)

When Joseph's opportunity finally came and he found himself in the presence of a Pharaoh perplexed by dreams, Joseph proceeded first to testify to divine guidance. Not only did Joseph interpret Pharaoh's dreams in detail, but he proceeded also to render advice based upon this interpretation. Evidently the sincerity and quiet confidence of Joseph entirely convinced Pharaoh, and he questioned neither the dream interpretation nor the soundness of the advice. It has been suggested that Pharaoh's acceptance of Joseph may have in part been prompted by a sympathy toward the God of Joseph that was the outcome of the monotheism of Akhenaten (or Ikhnaton) a one-time Pharaoh of Egypt. The word "kine" used in this account is our word cows, and corn would be any cereal grain such as wheat or barley.

Joseph's exaltation was immediate. Pharaoh discerned that this man with the wisdom to interpret was an ideal choice for the man who was to administer during the years to come. Joseph was not only appointed to this high post but also through his marriage to Asenath he was granted a kinship with Egypt's finest families. It is said that the expression "bow the knee" used in acclaiming Joseph at this time is a possible rendering of the word "Abrek" an adaptation of which is used to this day in Egypt by a camel driver when he wants his camel to kneel. The gold chain given to Joseph would be equivalent in our time to a distinguished service medal bestowed by the ruler of a state. In modern language, Joseph's new office would be described as that of "Prime Minister" or in Eastern terms "Grand Vizier." From a spiritual standpoint, Joseph's exaltation was partly of mixed benefit. His marriage to Asenath made him the son-in-law of Potipherah who was evidently the high priest of the idolatrous paganism of Egypt. Such a family influence undoubtedly was not a spiritual asset to Joseph.

During the seven years of plenty, Joseph's two sons, Ephraim and Manasseh were born. These lads were destined to become heads of Israelitish tribes, and the extra tribe was to serve to replace the Levites who were called to a spiritual ministry. The sequence of plenty and famine in ancient Egypt was not uncommon. Archaeologists report several descriptions of prolonged famine and the expedient of feeding the nation from storehouses previously provided. Likewise reported by archaeologists, is the finding of stories in Egyptian records of several Canaanites who were promoted to high rank in the court of Pharaoh. Joseph's exaltation was evidently not contrary to precedents of his day.

6. The First Trip of Joseph's Brothers to Egypt (Ch. 42)

Because the seven-year famine prevailed, not only locally but as far away as Canaan as well, the aged Jacob found it necessary to send his sons to Egypt in order to buy food. Thus Joseph once more found himself face-to-face with his brothers. In his relationship to these, his former persecutors, Joseph showed admirable restraint and penetrating insight. Though even at the outset, Joseph undoubtedly purposed to reveal himself to his brothers and re-establish his family ties, he chose to wait until his brothers had bared their hearts and given evidence of a salutary change of attitude. His actions in binding and imprisoning Simeon, and in returning the money, seem to have been calculated to disturb and confuse his brothers and to dispel any superficiality and hypocrisy. Perhaps also, Joseph sought to test and temper the heart of Jacob in order to teach him that a family of sons called for impartiality.

7. The Second Trip of Joseph's Brothers to Egypt (Ch. 43)

The brothers postponed the return to Egypt as long as they dared, but when the pangs of famine pressed too severely, they once again made the journey. This time they took Benjamin, double money for the corn, and a gift for Joseph. The gift was constituted of the delicacies of Canaan which even in time of famine would include: date honey, pistachio nuts, balm, almonds, and laudanum. These were useful and desirable items but they were not such as served as fare for everyday living. The eleven brothers were cordially received by the younger brother and he straightway proceeded to prepare to entertain them in a banquet. The brothers participated with considerable misgivings and not a little amazement at the apparent remarkable insight of the chief administrator of all Egypt. In the course of their associations with him, the entire group of eleven bowed down to Joseph and thus fulfilled his early dreams. In sitting apart from his brothers at the banquet, Joseph adopted the role of a native Egyptian, for Egyptians considered that they would be defiled if they allowed themselves to be too close to an alien. The show of favoritism to Benjamin at the banquet may have been for the purpose of testing the heart attitude of the brothers, and also it was Joseph's expression of his affection for his own true brother.

8. The Repentance of the Brothers (Ch. 44)

History records that it was the custom of Egyptian men of status to acquire a personal special cup. In the instance of the pagan Egyptians this cup would serve for divining purposes. It would be filled with water and then particles of gold, silver and precious stones would be added. The resulting designs would be read somewhat in the pattern of modern teacup reading. Although Joseph may not have used his cup for this purpose, his status in Egypt no doubt dictated that he should have one. There was thus considerable significance in the fact that it was this important personal object that was found in the sack of Benjamin.

Joseph's strategy in the matter of the cup resulted in impressive demonstration of change of heart in the brothers. Judah many years ago had urged concerning Joseph "Come, and let us sell him to the Ishmeelites, . . ." (Gen. 37:27). Now he stands before Joseph and in humility and tenderness describes the family circumstances and offers himself as Joseph's personal slave if only Benjamin might be granted his freedom. Sampey says, ". . . Judah's speech on behalf of Benjamin is the most pathetic in all literature. He, . . . is brought face to face with the doctrine of the cross; and he hesitates not, but bravely offers himself as a substitute for his guilty brother."3 Joseph now knew that his brothers had undergone a genuine inner change and that they sincerely regreted their past conduct. They now evidenced a devoted attachment to one another, including Benjamin, and they manifested a loving reverence and affection toward their father.

9. Joseph Reveals Himself to His Brothers
   (Ch. 45)

The time to make himself known had come. Hence, in privacy with the eleven, Joseph declared his identity. He somewhat attenuated his brothers' shock by proceeding to describe his plans for them for the future and commissioning them to bring their families and Jacob to the land of Goshen to live. Eventually the truth of the matter was impressed upon the brothers and they responded to the degree of exchanging with Joseph hearty brotherly demonstrations of affection. Joseph's lovely spirit at this time is revealed in his words, "now therefore be not grieved, nor angry with yourselves, that ye sold me hither: for God did send me before you to preserve life" (v. 5). Years later he affirmed the same outlook: "But as for you, ye thought evil against me: but God meant it unto good, . . . to save much people alive" (Gen. 50:20). Joseph's role

was indeed typical of the suffering and death of Christ that He might be mankind's Savior.

At Joseph's request the brothers returned to Canaan with the intention of bringing Jacob and their households to settle in Goshen. Joseph thoughtfully provided food for the family in order to meet their immediate needs. Also he provided clothing for his brothers and thus enabled them to dress as befitted their new status as close relatives of Egypt's chief administrator. Though, at first, Jacob was inclined to be skeptical of the brothers' story, he was convinced when he saw the Egyptian wagons, and he thus agreed to journey to Goshen. Scripture reports, "The spirit of Jacob revived; and Israel said . . ." The change of name within the sentence might be interpreted to indicate that at the evidence of the wagons the inner man of Jacob once more asserted himself. Joseph's parting words, "See that ye fall not out by the way" (v. 24) might be rendered, "Do not give way to emotion."

10. The Family Migrates to Egypt (Ch. 46)

God had instructed Isaac "Go not down into Egypt . . ." (Gen. 26:2). Thus Jacob (or Israel) appears to have had some reluctance in making the trip. However, God appeared to him and assured him "fear not to go down into Egypt." Thus it appears that in tenderness God was permitting the aged Jacob to be reunited with his son. Joseph journeyed to Goshen to meet his father, and Scripture touchingly describes the scene as at that place the two were reunited. Notwithstanding his many adventures and achievements in life, at this point Jacob discovered that his true greatness no longer existed in himself but rather in his relationship to his son Joseph. Although Jacob declared himself content to die as soon as he found himself once more united with Joseph, he lived for 17 years after his migration to Egypt.

In spite of the fact that shepherds were despised by Egyptians, Joseph instructed his brothers to be sure to tell Pharaoh that they were shepherds. Apparently Joseph wished to assure separation between his family and the Egyptians. The Israelites would be unlikely to mingle with the Egyptians and be absorbed into the population if there were emphasis upon this lowly calling. Some scholars have suggested that Egyptians despised shepherds at this time because they temporarily were being

---

3Sampey, op. cit. p. 41.

ruled by a family of alien shepherd conquerors. To the native Egyptian, a shepherd was a reminder of a galling foreign domination. If it were true that Pharaoh was a semi-shepherd or Hyksos King, then it is quite understandable why he would be kind to the Israelites who also were a semi-shepherd people.

There is some confusion about the number of Israelites that migrated to Egypt. In this chapter it declares that 66 persons and Jacob (a total of 67) were in the incoming caravan, and that Joseph and his two sons already there made 70. In Acts 7:14 the total is given as 75, a figure quoted from the Septuagint which adds five names. A further difficulty is the fact that in verse 21, ten sons of Benjamin are listed, and yet, since Benjamin was fourteen years younger than Joseph, at the time of the immigration Benjamin was still only in his mid-twenties. Some authorities consider that the number 70 is only a reference figure, and that some of those included in the group were not born until after the arrival in Goshen. On

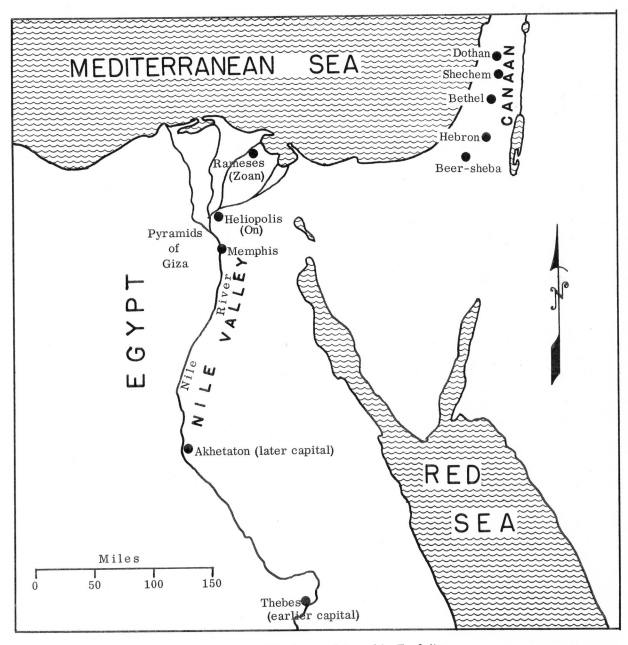

Figure 7 -- The Scene of Joseph's Exploits

the other hand, there is the viewpoint of Erdman who says, "It must not be supposed that
the migration from Canaan to Egypt was composed of only seventy souls named in the narrative. There were the sons of Jacob and
'households,' but the latter included wives,
children, grandchildren, and large numbers
of servants and retainers."[4]

11. Joseph Introduces his Family to Pharaoh
    (Ch. 47)

Though Joseph was the duly appointed
chief administrator of the land, he thought it
proper to have Pharaoh's approval upon his
final plans for the settlement of his family.
Thus, he brought five of his brothers, and
later Jacob, and presented them to Pharaoh.
An interesting comment is made by Sampey
at this point, "When Joseph led his father into
the palace to meet the king of Egypt, it was
not Jacob the wily supplanter, but Israel the
saint, who lifted his hands to bless Pharaoh--
Divine grace achieved a wonderful triumph in
the life of Jacob."[5] The Egyptian monarch
was favorably impressed by Joseph's family,
and he freely gave what Joseph asked. Goshen
was a desirable place to settle, for it was fer-
tile and it included ample grazing land; also,
it was somewhat isolated from the rest of
Egypt.

Joseph proved to be an unusually competent administrator, for he was able to
obtain for Pharaoh all of the wealth and
possessions of the Egyptian people. Nevertheless, he managed in no wise to antagonize or
offend his subjects. The outcome was that
thereafter, the Egyptian people, with the exception of the priests, leased back their lands on
a share basis with one-fifth of all their produce
being returned to Pharaoh. This arrangement
constituted a feudal system of land tenure.
Such a plan resulted in vast revenue for the
state yet apparently without the people feeling
oppressed by it. Joseph brought about a large
scale movement of the population (v. 21) and
thereby made easier the feeding of the people
from the store cities, and less public the lot

of former landlords who now became mere
tenants.

Since the family of Joseph had not come
into Egypt until the close of the second year of
famine (45:11), they need not have stayed
longer than five years. This chapter records
their activities (vs. 27-31) including the death
of Jacob which occurred after 17 years, or 12
years beyond the end of the famine. In spite of
the fact that Joseph and his family prospered
so freely in Egypt, undoubtedly they ought not
to have chosen to remain, for thus they exposed
themselves to the later oppression.

The plausibility of the events of the life
of Joseph in Egypt is confirmed by archaeological findings. The tomb of El Kab, a governor of an Egyptian province and a possible contemporary with Joseph according to some chronologies, contains an inscription that includes
the story of a great famine. The inscription
reports that the governor distributed to the
sufferers the wheat that had been stored in the
years of plenty.

12. Joseph's Sons Blessed by Jacob (Ch. 48)

At the news that the aged Jacob was ill,
Joseph proceeded to pay a call, taking with him
his two sons, Ephraim and Manasseh. The dying
patriarch was well pleased with his visitors, and
he announced to Joseph that the two boys should
be counted as his own sons. By this means they
were appointed as tribal leaders, and were specifically brought into the covenant as people of
God. Thus, in a sense, Joseph was granted a
double portion of his father's blessing. In bestowing the patriarchal blessing, Jacob deliberately placed his right hand upon the younger son,
thus signifying that the younger was to have preeminence over his brother. Perhaps owing to
his own experience, Jacob had a special sympathy for younger brothers and their rights of
heritage. Perhaps also, Jacob wished to illustrate that the blessing he was bestowing was
not given according to natural law. In later
history, the tribe of Ephraim became more
powerful than that of Manasseh, though Manasseh was actually the elder brother.

13. The Patriarchal Blessing (Ch. 49)

The occasion of Jacob's death is described as an impressive scene. The aged
patriarch gathered his sons about him and in

4Charles R. Erdman, The Book of
Exodus. New York: Fleming H. Revell
Company, 1949, p. 16.

5Sampey, op. cit. p. 39.

poetic form addressed each in turn. Noteworthy facts about the messages to each include the following:

a. Reuben. Although he was Jacob's first
born, he lost his privileges, and the tribe was
to be relegated to comparative obscurity. Reuben had demonstrated himself rash in his actions and he especially stood condemned because he had committed adultery with Bilhah,
his father's concubine.

b. Simeon. To be scattered in Israel so as
to become one of the weakest of the tribes.

c. Levi. To be divided in (or from) Israel.
Simeon and Levi had acted wrongly in the
treacherous murder of the Shechemites. They
had thus disqualified themselves from patriarchal commendation. In historical outworking, Simeon was largely absorbed by Judah and
the identity of the tribe was lost. The Levites
were, of course, destined to be the priestly
group who did not receive an individual tribal
inheritance.

d. Judah. To increase in strength until
Shiloh (peace-bringer) should come (probably
a reference to the Messiah). A sceptre was
a shiek's staff which indicated his right to
lead. The prophecy to Judah is actually the
heart of Jacob's pronouncement for Jesus
Christ was to be of this tribe and be known as
"the lion of the tribe of Judah." The figure in
verses 11 and 12 seems to portray prosperity
and abundance which would be the evidence of
divine approval upon the tribe.

e. Zebulun. To settle in the coastal regions
as a trader.

f. Issachar. A patient agricultural worker
pursuing a policy of appeasement.

g. Dan. Though provided a small inheritance, Dan was to become a leading tribe,
shrewd and clever, and by nature predators.

h. Gad. To be the victim of invaders, but
ultimately to triumph. (When the tribe settled
in the land it was located east of Jordan and
therefore particularly subject to plunderers.)

i. Asher. To enjoy prosperity and the blessing of God.

j. Naphtali. To be free and prosperous. A
special privilege provided to Naphtali in later
history was that it was in this tribal settlement
that Christ lived and performed His early ministry.

k. Joseph. To be numerous and blessed
above his forebearers and to maintain spiritual virtue. God, of course, had provided that
Joseph's two sons Ephraim and Manasseh actually partook of his inheritance and represented him among the tribes.

l. Benjamin. To be war-like and adventur-
ous, to be enriched of the spoils of victory. It
was this tribe that was to produce both Saul,
the king, and also Saul of Tarsus who became
Paul the apostle.

Jacob's last request was that he should
be buried in the cave in the Field of Machpelah
which had become the family burying grounds.
At the time of his death, Jacob was 147 years
old and as previously noted, he had lived in
Egypt for seventeen years. Jacob is remembered as the "most human" of the three patriarchs of Israel and there are those who are
quite critical of many aspects of Jacob's life.
Graham, for instance, notes that Jacob remained in Egypt twelve years after the famine
ended and he comments concerning his desire
to be buried in Israel "Let us note that it is
more pleasing to the Lord that we act in obedience while we live, than that we make bequest
concerning a post-mortem arrangement."[6]
Jacob's last request for the first time mentions
the fact that Rebekah and Leah were buried
with the other patriarchs and their wives in
the cave of the Field of Machpelah.

14. Joseph Buries His Father. His Last Days
(Ch. 50)

The body of Jacob was embalmed according to the skill of the Egyptians. The forty days
that were required for the embalming of Jacob
seemed to have been about the least time that
was allowed for the process. The procedure of
embalming included removing the internal

[6]James R. Graham, A Philosophy
of Scripture: A Connected Commentary on
the Book of Genesis. Butler: The Highway
Press, 1955, p. 318.

The Tomb of Joseph is to this day to be found at Shechem as a Muslim "weli" or shrine.
The site is particularly revered by the Muslim women who gather here for prayer. The
purchase of this "parcel of ground" is reported (Gen. 33:18-20), as well as the deposit
there of the bones of Joseph. (cf. Josh. 24:32; Acts 7:16).

organs and viscera and soaking the remains in a solution of sodium carbonate (washing soda). As a final step, the body was wrapped in many yards of linen cloth. In mourning for Jacob, the people of Egypt accorded him the customary 70 days that was usual in the case of death of a member of the royal family of Egypt. Mourning consisted of rending the garments, smiting the breast, and throwing dust upon the head. At the end of the mourning period, Joseph and his household, his brothers and the servants of Pharaoh made the 300 mile journey to Canaan to bury Jacob. The Egyptians were accustomed to great pompous funerals, and their influence is evident on this occasion even though they would never have buried one of their dignitaries in a foreign land.

Although the brothers feared retaliation at the hand of Joseph following the death of their father, their fears were wholly groundless. They were mistaken in measuring Joseph by themselves. Joseph maintained his kindly virtue and lived to be 110. It is reported to have been an Egyptian tradition that the age of 110 was the ideal length for a happy and prosperous life. Scripture passes over the events of the latter years of Joseph's life, although there is record that he had the pleasure of seeing in his own lifetime the growth and maturity of his grandchildren.

Before his death, Joseph secured from his family the promise that he should be buried with his forefathers. The book of Genesis, therefore, closes with the statement that Joseph died, was embalmed and "put in a coffin in Egypt." Such a statement is in striking contrast with the sublime opening words of this great book, but it stands as an all too apparent evidence of the destructive effects of sin. The Egyptian idea of a coffin was no doubt a mummy case and its presence with the tribe in their later migrations served as an abiding testimony of the persistent faith of Joseph.

So far as the Scriptural report sets forth, Joseph represents the outcome of all the spiritual lessons learned by the patriarchs. The events of his life set forth the truth of the 'nothingness' of mere human attainment. Only once is Joseph mentioned in the New Testament, and in this citation neither his great honors nor high administrative posts are mentioned. Instead: "By faith Joseph when he died, made mention of the departing of the children of Is-

rael; and gave commandment concerning his house" (Heb. 11:22). The significant fact in Joseph's outlook singled out by the New Testament writer was that at his death he was committed in faith to God's plan providing for the departure of the people from Egypt. Obviously, no matter how great man's achievement, none is greater than the fact that he achieves the exercise of believing faith in God.

Of all of the individuals in Scripture, Joseph is the most nearly perfect type of Christ. Those aspects of his life that compare with the life of our Lord may be set forth as follows:

JOSEPH	CHRIST
Loved by the father. Gen. 37:3	"This is my beloved Son." Mt. 3:17
Brethren did not believe him. Gen. 37:5, Brethren hated him. Gen. 37:4	Neither did His brethren believe in Him. Jno. 7:5 ". . . They hated both me and my Father." Jno. 15:24
Brethren rejected his reign. Gen. 37:8	"We will not have this man to reign over us." Lk. 19:14
Conspired against him. Gen. 37:23	Took counsel against Him. Mt. 27:1
They stripped him. Gen. 37:23	They stripped Him. Mt. 27:28
Sat down and watched him. Gen. 37:25	Sitting down they watched Him. Mt. 27:36
Sold for silver. Gen. 37:28	Sold for silver. Mt. 26:15
Everything prospered in his hand. Gen. 39:3	". . . and the pleasure of the Lord shall prosper in His hand. Isa. 53:10
All things were put into his hand. Gen. 39:4-8	Hath given all things into His hand. Jno. 3:35
Tempted and did not sin. Gen. 39:9	Tempted, yet without sin. Heb. 4:15

····· continued ·····

Joseph	Christ
Bound and imprisoned. Gen. 39:30	Bound and led away. Mt. 27:2
With two malefactors. Gen. 40:2, 3	With two malefactors. Lk. 23:32
One received message of life, other died. Gen. 40:21, 22	One thief penitent-- "Today shalt thou be with me in paradise." Lk. 23:43
None so discreet and wise. Gen. 41:39	"In whom are hid all the treasures of wisdom and knowledge." Col. 2:3
They bow the knee to him. Gen. 41:43	Every knee shall bow. Phil. 2:10
Thirty years old. Gen. 41:46	About thirty years old. Lk. 3:25
God used Joseph's suffering to save. Gen. 50:21	God used Christ's suffering to bring blessing. Rom. 5:8
Given power over all Egypt. Gen. 41:42-44	All power given unto Jesus Christ. Mt. 28:18

····· continued ·····

Joseph	Christ
Gentile bride to share his glory. Gen. 41:45	The converts of Christ will share His glory eternally.
God promised a place of rulership. Gen. 37:8	"The government shall be upon his shoulder. . ." Isa. 9:6
Cast into a pit, but delivered out of it. Gen. 37:24, 28	"Now he that ascended, what is it but that he also descended first into the lower parts of the earth?" Eph. 4:9
Imprisoned on false charges. Gen. 39:19, 20	"For many gave false witness against him . . ." Mk. 14:56
Joseph dealt with his brethren so as to bring them to repentance. Gen. 42:7	"If they shall confess their iniquity. . . Then will I remember my covenant . . ." Lev. 26:40, 42
Joseph revealed himself to his brothers during their imprisonment. Gen. 45:1	". . . in their affliction they will seek me early." Hos. 5:15

THREE: The Book of Exodus

The book of Exodus, the second book of the Bible, is concerned with the continuation of the story of Israel, and the outworking of the plan of God for the nation. In the original, this book is joined to the preceding by the common conjunction "and," though in our version it is translated "now." The book introduces one of the greatest Biblical characters--Moses, and it presents one of the greatest migrations of history--from Egypt to Sinai. Says Manley of this book:

> Whereas the book of Genesis begins with the creation of man in conditions of innocence and beauty, and tells of his fall and continuance in sin, this second book of the Bible tells the story of Israel's bondage and redemption, and provides many pictures of the salvation wrought by our great High Priest.[1]

Manley points out that Christ is prefigured in Exodus in: the Passover (1 Cor. 5:7), the Manna (John 6:32), the Smitten Rock (1 Cor. 10:4), and the Levitical Offerings (Heb. 10: 11, 12).

The Name of the Book

The Jewish name for Exodus consists of the first two words in the Hebrew, and it means "and these are the names." Our name "Exodus" means "going out" or "pathway out," and it comes to us from the Septuagint by way of the Vulgate. The Hebrew name is merely accidental, and even ours is only partly justified. The book contains a good deal more than the account of the departure of Israel from Egypt.

The Theme of Exodus

The book is concerned with the establishment of Israel as a nation and its recog-

nition as such both by God and by contemporary peoples. The redemption of the Israelites from the Egyptian bondage and the establishment of the covenant at Sinai were two vital factors in the achievement of this goal. Within the era of this book, Israel expanded from being a mere family to being a sovereign nation united under a divinely given constitution (the Sinaitic Law). The exodus of chapter 12 marked the beginning of Israel as an independent people; the bestowment of the Law in chapter 20 marked the consolidation of the people into a nation.

Foreshadowings in Exodus

The events of this book serve to foreshadow the fortunes of Israel throughout her history. The years of bondage speak of the entire "times of the Gentiles" during which the Jews have consistently suffered. The afflictions upon the Egyptians during the plagues represent the afflictions to fall upon the Gentile kingdoms during the tribulation period. The deliverance of Israel in spite of Pharaoh's efforts parallels Israel's preservation during the tribulation and her preparation for possessing her national home.

The Chronological Relationship of Genesis and Exodus

The narrative of Genesis closes with the death of Joseph, that of Exodus begins virtually with the account of the birth of Moses. Between these two events there is the indefinite period of time during which Egypt's Pharaohs began their campaign of persecution. Though 12:40 states: "Now the sojourning of the children of Israel, who dwelt in Egypt, was four hundred and thirty years," uncertainty arises because the beginning of the period of sojourn is not identified. Traditionally it has been customary to assume that the 430 years began when Abraham left Ur and the "shorter chronology" of Ussher, which provides only half of the period for the actual bondage, is figured on this assumption. However, the tendency of evangelical scholars today is to begin the 430 years with Jacob's migration to Egypt and to

---

[1]G. T. Manley, The New Bible Handbook. Chicago: The Inter-Varsity Christian Fellowship, 1948, p. 134.

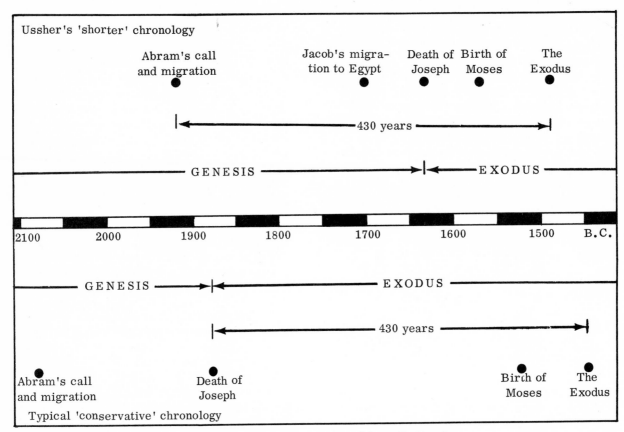

Figure 8 -- Two Chronologies of Israel's Bondage

extend Abraham's call as far back as necessary.

Further complications in the subject of the chronology of these events include: 1) uncertainty concerning the date of the Exodus: Ussher dated it at 1491 B.C., contemporary evangelicals likely agree to within a few decades, but datings from the 18th to the 12th century may be found, 2) uncertainty concerning the Bible record of the duration of the bondage: Sometimes the Bible lists the bondage as 400 rather than 430 years (e.g. Gen.15:13; Acts 7:6). Usually this latter problem is resolved by concluding that these writers were merely contenting themselves with round numbers and thus no real contradiction exists. The "shorter chronology" is based upon the fact that the genealogical tables list just one individual between the original seventy immigrants to Egypt and the generation of Moses. However, it is suggested that the genealogical tables are not meant to burden the reader with the enumeration of every generation. They simply name key individuals which, though in direct line, are not father and son, but several generations removed.

ANALYSIS AND EXPOSITION

I. ISRAEL IN EGYPT (Chs.1-12:36)

1. The Egyptian Bondage (Ch.1)

The increase of the population of the Israelites was so striking a fact that the author, in verse 7, uses five forceful adjectives to describe it. In this chapter (v.5) and in Genesis (46:27) it is noted that seventy individuals came into Egypt in the time of Jacob. However, of the seventy (Gen.46:8-25) who are enumerated as coming into Egypt in the time of Jacob, all but two are males. Since each of these could be presumed to take at least one wife, the vast increase in population is the more understandable. The success and prosperity of the Israelites were the causes of their undoing. The Egyptians noting such a rapidly increasing minority group felt that their supremacy was threatened. Their tactic of oppressing Israel constitutes the beginning of antisemitism which has proved to be a periodic phenomenon among the Gentile nations of the world.

The "new king over Egypt, which knew not Joseph" is thought to have been ruler of another dynasty from that which was in power in Joseph's day. It is generally concluded that experiences of the Israelites coincided with the rule of the Hyksos in Egypt. These hardy Asiatic nomads invaded the land beginning at about 1900 B.C. and until about 1580 B.C. they intermittently overthrew the native Egyptian dynasty and assumed rule of the land. It has already been noted that there are many uncertainties concerning the chronology of this era, but it may be assumed that the Pharaoh of Joseph's day was the Hyksos dynasty while the Pharaoh of Moses' time was a native Egyptian. Josephus declares that the Hyksos actually were Israelites, but on the basis of historical and etymological studies this claim seems to have little support. Rather, it is concluded that in being alien Semites, the Hyksos would befriend the Israelites whereas the native Egyptians would understandably identify the Israelites with their despised former oppressors.

Uniformly in Scripture, Israel stands as a type of God's people and Egypt represents the secular worldly system. Thus, the fate of the Israelites in Egypt is typical of the fate of Christian believers in the world system. It is significant that it is but a short step from the time when Joseph was Lord over all the land to the time when his descendants were writhing in cruel bondage. The step from acclaim in this world to flagrant rejection is equally as short.

The cities of Pithom and Raamses were designated as "treasure" or "store" cities, and they were built to be warehouses for items of trade or army stores. Excavations in Egypt at what may be the site of ancient Pithom reveal a city composed almost wholly of storehouses. Bricks used in such structures are commonly large blocks about a foot long and a little more than a half foot high. Some are found made with straw and some without. Although Nile mud does not demand straw as a binder in making bricks, it has been demonstrated that with the addition of organic matter such as straw or stubble, the mud is easier to work. Even the use of water in which straw has been soaked (or cooked) seems to help.

The city of Raamses (or Rameses) had previously been known as "Avaris" and later in history the same city was called "Tanis" or "Zoan." Egyptian monuments confirm the fact

that public works were frequently performed by forced Asiatic labor. It has been conjectured that one reason for the great building projects of the Pharaohs was simply a desire to use oppresive labor to crush the spirits of subject people. In Israel's time, not only were the people forced to serve as state slaves, but Pharaoh also decreed that all their male children should be destroyed. The God-given convictions of the midwives nullified the cruel order of Pharaoh and assured that God's plan for the emancipation of Israel proceeded even though Pharaoh plotted the nation's extermination. The fortune of the midwives illustrates the text, "Them that honor me I will honor" (1 Sam. 2:30). These women were rewarded, not because they deceived Pharaoh, but because they honored God. Their names Shiprah and Puah are names common in ancient Egypt; the name Shiprah is found in an 18th century B.C. Egyptian list of slaves; Puah is found in the Ras Shamra texts.

2. The Early Life of Moses

Moses was born to Amram and Jochebed (cf. 6:20) at a time when all male Israelitish children were to be destroyed. His parents were both of the tribe of Levi. In hiding her little son in the reeds along the river's edge, Jochebed combined faith in God with common sense. Someone has commented concerning the situation at this time "The heart of every woman was in a plot against Pharaoh." The writer of Hebrews reported "By faith Moses, when he was born, was hid three months of his parents . . ." (Heb. 11:23). The exercise of faith transformed a river that was intended to be a place of death for male Israelite children into a place of life for Moses.

Tradition says that Pharaoh's daughter who found the ark, was named Thermoutis. Many commentators consider that in all likelihood Pharaoh's daughter clearly saw through the thin plot of which she was a part. Her natural feminine concern for a human child prompted her to take the action that she did. The outcome was a rather amusing situation wherein the royal treasury of Egypt paid money to a mother to raise her own son; while actually, Pharaoh had decreed that no such children should live. By virtue of having a royal foster mother, Moses was assured the finest possible education of the day. Scripture reports "Moses was learned in all the wisdom of the Egyptians" (Acts 7:22). Among other arts, the Egyptians had developed hieroglyphic writing and they possessed advanced insights into mathematics, astronomy and chemistry. Also they knew and enjoyed music.

Moses was forty years of age when he slew the Egyptian and thereby incurred the wrath of Pharaoh. Moses' flight to Midian was the choice of faith as well as the expediency of the moment: "By faith he [i.e. Moses] forsook Egypt, not fearing the wrath of the king: for he endured, as seeing him who is invisible" (Heb. 11:27). According to Hebrews the over-all course of action of Moses was by deliberate choice. "By faith Moses, when he was come to years, refused to be called the son of Pharaoh's daughter; choosing rather to suffer affliction with the people of God, . . ." (11:24, 25). It is evident that though Moses made a wise choice of that which was right, he at first undertook to endorse it with premature action that was rash and foolish. Thus, his ill advised zeal resulted in forty years of exile but in no wise detracted from the rightness of the choice. F. B. Meyer describes Moses' actions at this point as: "The great renunciation" and he comments "An Exodus and the birth of a nation of free men were the outcome of this great renunciation."

In Midian, Moses befriended the priest Reuel (later called Jethro), and received Zipporah, Reuel's daughter, in marriage. It is here recorded that she bore him his first son, Gershom. In the later unfolding of history, the family of Moses achieved negligible status among the people of Israel, and in fact in later times it was Moses' grandson who was responsible for a dangerous schism (cf. Judg. 28:30). Moses remained in Midian for forty years, and evidently underwent an educative process just as important as his previous forty years in Egypt. The impetuous, desperate, self-appointed deliverer was transformed into a man, modest, humble, and meekly dependent upon God's empowering. Mackintosh comments: "The man whom God educates is educated and none other."

3. The Call and Commission of Moses (Ch. 3)

The phenomenon of the burning bush and subsequent calling of Moses took place at Mt. Horeb, the site where the Ten Commandments later were given. The bush that burned without being consumed provided the setting for the appearance of the angel of the Lord. Although Scripture does not report that the cry of the Israelites had been directed toward God, the

angel reported that God had indeed heard their cry. No doubt the burning thorn bush was a type of persecuted Israel in Egypt enduring the fires of affliction.

The Lord's command to Moses to remove his shoes served to impress him with the sacredness of the spot. Easterners, such as the Brahmans and Muslims, typically remove their shoes in religious exercises to show respect. Although the bush burned in the remote corner of the desert of Midian as Henry Ward Beecher once wrote, "Wherever a man's soul is brought into the presence of God Almighty the ground is sacred, whether it be in a church or on a ledge, on a crag or in a cathedral."

At this time, God revealed Himself by the name "I AM." The form is appropriate since the basis for the name Jehovah is the verbal expression "I am." Such a name implies: 1) the all-sufficiency of God, 2) the eternal existence of God, and 3) the self-sufficiency of God. Says Mackintosh: "Jehovah, in taking this title, was furnishing His people with a blank check, to be filled up to any amount." Someone has written:

When God would teach mankind His name
He calls Himself the great "I AM,"
And leaves a blank--believers may
Supply those things for which they pray.

The Lord Jesus revealed Himself as "I AM" in John 18:6 and the revelation temporarily stunned His would-be captors. The name "Jesus" itself is an adaptation by way of the Greek influence upon Hebrew of the declaration "Jehovah [or the I AM] the Savior."

God indicated to Moses that the exodus of Israel would involve the plundering of the Egyptians. The people were to "ask" (or "beg" or "request") jewels of their captors. Egypt had spoiled Israel by forced labor, and now Israel was to spoil Egypt. This transaction illustrates relationships under the law rather than those expected of Christians. The Christian believer is not entitled to take law into his own hands, but must leave all ultimate judgment and recompenses with God. He is soundly impressed that for him, in relating to men of the world, two wrongs cannot possibly make a right. The Christian believer typically is instructed: "Recompense to no man evil for evil. Provide things honest in the sight of all men" (Rom. 12:17).

4. Moses' Objections Met (Ch. 4)

In objecting to his fitness to fulfill the Lord's call, Moses revealed himself as a man who had undergone a great change. Apparently the man who once had tried in his own strength and had miserably failed now had learned his lesson. He who once presumed to go un-sent now when sent almost presumes not to go. He who had previously run before God now timidly lags behind Him. Moses' excuses indicated that he was more fearful of his reception by his own people than his reception by Pharaoh. Evans says, "Moses' excuse of timidity and lack of speech was wrong. There is a time when timidity is sinful." God met the objections by providing His servant with the power to work supernatural signs, assuring him that He would be with his mouth, and providing Aaron as his speaker. The outcome is reported in v. 18 "And Moses went . . ." Comments Erdman, "It should be noted that the promise of the sympathy and companionship of a brother did what the promise of the presence of God failed to do."

With Jethro's approval, Moses and his family, with the rod of God, set out for Egypt. It may be understood that along the way, Moses suddenly suffered a violent illness at the hand of God that he might be dramatically reminded of his neglect of the right of circumcision. Zipporah's behavior on this occasion seems to be that of abject revulsion. Commentators frequently conclude that as an outcome of this incident she separated from Moses to return to her father in Midian and was not again united with her husband until the victory over Amalek. (cf. Ex. 18:1, 2). As Moses, probably now without his family, drew near to Goshen, he was met by Aaron at what is called the Mount of God. The two brothers enjoyed a time of fellowship and then proceeded into the company of their people. At this stage the two deliverers-elect found a ready acceptance for the people responded by a display of devout worship.

5. The First Appearance before Pharaoh.
   Its Consequences (Ch. 5)

The first step in the effort to secure freedom for Israel was an audience with Pharaoh. Inasmuch as the Egyptians were committed to the doctrine that Pharaoh was the offspring of the sun, and thereby God personified, such an appearance was a major undertaking.

Historians usually note that the Pharaoh of the oppression who had ruled in Moses' youth was a different individual from the Pharaoh of the Exodus who now ruled. In the presence of this Pharaoh, Moses and Aaron requested permission for a three day journey into the wilderness. Although three days may have had religious significance to Pharaoh it would no doubt be clear that since this was sufficient to take the Israelites beyond the borders of the land, the request was actually a euphemistic petition for the freeing of the Israelites. In three days the Israelites would have learned the sweetness of freedom, they would have developed national unity and organization and they would never again have been willing to submit to Egyptian bondage.

Pharaoh's response was to order an increase in the burdens that were being imposed upon the Israelites. He who was the offspring of the sun could not agree to obey the injunctions of Jehovah. Pharaoh inferred that if the people considered that they had time to engage in religious exercises, they must not be sufficiently burdened in their tasks. The command to produce the same quota of bricks without the supply of straw caused confusion and anguish in the ranks of the Israelites. When the people failed to meet their quota their leaders were cruelly beaten. A typical Egyptian procedure was to beat the victim with a rod on the soles of his feet. The Israelites suddenly found themselves with their troubles greatly multiplied by virtue of the intervention of Moses and Aaron.

The leaders of the Israelites proceeded into the presence of Pharaoh and sought to appeal his harsh demands. Their appeal was firmly rejected. Accordingly, the Israelite leaders took their protests to Moses and in turn they charged him with the responsibility for their new burdens. In their presence, Moses was chastened and humbled. He fled into the presence of the Lord and in a pathetic plea set forth his troubles. This man who had undertaken to obey the call of God was finding that by no means does God guarantee to His servants a life of unchallenged ease.

6. Jehovah's Answer to Moses (Ch. 6)

God magnificently answered the prayer of Moses, and granted a new revelation of Himself as the great JEHOVAH. He commanded Moses and Aaron once more to appear before Pharaoh to request Israel's freedom and He promised to be active on their behalf. By speaking of himself as one of "uncircumcised lips" (v. 12), Moses implied that whereas circumcision was the sign of the renewal of nature, his lips were uncircumcised in the sense of being still in bondage to the natural man and incapable of holy doings. On this occasion, Moses indicated for the last time his reluctance to obey the Lord's commission.

The genealogy in this chapter serves to establish the prerogatives of Moses and Aaron by virtue of their family ties. In v. 20 it is stated that Jochebed was Amram's aunt as well as his sister. The fact that God so carefully guided the detailed preservation of genealogies is evidence of His vital interest and concern for frail mankind.

7. The Renewed Commission. Pharaoh's Heart to be Hardened (Ch. 7:1-13)

The Lord appointed Moses as "a god to Pharaoh" in the sense that Moses was given divine authority and power over Egypt's ruler. On the basis of Pharaoh's acceptance or rejection of Moses, the ruler was to be judged. Aaron was designated as the prophet or spokesman for Moses.

God promised (v. 3) to harden Pharaoh's heart that thereby there might be occasion for His signs and wonders to be wrought in delivering the people from bondage. The intervention of God to harden Pharaoh's heart concerned the ruler's administrative policy and was not a matter of Pharaoh's personal salvation. Although God at this place promised that Pharaoh's heart should be hardened, it was not until the sixth plague had occurred that Pharaoh's heart actually was hardened. Scripture divides its emphasis between stating that Pharaoh hardened his own heart and stating that God hardened his heart.[2] Pharaoh was not made more wicked by the hardening of his heart, he was simply made adamant in his wickedness. In

---

[2]The hardening of Pharaoh's heart is attributed to God in 4:21, 7:3, 9:12, 10:1, 10:20, 10:27, 11:10, 14:4, 14:8, and 14:17. It is attributed to Pharaoh himself in: 7:3, 7:14, 7:22, 8:15, 8:19, 8:32, 9:7, 9:34, 9:35, and 14:5. In each case there are ten references, although some of the texts in the second list are debatable.

spite of the divine involvement, Scripture makes clear that Pharaoh was fully responsible for his conduct; hence the final four plagues, after the time that God hardened Pharaoh's heart, were strokes of penalty upon Pharaoh rather than efforts in disciplining him.

In general, it may be said that Pharaoh's hard-heartedness came about as an outcome of his rejection of divine grace. The occasion of this rejection was God's mercy in offering His grace. Pharaoh hardened his own heart, but the workings of God provided the occasion in which Pharaoh was called upon to take a stand in relation to God. Pharaoh's heart was of such a quality that the divine moving resulted in its being hardened just as sunshine hardens clay. Pharaoh might have inclined his heart to be softened in God's presence just as the same sunshine may soften wax. The withdrawal of God's Spirit from one's heart and life results in a hardening, but God's Spirit does not withdraw until He is forced to do so by the stubborn sinfulness of the one from whose heart He has been driven.

Moses and Aaron proceeded once more before Pharaoh, and on this occasion became involved in a contest with the magicians. Though these latter were able to duplicate the feat of Aaron and likewise produce serpents, the swallowing of their rods established the superiority of God and His messengers. The New Testament tells us that these magicians were named Jannes and Jambres. (cf. 2 Tim. 3:8). They likely worked by satanic power, though their feats could have been mere sleight-of-hand. Some authorities believe that what is here called "Aaron's rod" was the "rod of God" that Moses had brought from Midian. Pharaoh remained unimpressed by this display of miracles, and apparently he concluded that Moses and Aaron were simply a little more clever than his magicians. The fact of so ready a display of miracles makes evident the fact that miracles do not prove that a teaching is sacred, they prove only that it is supernatural.

8. The First Nine Plagues Upon Egypt (Chs. 7:14-10:29)

In the face of the continued enforced bondage of the Israelites, God resorted to the plagues. As the plagues progressed, Moses became increasingly aggressive and militant, and Aaron increasingly dropped into the background. Evans discusses the purpose of the plagues upon Egypt and he makes the following points: [1] that the Egyptians might know Jehovah (7:5), [2] to administer judgment upon the gods of Egypt (12:12), [3] to honor Israel (8:22, 23), [4] to reveal the holiness, justice, and power of God (7:3, 5; 9:15, 16, 27), and [5] a testimony to future generations (10:1, 2).[3] Although catastrophes of the order of the plagues might occur in Egypt at any time, these were especially notable because they were specifically predicted, they were administered specifically as a punishment, and for the most part, they were much more intense than the usual rampages of nature. It is probable that the first three plagues fell equally upon the Israelites, but thereafter Israel was free from the plagues and thereby their separation from the Egyptians became more conspicuous.

On four occasions, Pharaoh temporarily repented and in each case, he made a compromising offer to the Israelites. However, so far as lasting effects were concerned, neither God's severity in inflicting the plague, nor His goodness in withdrawing it, really achieved any real difference in Pharaoh. Pharaoh's compromising offers were as follows: 1) "Go ye, sacrifice in the land." (8:25), 2) "Sacrifice . . . in the wilderness: only ye shall not go very far away:" (8:28), 3) "Go now ye that are men, and serve the Lord;" (10:11), and 4) "Go . . . only let your flocks and your herds be stayed:" (10:24). In each instance the offers of Pharaoh were inadequate and they would have provided emancipation in name only and not actually. The same kind of separation upon which Moses insisted is the separation that Christian believers must exercise today in relation to the world of carnal mankind.

The plagues were not only a punishment and a nuisance to the Egyptians, but they also exposed the weakness of the gods of the land. Almost every realm of life and daily concern were one way or another touched by the plagues, and all citizens were affected. The Egyptians in their pantheism had assigned a different god to each realm or area of being, and yet successively they saw these gods made foolish. It is judged that in view of the sequence and variety of the plagues, a total of nine months would have elapsed from their beginning until they ran their course.

---

[3]Evans, op. cit. pp. 148, 149.

It is interesting to note the manner in which the plagues divide into groups of threes:

GROUP ONE	
Plague 1 warning in morning	Aaron
Plague 2 pre-announcement	used
Plague 3 no pre-announcement	rod
Each of the plagues in this group may be described as "merely loathesome."	

GROUP TWO	
Plague 4 warning in morning	rod
Plague 5 pre-announcement	not
Plague 6 no pre-announcement	mentioned
Each of the plagues in this group involved pain and loss upon their victims.	

GROUP THREE	
Plague 7 warning in morning	Moses
Plague 8 pre-announcement	used
Plague 9 no pre-announcement	rod
Each of the plagues in this group involved dramatic upheavals of nature.	

The first plague concerned the sacred Nile and all water sources derived from it and all its tributaries. It would appear from Ex. 7:24 that well water remained uncontaminated, and only by this means were the people able to survive. In ancient times frogs in Egypt were emblems of the goddess of fertility, and being sacred, were not to be destroyed. It is said that to this day, frogs in Egypt are noisy, repulsive creatures. If the third plague constituted lice, these insects would disastrously contaminate the Egyptians and complicate the elaborate purification processes that their worship involved. It may also have been possible that the insects were some type of mosquito. The insects of the fourth plague were perhaps some mixed species and may have been a type of biting beetle. It was not until the occasion of the seventh plague, the hail, that the Egyptians actually believed that it was coming and attempted to take precautionary measures. Egyptians normally had little contact with locust plagues, for while not unknown, locusts were comparatively rare in Egypt. Pharaoh declined to heed to remonstrances of his advisors in the face of this threat. The prolonged darkness was probably made the more severe by the accusing conscience of the Egyptians during this period.

9.   The Tenth Plague Announced (Ch. 11)

At the Lord's instruction, Moses once more proceeded before Pharaoh and conveyed the word of the forthcoming death of the firstborn. However, even in the face of news such as this, Pharaoh remained unimpressed and impenitent. Moses was so affected by such a callous rejection of the wonders of God's moving that "he went out from Pharaoh in a great anger" (v. 8). The death of the firstborn would affect every family in Egypt and give evidence that God had the power to destroy the entire nation. In the face of all this destruction, God assured Moses that he would "put a difference between the Egyptians and Israel" so that, "against the children of Israel shall not a dog move his tongue."

Once more, God instructed Moses to request the people to borrow or ask jewels from their Egyptian captors (cf. 3:22). The riches thus obtained were to enrich the Israelites and achieve the fulfillment of the prophecy "and afterward shall they come out with great substance" (Gen. 15:14). The word that is here translated "borrow" is the same word in the original that is used in the case of Solomon asking God for wisdom, or Sisera asking Jael for water. In the era of the early church, St. Augustine used this incident of the jewels of Egypt to justify the application of Greek philosophy to Christian theology. He concluded that all truth regardless of its source led to God and therefore he urged Christian scholars freely to adapt secular learning that they might "spoil the Egyptians."

10.   The Passover Instituted (Ch. 12:1-36)

God's provision of the Passover became the birthday of the nation of Israel. God undertook at this time, not the mere deliverance of the Jews from their bondage, but the establishment of a national people with a miraculous historical event as a vital factor in their new national heritage. The word "Passover" is derived from the statement of Scripture "When I see the blood, I will pass over you, . . ." (Ex. 12:13). Although all people

including both Egyptians and Israelites may have deserved divine judgment. God thus provided that the stroke was to fall not upon His people but upon the lamb that was to be the atonement.

Comparisons between the Passover and the sacrifice of Jesus are as follows:

PASSOVER LAMB	JESUS CHRIST
The slain, not the living lamb availed. (12:6)	"Jesus Christ, and him crucified." (1 Cor. 2:2)
The lamb was without blemish. (12:5)	"Christ as . . . a lamb without blemish and without spot:" (1 Pet. 1:19)
Blood to be shed. (12:7)	". . . came there out blood." (Jno. 19:34)
Blood to be sprinkled. (12:22)	"Our hearts sprinkled from an evil conscience." (Heb. 10:22)
No bone broken. (12:46)	"A bone in him shall not be broken." (Jno. 19:36)
If the lamb did not die, then the firstborn would. (12:3, 20)	"The wages of sin is death." (Rom. 6:23)
Those redeemed by the lamb to be sanctified to the Lord. (13:2)	"Ye are not your own . . . For ye are bought with a price:" (1 Cor. 6:19, 20)

The Passover called for the shedding of blood and the sacrifice of life. The blood upon the lintel (top crosspiece of a door frame) and the two single posts caused the house and its dwellers both to be atoned for and to be consecrated. Here, as always in Scripture, hyssop is associated with religious purification. In the acts that he performed in connection with the Passover, the Israelite learned vital lessons concerning God's mode of expiation. The

PLAGUE	TEXT	WARNING	PHAROAH'S HEART	EGYPTIAN GODS MOCKED	REMARKS
water to blood	7:14-24	Yes	heart was hardened	The Nile Gods. The Nile was sacred.	Remained 7 days. Magicians imitated but could not undo the damage.
frogs	8:1-15	Yes	hardened his heart	Ptha-the frog-headed god. Heka-frog goddess.	To the Egyptians, the frog represented human life in embryo.
lice (fleas or gnats)	8:16-19	No	heart was hardened	Leb-earth god.	Magicians acknowledged: "This is the finger of God."--it was outside human control.
flies (dog-flies These bite the edge of the eyelid!)	8:20-32	Yes	hardened his heart	Khepara-beetle god.	Israel immune. FIRST offer from Pharaoh. SECOND offer from Pharaoh.
murrain	9:1-7	Yes	heart was hardened	Apis (or Sera-phis)--sacred cattle god at Memphis.	Some cattle survived. Murrain is a general term implying a plague upon domestic animals.
boils (an eruptive disease that turned into an open sore.)	9:8-12	No	Lord hardened his heart	Neit-the goddess queen of heaven.	Even magicians affected and rendered unclean to worship Neit.
hail	9:13 35	Yes	hardened his heart	Iris-water deity. Osiris-fire deity.	Those smitten who neglected the warning.
locusts	10:1-20	Yes	Lord hardened his heart	Shu-god of air. Sebek-insect god.	THIRD offer from Pharaoh. Egyptian officers pleaded with their ruler.
darkness	10:21-22	No	Lord hardened his heart	Ra (or Atun-Re) sun god the supreme deity.	FOURTH offer from Pharaoh. Darkness remained 3 days. The name "Pharaoh" means sun.

evangelical Bible scholar would see no ground for identifying the institution of the Passover with the Canaanitish spring rites of purification that conventionally were practised among Israel's pagan neighbours in ancient times. However, it is usually considered that Christianity represents the transposition of the the Old Testament Jewish Passover into the Christian ordinance of the Lord's Supper.

The death angel proceeded to perform his mission at midnight. No doubt a violent reaction was promptly forthcoming. In Eastern fashion the death of the firstborn in the home is the occasion for the women of the household to rush outside and to rouse the neighborhood with a piercing wail. In this instance, as one household after another was disturbed, each would add its quota of cries. Upon this night in Egypt the entire inhabited land must have been an ever-rising chorus of chilling death cries. In a few short hours the cries of the Egyptians may have more than equaled the centuries of Israel's sighing and crying during her bitter bondage. At this point, Pharaoh unhesitatingly agreed to the departure of Moses and his people and he even requested that they would pronounce blessing upon him (v. 31, 32). Pharaoh's people likewise joined in encouraging the Israelites to leave and actually sharing with them their riches and jewels that the costs of the journey might in part be provided.

Egypt has been a fruitful archaeological field, and it would be a matter of some interest to find archaeological confirmation and elucidation of the Egyptian bondage. Several factors have been alluded to from time to time thus far, but in the interests of precise scholarship, some caution is probably necessary. Finegan, a competent archaeologist but a liberal theologian, says at the close of his chapters concerning archaeology in Egypt:

In conclusion we may say that Egypt has afforded us no direct evidence of the sojourn of the Israelites, but it has revealed much which makes that sojourn and the Exodus which followed entirely credible. . . . It was not uncommon for Asiatic people to find refuge in Egypt nor for them to be set at heavy labor on the great building projects of the Pharaohs. Without doubt the children of Israel were in Egypt in the days of the Hyksos, and their oppression and Exodus fell under Rameses II. [4]

Egyptian history of this era remains a challenge to chronological research.

_____

[4]Jack Finegan, Light From the Ancient Past. Princeton: Princeton University Press, 1959, p. 134.

II. ISRAEL'S JOURNEY TO SINAI (12:37-18:27)

1. The Journey Begun. Further Instructions Concerning the Passover (12:37-51)

The Israelites first gathered at Rameses and then proceeded with their great migration by journeying to Succoth. The company is described as numbering 600,000 men (cf. a year later it numbered 603,550 men of military age [Num. 1:46]). It may be assumed that with women and children the entire group numbered upwards of three million people. The mixed multitude (literally: swarm of foreigners) appears to have consisted of discontented and unhappy people of all nations. This group later was the cause of many of Israel's troubles in the wilderness. The possibility of a mass migration of so large a group frequently is disturbing to scholars and various theories have been suggested that would interpret the Bible so as not to require so large a group. It has been suggested for instance that instead of reading 600,000 we should read 600 families. However, few evangelicals would be impressed by such a theory. As a parallel to the Bible story, history reports that in January 1771 a company of upwards of 600,000 Kalmuks staged a secret migration from Czarist Russia. In five months of time, beginning in the dead of a Russian winter, they travelled a total of 2,100 miles carrying their infants and little children and their old people and at the same time maintaining constant military action against the pursuing Cossack army that followed. They eventually successfully and safely arrived at their destination in China.

There is no general agreement concerning the date of the exodus. The chronology of Solomon's reign would permit this event to be calculated at about 1446 B.C. (cf. 1 Ki. 6:1). Such a date would coincide nicely with the generally agreed date for the destruction of Jericho which was very close to 1400 B.C. and thus just about 40 years after the Exodus. However, this date would not put the migration of the Israelites in Joseph's time in the Hyksos period as the facts seem to indicate. Further, it would require that the Egyptian capital be still located on the upper Nile rather than in the Delta region where it seems to be during the time of events of the Bible. The concern over the location of the capital has led some scholars to prefer to assign the Exodus to 1250 B.C. and leave unanswered the problem of explaining the destruction of Jericho. The dating in Ex. 12:40 identifies the time "the sojourning of the children of Israel" and this period is usually thought to have begun with Abraham's entrance into Canaan. The same 430 year period is mentioned in Gal. 3:7. As discussed previously, the period is described as an even 400 years in Acts 7:4. Some scholars feel that this is dating from the occasion of the weaning of Isaac which probably was some 30 years after Abraham's arrival in Canaan. In the light of evidence presently available, it would appear that dogmatic views concerning the date of the Exodus are not adequately warranted.

Though the Passover had already been prescribed as an annual ordinance, the Israelites were now given confirmation and additional information concerning the manner of its observance. One must be either an Israelite by birth or a duly circumcised proselyte in order to partake of the Passover. Thus any Gentile who wished the privileges of Israel might enjoy them provided he was willing to be circumcised.

2. The Sanctification of the Firstborn. The Journey Continued (Ch. 13)

The instructions for the dedication to God of the firstborn are here interwoven with the description of the permanent ordinance of the Passover. God had a special claim on the firstborn, both because He had spared them on the night of the Passover in Egypt, and because He had adopted Israel as His firstborn son. (cf. "Thus said the Lord, Israel is my son, even my firstborn" [4:22].). All firstborn males fit for God's service were to be devoted to Him, those not fit were to be redeemed. At that time just as in all times, God sought for His service the best of the people. Later, of course, he allowed the tribe of Levi to substitute for the firstborn as his chosen workers.

The idea of the Jewish phylacteries (from Gk. phylassō--I guard) is apparently based upon verses such as v. 16 "And it shall be for a token upon thine hand, and for frontlets between thine eyes: . . ." A phylactery is a small box containing pieces of paper inscribed with certain passages of Scripture. On occasions of worship, pious Jews wear these boxes upon their forehead or in the bend of the right arm. A leather thong serves to hold them in place. It is evident that God intended, not to prescribe usage of amulets in the manner of the heathen, but He meant that His law was always to guide man's viewpoint and direct his actions. Murphy says of phylacteries, "This custom was not prescribed by the . . . passage and can only be regarded as an indication of a feeble and declining piety."

Israel next journeyed from Succoth to Etham. They were led by the emblem of God's presence: the cloud and the fire. It is likely that there was only one pillar, but that its difference as cloud or fire depended upon how it was seen (cf. 1 Cor. 10:4). The prophet Nehemiah commented, "Thou leddest them in the day by a cloudy pillar; and in the night by a pillar of fire, to give them light in the way wherein they should go" (Neh. 9:12). Insofar as the pillar of cloud and fire guided the people in the way that they should go, it is a type of the Holy Spirit; He today guides Christian believers in their daily walk. "For as many as are led by the Spirit of God, they are the sons of God" (Rom. 8:14). Inasmuch as the pillar of cloud led the Israelites to Etham the people might clearly have understood that God planned otherwise than that they take the shortest route to the promised land.

3. The Crossing of the Red Sea (Ch. 14)

The site of Pi-hahiroth, where God next led the people constituted a strategic trap for the fleeing Israelites. On either side were mountains and desert. Before them was the Red Sea. As God intended, within a day or two this predicament invited pursuit by Pharaoh and his company of chariots. In such an hour of extremity, Moses exhorted the fearful people, "Fear ye not, stand still, and see the salvation of the Lord." Thus God intervened to provide for the crossing of the Red Sea. Some scholars feel that since the original implies this was a "Reed Sea" the body of water actually was not the gulf of Suez but a northern inland lake that is now extinct. It is evident that it is no insignificant body of water, for the entire army of Egypt was destroyed by the returning waves. Scripture points out that before long the bodies of dead Egyptians littered the shore and Josephus reports that the Israelites armed themselves with weapons that were salvaged on this occasion.

In order to accomplish the events described in Scripture the body of water crossed would necessarily be several miles in width. The dividing of the waters seems to have been accomplished by causing them to congeal (as if they were frozen) and thus stand as a wall on either side of the marching Israelites. Elsewhere Scripture comments "He divided the sea, and caused them to pass through; and he made the waters to stand as a heap" (Psa. 78:13). Scripture describes the role of the wind in connection with this division but it is to be noted that although a strong wind will somewhat influence the ebb or tide of a body of water no natural wind has been known actually to divide waters. Evidently the wind was only one aspect of God's working and not the whole means of His divine operation.

The crossing of the Red Sea is a type of water baptism for the Christian. St. Paul wrote ". . . all our fathers were under the cloud, and all passed through the sea; and all baptized unto Moses in the cloud and in the sea" (1 Cor. 10:1, 2). In crossing the Red Sea, the Israelites who already were redeemed by blood now left Egypt forever and officially and determinately took on a new life and a new leader. Their slavery in bondage in Egypt was typical of the sinner's ensnarement in the bondage of sin. In effect, a nation of slaves now were a nation of freed men and in standing on the further shore of the Red Sea they were standing upon the shores of a new continent.

4. The Song of Redemption (Ch. 15:1-21)

The song of Moses commemorating this victory is the first major song in the Bible, and among the oldest of known poems. (but note the "Song of Lamech" [Gen. 4:23]). It is mainly occupied with God rather than with man. As well as breathing praise and worship to their Deliverer, it also is prophetic, and it declares that God will repeat His conquering acts. The composition is arranged into alternate long and short stanzas; the long stanzas refer to the Lord and His ransomed people, and the short stanzas to their defeated or dismayed opponents. It both begins and ends with a long stanza.

Probably this song was sung antiphonally, with the men led by Moses, singing the main lyrics, and the women led by Miriam, replying with the refrain, "Sing ye to the Lord, for he hath triumphed gloriously; the horse and his rider hath he thrown into the sea" (v. 21). The women also danced in an unrestrained expression of their sacred joy. The entire performance must have been both impressive and inspiring. Here were a people, who only a few days before were a groaning race of slaves, now totally delivered out of judgment, placed beyond the power of the enemy, and miraculously set free. Their exuberant worship and praise is genuinely understandable. The words "I will prepare him an habitation" (15:2); have been thought by some to be an intimation of the future construction of the tabernacle.

5. From the Red Sea to Elim (Ch. 15:22-27)

When Jehovah's glorious victory was duly commemorated, the Israelites struck camp and pursued their journey southward. Across the Red Sea, they were now out of Egypt and journeying on the Sinaitic peninsula. For the first three days they travelled in the area known as the Wilderness of Shur. This region was barren land with insufficient rainfall for agriculture, but with some pasturage so as to support the flocks and herds of the Israelites. In recent times, archaeologist Nelson Glueck travelling in these regions reports regular daytime temperatures of at least 113 degrees.

By the time the people arrived at Marah, they were excessively thirsty, and thus the discovery that the water there was alkaline and unfit to drink was a bitter disappointment. The people commenced the first of a series of wilderness murmurings. Comments Meyer: "From minstrels they became mutineers." Moses' appeal to God brought the information that a certain tree cast into the waters would sweeten them. Hence, God's servant was vindicated and the Lord had opportunity to reveal Himself as the Jehovah-Rapha--"the Lord that healeth." It is not likely that the tree actually sweetened the waters, rather, casting it in became the act of faith which was the occasion of the manifestation of the Lord's healing. One site that is sometimes thought to be Marah is Huwara which is plausibly located in relation to known geography. There is there a natural well which to this day contains bitter alkaline water.

At Elim, the next stopping place, there were twelve wells of water and seventy palm trees. An oasis site known as Wady Ghurundel

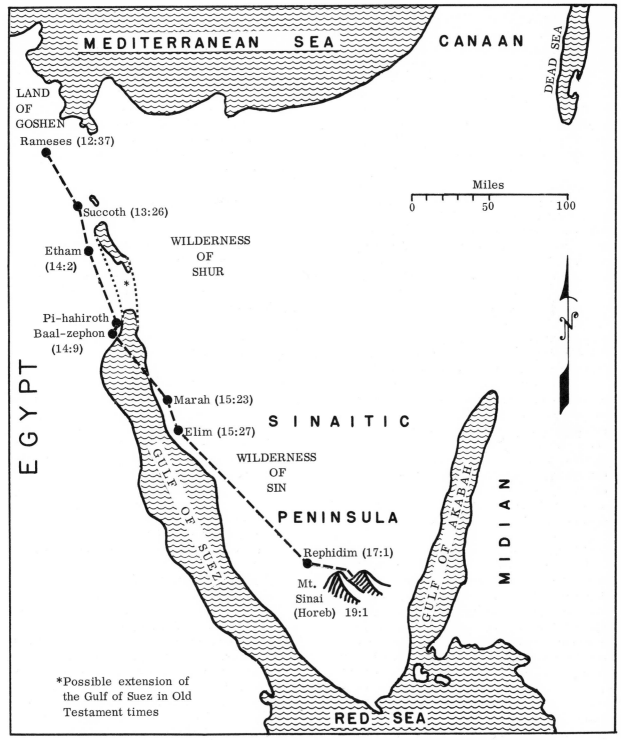

Figure 9 -- Israel's Journeys as Recorded in Exodus

is identified with the ancient Elim. Today it supports not only palm trees, but also tamarisks and acacia. The experience at Elim typifies the Christian experience: although there may be times of suffering, in general for each such occasion the believer may look forward to multiplied times of blessing. Only by enduring Marah and treading the desert were the Israelites able to come to Elim. The people remained in this lovely spot for three weeks and no doubt morale was thus restored.

6. Events in the Wilderness of Sin (Ch. 16)

The Wilderness of Sin, into which Israel next journeyed, was a geographical area believed to be in the southwest section of the Sinaitic peninsula. The people again found cause for complaint, and in their second wilderness murmuring, protested that their food supply was inadequate. God's response was His promise to provide manna, and also His provision of the quails.

Manna is here described as "a small round thing" . . . "like coriander seed, white; and the taste of it was like wafers made with honey" (vv. 14, 31). Elsewhere, Scripture reports: "And the people went about, and gathered it, and ground it in mills, or beat it in a mortar, and baked it in pans, and made cakes of it . . ." (Num. 11:8). Manna, as its name implies, differed from anything the Israelites knew (the name means "What is this?), and to this day it is an unknown substance. Though the natives of Palestine are known occasionally to eat dried white lichen swept into piles by the wind, and also the exuded gum of the tamarisk shrub (which like the manna must be gathered early before the sun can melt it), neither of these substances has the qualities or uses ascribed to manna in Scripture. In both its nature and provision, the manna obviously was something miraculous. An omer of manna (about 2 pounds or 3-1/2 quarts) was laid aside as a reminder of God's provision in this hour of need.

In many aspects, God's provision of the manna is rich in typical teachings. The smallness of the manna depicts the lowliness of the incarnate Jesus Christ. The roundness speaks of His universal accessibility. That the manna was white speaks of the spotless humanity of Jesus; that it was sweet indicates the nature of Christ to the one who appropriates Him. Just as the manna was associated with the dew, so Christ is associated with the Holy Spirit. It was necessary to gather the manna daily just as it is necessary daily to relate to Christ. The manna provided sustenance for all; Christ is sufficient for all as the Bread of Life. Our Lord particularly identified the manna with Himself in being sent down from heaven by the Father. (cf. Jno. 6:31-35).

The mention of the Sabbath in v. 23 is the first Biblical use of the word and, apart from the creation story, the earliest hint of the observance of this day. Though some of the people at first disbelieved the fact of the divine provision of the day, they soon learned that God meant what He said. "So the people rested on the seventh day" (v. 30). This incident makes plain the fact that even prior to the Law, the Sabbath was being observed. It cannot be maintained that the observance of Sabbath is exclusively a legal function without any other significance or precedence.

7. Events at Rephidim (Ch. 17)

The Israelites arrived at Rephidim and promptly began once more to murmur--the third murmuring of their journey. Once more the objection concerned the lack of water, and once more Moses took the matter to the Lord in earnest prayer. The Lord made provision by having Moses smite the adjacent rock of Mount Horeb and at that spot sending forth abundant water. This was not the occasion of Moses' sin, though the latter incident was similar (see Numbers 20:7-13). The theme of the smitten rock is repeated in the New Testament: ". . . They drank of that spiritual Rock that followed them: and that Rock was Christ" (1 Cor. 10:4). It is said that this incident was the inspiration for the hymn "Rock of Ages."

While Israel was encamped at Rephidim, the plundering Amalekites attacked, and the Israelites, for the first time, had to engage in warfare. They were granted ample divine aid, however, particularly when Moses held aloft his hands in a gesture of intercession. When Moses tired he was aided by Aaron and Hur just as all of God's leaders should be aided in their battle for the Kingdom. The leader of Israel's victorious forces was Joshua, who is here mentioned for the first time in Scripture. Josephus comments that Joshua was forty-five years old at the time; Bible scholars are inclined to accept this figure. On this occasion, the Lord was made known to Israel as "Jehovah-nissi" which means "the Lord our banner," and implies "the Lord our victory!" Amalek's attach against the Israelites was the beginning of a long series of harassments by these people against the people of Jehovah. Not until David's time were they wholly subdued. (cf. 2 Sam. 8:12). In Gen. 36:12 Amalek is named as the grandson of Esau. Whereas Egypt typically represents Satan in his attack, Amalek is a type of the flesh in its attacks.

8. The Meeting with Jethro (Ch. 18)

Moses' wife Zipporah, and his two sons, Gershom and Eliezer, had begun the journey with Moses from Midian to Egypt, but at some point they apparently had turned back. With Israel encamped at Rephidim, however, the time seemed favorable for a family reunion, and hence Jethro came, bringing them with him. Jethro was profoundly influenced in favor of worship of Jehovah (vv. 9-11), but it is not clear whether or not he was a true believer. On the occasion of this visit he made the very practical suggestion that Moses should appoint some deputies to assist him in his work. It appears that Jethro's suggestion was taken up by the people so that this organizational development was later described as being by popular demand. (see Deut. 1:13). The appointment of rulers of thousands, hundreds, fifties and tens served effectively to relieve Moses of detail work, though God later made a modification of this system by the appointment of the seventy elders. (Num. 11:16, 17).

III. ISRAEL AT SINAI (Chs. 19-40)

1. Arrival at Sinai. Preparation for the Giving of the Law (Ch. 19)

The departure from Egypt had been on the fourteenth day of the first month (12:2, 6), and the arrival at Sinai is now reported to have been on the first day of the third month. Since there were five days of instruction and preparation before the giving of the Law, the total time from the exodus was exactly fifty days. Evidently Israel received the Law on the same day that was later designated as the Feast of Pentecost. The site at which the Law was given is named Sinai thirty-five time in Scripture and Horeb seventeen times. No effort seems to be made to distinguish between these two names. Traditionally Sinai is identified with Jubal Musa (an Arabic name meaning "The Mount of Moses"). The mount is 7,370 feet high.

As a preparation for the giving of the Law, God called Moses into His presence and instructed him to make clear to the people the nature of the covenant which He was about to impose. The people listened to Moses with only moderate concern and they glibly

promised, "All that the Lord hath spoken we will do" (v. 8). In giving the Law to Israel, God's purpose was that they might be priestly-mediators to all mankind. It was not God's plan that the nation should become narrow and selfishly exclusive in her religion as she did in later years.

Before the Law was actually given, there was a three-day period of additional prepparation. During this time, all the people were to be spiritually and physically cleansed so as to be the best possible subjects for the visitation of God. Even the mountain from which the Law was to be given was made holy, and there was a great demonstration of supernatural phenomena including: lightning, thunder, a trumpet blast, smoke, fire, and an earthquake. In Old Testament times the principle prevailed whereby external events were made the symbol and type of things internal; to be cleansed externally was the mark of being cleansed internally.

2. The Decalogue (Ch. 20)

The ten commandments otherwise known as the "decalogue," the "greater law" or the "ten words" was not radically unique in the requirements that were set forth; this statement represents only reasonable moral laws that are essential if man is to live in a harmonious society. Rather, the unique aspect of the ten commandments was the association of moral precepts with spiritual religion. Among the known ancient nations, it was the nation of Israel who uniquely coupled civil law with the requirements of God, and freed such law from the arbitrary capriciousness of mere human whim.

Typical of existing moral codes prior to the time of Moses is the well-known code of Hammurabi. This legal code dated several centuries before Sinai has been found in modern times at Shushan carved upon a handsome stone column about seven feet high. Hammurabi is identified as a ruler of Babylon, probably in the seventeenth century B.C. The Code contains a total of 247 laws and at least superficially they are very similar to the Biblical Law. However, whereas Moses stressed the dignity of the individual man, Hammurabi stressed the protection of property. Hammurabi's Code distinguishes between rich and poor, includes bodily mutilation as a prescribed punishment and it prescribes capital punishment for a total of thirty-two crimes, many of them civil crimes rather than moral. It is evident that the sense of human equality and universal human rights that constitute the basis of laws in western civilization today is to be found uniquely in the laws of Moses and not in these typical secular sources.

The Law of Moses is essentially a religious pronouncement and it is ascribed directly to God. The laws are intended to contrast the sinfulness of man and the holiness of God so that man might be moved to cast himself upon divine mercy. God orally spoke the laws to Moses, but in addition, He personally wrote them upon two tables of stone (cf. Ex. 32:16). It is a fact of significance to pious Jews that only this portion of Scripture can claim to have been personally inscribed by God.

The commandments are mainly negative, with only two positive commands and eight prohibitions. Only one, the fifth commandment contains any promise of blessing for obedience. The first four state man's duty to God: I. All other deities and pagan religious systems are categorically condemned. The fact of the one true sovereign God is unequivocally asserted. II. The true God is to remain invisible and indescribable and with no physical representation. The presence of God was to be understood spiritually and in no manner whatsoever represented by an image. Judaism was to be uniquely distinctive among pagan religions in rejecting the conventional carved stone monuments, the bronze images and clay figurines that were frequently used. Israel's stand has been described as "aniconic." III. The name of that which is lofty and exalted is not to be used in a way that is empty and meaningless. IV. The Sabbath rest is to provide opportunity for worship, fellowship, and moral culture. This commandment alone is not reaffirmed in the New Testament and is not enjoined upon Christians.

The remaining six commandments refer to man's duties to his fellows. V. One's parents are his only natural superiors and in the home in which father and mother are reverenced, foundations are laid which even revolution cannot overthrow. VI. Human life stands sacred in God's sight. VII. The household is to be kept pure. Marriage is sanctioned, but all unchaste acts are forbidden. VIII. One man may not take what another has justly earned. IX. One cannot misrepresent his fellows and expect to have God in his life. X. Improper desire is the root of all evil; envy, jealousy, and hunger for that which is another's are all a violation of God's requirements for man. It is God's intention that man manifest righteousness of attitude as well as righteousness of act.

On this occasion, also God formally instituted the altar as a place of worship and sacrifice, and a site where man might meet God. Although altars had previously been used for this purpose there had not been explicit divine approval. God prescribed that the altar might be constructed in as simple a manner as possible to avoid any intimations of idolatry. Paganism favored elaborate construction and ornamentation and God's people were to be different.

In general, Christians consider that the Law for them is not binding, but that its principles serve to reveal the nature and will of God. A Christian is to conform to the higher Law manifested in the Holy life of Jesus, and thereby he will more than accord with all of the Mosaic legal requirements. St. Paul wrote: "Therefore we conclude that a man is justified by faith without the deeds of the law . . . . Do we then make void the law through faith? God forbid: yea, we establish the law" (Rom. 3:28, 31). Erdman expresses the view of many when he says:

> The followers of Christ are not under obligation to keep the ceremonial laws of Moses, but they accept the standards of the moral laws as rules of life. They are "free from the law" as a ground of acceptance with God, they are not free to break the law He has ordained for men. They fulfill its requirements out of gratitude to Christ and by the power of His spirit.[5]

3. Judgments Pertaining to Personal and Property Relations (Chs. 21, 22)

The Mosaic judgments and statutes constitute a sane and practical prescription of civil law and right relations with one's neighbor. The

---

[5]Charles R. Erdman, The Book of Deuteronomy. New York: Fleming H. Revell Company, 1953, p. 31.

judgments (21:1 - 22:17) are religious enact-
ments set forth as if they were pronouncements
or decisions of the court. They are made au-
thoritatively at this time and they apply to similar cases in the future. Statutes constitute
permanent rules of conduct which are basically
matters for the conscience more than matters
for the judge. Bible content from 22:21-23:19
may be considered to be statutes. To violate a
statute incurs not so much a legal penalty as
the personal displeasure of the Lord. Among
the subjects included in the judgments and statutes were: servitude (21:1-11); homicide and
personal injury (21:12-32); civil and criminal
liability (21:33-22:15); marriage (22:16-24);
and usury and sacrifice (22:25-31).

Two principles stressed by God included
the dignity of labor and the subordination of
property to personal right. Pagan society of
those days looked upon slaves as mere "ani-
mated tools." Work of any type was dishonor-
able and slaves had no human claims or rights.
Property values took precedence over human
values. Debtors could be imprisoned privately,
chained, sold into slavery, or even slain by the
creditor. Among the specific concepts set forth
in this section are the following: 1. After six
years a Hebrew bondman must be freed. 2. A
bondman could elect to refuse freedom and commit himself to his master for life. His ear lobe
was pierced as a voluntary servitude sign. 3. A
master should assume the responsibility to guarantee that the personal virtue of a bondwoman
should not be violated. 4. Capital crimes included: premeditated murder, kidnapping, and
the cursing of one's parents. 5. Damages shall
be payable in the case of injuries inflicted upon
another deliberately or through carelessness,
the amount depending upon the extent of the injuries. 6. The owner of an animal was responsible for its misdeeds. 7. Restitution for crimes,
included not only repayment, but sizeable penalty compensations in addition. 8. The weaker
was protected from the stronger who might take
unfair advantage. 9. God was to be put first in
all enterprises.

The judgments emphasized the difference
between accidental and deliberate, and between
spontaneous and premeditated injury to another.
The law specifically made provision for legal
immunity to provide for a fair trial and due legal process in contrast with the typical precipi-
tous acts of justice in pagan society. On the
other hand, there is no immunity for the willful

murderer even though he tried to cling to the
altar (21:12, 14). Civilized men everywhere
have recognized that the standards and patterns
set forth in the law of Moses have abiding validity in ordering the relationships of mankind.
The decalogue and its judgments remain in
force in almost all civilized human society.

Critics sometimes condemn the provisions of 21:23-25 as being unworthy of a benefi-
cent God. (cf. "Eye for eye, tooth for tooth,
hand for hand," etc.). However, it is evident
that the Israelites never followed the practice
of physical mutilation literally, and it would
have been a perversion of Judaism to do so.
Likewise, there is no evidence that the Jews
used 22:18 as an excuse to torture and murder
eccentric females. (cf. "Thou shalt not suffer
a witch to live."). In Leviticus 20:27, God indicated that the penalty for the practice of black
arts was death by stoning, but this provision
engendered no hysterical witch-hunt.

4. Precepts for Right Living. Divine Ordinances. (Ch. 23)

The first nine verses of this chapter add
twelve miscellaneous laws or judgments to those
of the preceding two chapters. The judgments
in this section concern such topics as: gossip,
mob violence, justice, good neighborliness,
bribes, and humanitarianism.

The sabbatic year is here mentioned
(v. 11) for the first time; while the observance
of the sabbath day is emphasized anew. The
necessary extra harvest in the sixth year was
to be provided by God in specific divine intervention, and was not to be merely a chance outcome. Most of the regulations concerning the
sabbatic year are found in Leviticus 25:1-7. The
three feasts which all Israelites were required
to observe also are mentioned here: Unleavened
Bread(this feast included the Passover), First-
fruits, and Ingathering (also called Tabernacles) and their significance briefly set forth.
More information concerning these feasts is
found in Leviticus 23.

It is believed that the Israelites were
forbidden to "seethe a kid in his mother's milk"
(v. 19, cf. 34:26), because the milk was that
which provided life for the kid and to use it to
prepare the young animal for food was to engender an outlook that was warped and hardened.
Furthermore, according to the Ras Shamra

tablets, such a ceremony had significance in pagan worship. Among the Canaanites it was practiced as a magical fertility technique that was intended to produce the early rains. Orthodox Jews today consider these verses to be the basis of their "laws of kashrut" which prescribe that dairy foods and flesh foods shall not be eaten at the same meal and that pots, pans and dishes used in preparing each shall not be mixed.

The chapters of judgments and ordinances (which contain a total of 70 judgments) close with God's promise of the guiding Angel, victory over foes and usurpers of the Promised Land, and the promise of abundant prosperity. The Angel is referred to elsewhere as the "angel of his presence" (Isa. 63:9) and is thought to be a theophany of the Lord Jesus.

5. The Covenant Sealed. The Leaders Worship (Ch. 24)

The Israelites' vow to obey the Law of the Lord was made the more solemn by the enactment of a blood covenant. The fact that the blood of the sacrifice was sprinkled partly upon the people and partly upon the altar indicated that both man and God were being bound by ties of blood.

On this occasion, Moses, Aaron and his sons, and the elders of Israel are said to

have seen God. What they apparently saw was some symbol or phenomenon of God's presence, or perhaps a theophany of some sort. Moses later declared, ". . . for ye saw no manner of similitude on the day that the Lord spake unto you in Horeb, out of the midst of the fire" (Deut. 4:15). Keil and Delitzsch say, "We must regard it as a vision of God in some form of manifestation which rendered the divine nature discernible to the human eye."[6] It is not that Scripture does not here, and in a number of other references (e. g. Gen. 18:1; Judg. 13:22; Isa. 6:1), report "seeing" God, but in comparing Scripture with Scripture it seems necessary to consider this to be a special usage of "see."

Following the worship with Aaron and the elders, Moses went up into the mountain and there he remained for forty days. He left Aaron and Hur in charge during his absence. It is evident from 32:17 that Joshua was with Moses on the mountain, but 24:2 and 33:11 would indicate that only Moses went into the presence of God. For six days Joshua waited apart, but it was nevertheless his privilege to be closer than any other man to the vital events on Sinai. To a large degree, he shared with Moses the thrill and blessing of these hallowed moments.

6. The Tabernacle and its Furnishings (Chs. 25-27, 30, cf. Chs. 36-39)

The tabernacle, which has been called "The Gospel of the Eye," was the symbolic dwelling place of God among His ransomed people. It constituted an expansion and completion of that which was represented in the passover lamb and in its every part spoke of Jesus Christ. This home in which God dwelt, or tabernacled, in Old Testament times was

---

[6]C. F. Keil and F. Delitzsch, Biblical Commentary on the Old Testament (Vol. II, The Pentateuch). Edinburgh: T. & T. Clark, 1878, p. 159.

Bas-relief of a wagon carved in stone, with a representation of the Ark of the Covenant. This carving is from the synagogue at Capernaum. While not all scholars agree, there are many who hold this to be a picture of the ancient Ark containing the scrolls of the Torah. It is held that the Ark was movable during a certain period of Israel's history.

Carved stone relief showing an ancient Hebrew menorah or seven-branched candlestick. This carving, from an unspecified source, is on display at the Palestine Archaeological Museum in Jerusalem, Jordan. Representations of the menorah in classical design are not common in Bible lands today.

planned by God Himself. It is described as: ". . . the true tabernacle, which the Lord pitched" (Heb. 8:2), and the origin of the plans given to Moses is said to have been:". . . the pattern shewed . . . in the mount" (Heb. 8:5). Moses was instructed to duplicate that which he had been shown. Except for the atonement money (30:11-16), all of the materials of the tabernacle were given as voluntary offerings by the people. The people gave specific materials for construction according to the careful directions of the Lord.

The Ark (25:10-22 37:1-9)

Because the description of the tabernacle begins from the inside and proceeds outward, the ark is the first article of furniture mentioned. It would have been the last article met by the approaching worshipper. The ark may be thought of as the most important of all the furniture and the central object towards which everything else pointed. In construction, the ark comprised a chest or trunk within which the tables of the law might be preserved. In size it was three feet nine inches long and two feet three inches deep and wide (assuming a cubit was eighteen inches). It was made of shittim wood (Acacia vera--hence popularly known as acacia) and was covered within and without with an overlay of pure gold. It was the only piece of furniture thus lined within of gold. There was a golden rim or border about the top and at each corner there was a golden ring through which the carrying staves were passed. It has been pointed out that the wooden box overlaid with gold speaks of the incarnate Christ with deity enshrined within humanity. Desert acacia is thought to be the reference in the phrase "root out of dry ground" (Isa. 53:2).

The top or lid of the ark was a slab of pure gold, and it was known as the mercy seat. It typically represented the throne of God. The Psalmist thus expressed himself: "The Lord reigneth; . . . he sitteth between the cherubim; let the earth be moved" (Psa. 99:1). It was

there that the blood was sprinkled as a symbol of the appeasement of God through sacrifice. Though the sinner deserved condemnation, God looked at him by way of the blood-sprinkled mercy seat and on that basis granted pardon and blessing. The word 'mercy seat' has a dual meaning and may be rendered: 'propitiation, place of atonement, or covering over of sins.' Thus, "Whom God hath set forth to be a propitiation [or mercy seat] through faith in his blood . . ." (Rom. 3:25). The New Testament believer understands that Christ is the meeting place between a Holy God and a penitent sinner just as the mercy seat was Israel's place of meeting with God. As the shed blood of Christ, so the sprinkled blood upon the imperishable golden lid, rendered God favorable to one who deserved only destruction. At the mercy seat, the Old Testament believer learned that sin could be covered and God might be propitiated.

On the basis of 1 Kings 8:9 and 2 Chron. 5:10, it is usually considered that, at least in the temple, the ark was used as a repository for nothing except the two tables of Law. However, perhaps during the time of the tabernacle the pot of manna and Aaron's rod were also placed there. "So Aaron laid it [i.e. the pot of manna] up before the Testimony, to be kept" (Ex. 16:34). The description of the tabernacle in the book of Hebrews definitely described these items as being in the ark. ". . . wherein was the golden pot that had manna,   and

Aaron's rod that budded, and the tables of the covenant" (Heb. 9:4). It is probable that Spink is correct when he says: "The golden pot of manna was removed from the ark in the Temple--no need for wilderness fare in Glory!" The word "Testimony" is another name for the two tables of Law. (cf. Ex. 31:18).

The cherubim which were formed upon the mercy seat typically represent the judgment of God. Their position indicates that God's judgment upon Israel was averted because of the blood-sprinkled mercy seat. Just as these golden replicas looked down upon the sprinkled blood, so heaven's citizens witness the solemn blood covenant between God and any man who identifies himself with Christ's atoning sacrifice. Just as in the tabernacle, the meeting place between God and man was one of mercy and not of judgment, so today, penitent men may meet God at the cross and there find abundant mercy and grace. The added advantage of the New Testament believer is that his sin is forever put away, whereas in Old Testament times sin was merely covered over.

The Table of Shewbread (25:23-30, 37:10-16)

The table where the shewbread was to be placed was about the size and proportions of a modern coffee table. Its dimensions were probably 3' long, 1'6" wide, and 2'3" high. It, just as the ark, was made of durable desert acacia wood covered with gold, and decorated with a border of gold about the top. There was a ring at each corner for the carrying staves.

The table served to display (or shew[7]) twelve small, flat, round loaves that were laid out in orderly fashion so as to be displayed, and then liberally sprinkled with frankincense. Each Sabbath day, new loaves were provided. The priests were entitled to eat the old loaves if they chose, though they were required to do so in the Holy Place. The frankincense that was removed each week was burned as a special oblation (offering) to God. Also on the table, in addition to the bread, were: dishes

(bread plates), spoons (to sprinkle frankincense), covers (literally "cups, flagons"-- probably containers for liquid offerings), and bowls (vessels containing the frankincense).

The shewbread, in serving as nourishment for the priests, represented Christ the Bread of Life who nourishes believers. As the bread was laid out upon this table, it was evident both to God and to all men who would care to look. Thus, the shewbread is also known as "the bread of his presence." The bread brought God and man face to face, for thus man partook of that which was dedicated to God, and mutually God and man enjoyed reconciliation and fellowship. The twelve loaves spoke of the twelve tribes, and typically embraced all of the people of God. The fact that a table was used speaks of fellowship, feeding, and communion. The fragrant frankincense speaks of the sweet savor of Christ's righteous life.

The Golden Candlestick (25:31-40, 37:17-24; Num. 8:1-4)

The candlestick, or lampstand, was made of a talent of pure gold which was shaped and tempered by beating. It weighed well over one hundred pounds, and according to tradition, stood three cubits high. From the massive base there arose a central shaft with three branches on each side to provide seven lamps in all. Although tradition depicts the lampstand with each lamp at the same level, many authorities feel that on typical grounds they necessarily would have been stepped, with the center light rising above those at the sides. Each arm and lamp socket was attractively formed so as to represent a flowering and fruit-bearing almond branch. This type of beaten work in metal is known as repoussé. The bowls, knops, and flowers mentioned in Scripture suggest the successive stages in the process of the developing almonds. The lamp was designed to use oil for fuel, with a wick for each of the seven flames. At today's prices the value of the metal in the lamp would be at least $30,000.

The candlestick speaks of the sevenfold perfection of the illumination of the Spirit who witnesses to and through Jesus Christ, the Light of the world. Scripture speaks of "Seven lamps of fire burning before the throne, which are the seven spirits of God" (Rev. 4:5). The lampstand produced the only light in the Holy Place, for there natural light was excluded. The ministry and service of the priests in the tabernacle was

---

[7]In pronunciation and primary meaning this word is identical with our word "show." The form "shew" is found in the Bible simply because that was the spelling of the word "show" when our version was originally prepared in 1611.

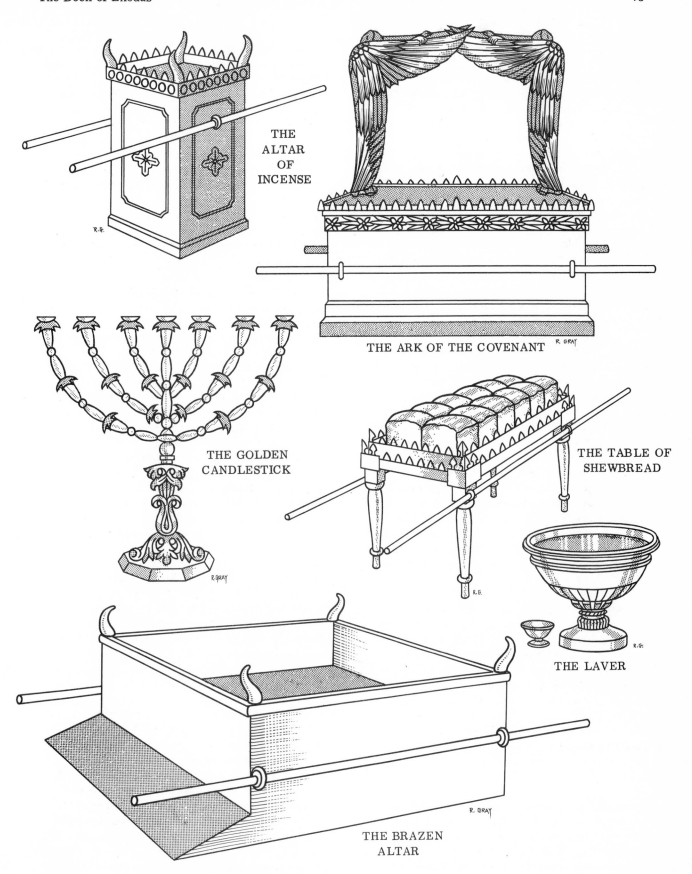

THE
ALTAR
OF
INCENSE

THE ARK OF THE COVENANT

THE GOLDEN
CANDLESTICK

THE TABLE OF
SHEWBREAD

THE LAVER

THE BRAZEN
ALTAR

Figure 10 -- The Furnishings of the Tabernacle

dependent upon this light, just as the ministering believer is dependent upon Christ's illumination. Auxiliary equipment used with the
lampstand included the golden tongs to trim
and adjust the wicks and the golden snuffers to
extinguish the flame during the brief time each
morning when the individual lights were re-
fueled and trimmed. The lamp as a whole
was kept burning perpetually (27:20). It should
be realized, that not withstanding the use of
the word 'candlestick,' this object was strictly
a lampstand. The Hebrew word translated
'candlestick' is menorah, and it means literally 'light-holder.' Nowhere in Scripture are
candles ever mentioned in any aspect of religious worship.

The Curtains of Linen (26:1-6, 36:8-13)

The ten linen curtains were each long
enough to extend across the ceiling from wall-
to-wall and hang down the wall on each side to
within one cubit of the ground. When all ten
were attached side-by-side, the composite curtain so constructed was adequate to extend from
the front of the building to the back, with enough
to spare to form a hanging to cover the entire
back wall in the Holy of Holies. Is is generally
held that the arrangement of hooks and clasps
provided for the linen curtains to hang down inside the walls so that they formed not only the
ceiling of the tabernacle, but the wall tapestry
as well. Thus, these curtains would be primarily what the priests would see inside of the
tabernacle. However, the gold covered plank-
ing would be visible beneath the curtains to a
height of one cubit. In their basic fabric of
fine twined linen, the curtains spoke of the
righteousness of Jesus Christ. Their ornamentation in blue, purple and scarlet, with figures
of cherubims worked upon them, would in part
speak of the judicial ministry of Christ (cherubims are the emblem of justice). The combination of ten curtains indicates harmony, con-
sistency and unity; while the colors indicate
God's redeemed people (scarlet speaks of re-
deeming blood) in the heavenly Jerusalem
(blue speaks of heaven) reigning with Christ
(purple speaks of royalty).

The Curtains of Goat's Hair (26:7-13, 36:14-18)

A total of eleven sections instead of ten,
and an increase of two cubits in the length of
each section, made the combined curtain of
goat's hair longer and wider than the linen cur-

tain. The extra material was no doubt arranged
to overhang so as to provide additional curtain-
ing effect. Inasmuch as the curtain of goat's
hair was visible from without, and since goat's
were a common animal of sacrifice, (a goat was
sacrificed as a sin offering on the day of atonement), this curtain would stand as an invitation
and encouragement to all worshippers to be free
to draw near to God. Just as in the time of
Adam and Eve, the use of animal skins neces-
sitated the shedding of the animal's blood and
served as an object lesson of the divinely prescribed method of atonement. Since oriental
goats are usually black, the entire curtain was
probably black.

The Skin Coverings (26:14, 36:19)

Two additional coverings, one of rams'
skins dyed red, and the other of badgers' skins.
were to be placed over the coverings already
described. The ram's skins, with their distinctive color, speak of Christ's atoning devotion
in His life, and the shed blood of His death. The
outer skins, in being plain and unadorned, speak
of Christ the lowly one without form or comeli-
ness (Isa. 53:3). The description "badger skins"
is simply the guess of the translators who identify the Hebrew word tahash with the Latin taxus
in order to derive the name of a known animal.
However, scholars generally agree that the
identification is at best uncertain. A plausible
alternate for badger may be "dugong skin left in
a rough undressed state." The dugong is an
animal like a dolphin or porpoise which lives in
the coastal waters of the Red Sea and feeds on
seaweed. It grows up to nine feet long and has
a fine waterproof hide which would have provided the tabernacle with protection from rain.
Normally the Israelites used this same material
for their shoes. (cf. Ezk. 16:10).

The Boards and Sockets (26:15-30, 36:20-34)

Each of the sides of the tabernacle consisted of twenty wide planks standing on end;
while the back consisted of six such planks. The
detail of the construction at the corners is not
clear, but there may have been a massive pil-
lar-like plank in each corner. Each plank
rested on two sockets of silver, and the whole
was made solid by five horizontal bars which
connected the boards together. The center bar
ran the full length of the tabernacle and either
passed through rings anchored to the planks in
the manner of the other bars, or through a hole

in each plank so that it was concealed from view. Both the planks and the bars were overlaid with gold.

In that the planks were made of acacia wood, a desert growth, and that they were assembled to constitute a building of God, they represent believers who are redeemed from an empty and vain life and placed in the Church of Jesus Christ. Former strangers and foreigners may grow "unto an holy temple in the Lord: In whom ye also are builded together for an habitation of God through the Spirit" (Eph. 2:21, 22). The visible bars represent the outward forms of Church government and organization; while the invisible bars (assuming that the center bars were invisible) represent the hidden bond or unity of the Holy Spirit.

The silver sockets upon which the planks rested were made from the half shekel of atonement money which had been contributed by each male. (cf. Ex. 30). Thus, the boards rested upon the atonement money of more than 600,000 males, and these foundations would have constituted an amount of silver weighing more than five tons. Since silver is always the emblem of atonement or redemption, it is evident that typically the entire tabernacle found its basis in atonement. The parts of the tabernacle were able to take their place in belonging on the basis of atonement, just as the human members of the true Church may take their place only on the basis of salvation.

The Inner and Outer Veil (26:3-37, 36:35-38)

The inner veil was made of finely spun linen in colors of blue, purple, and scarlet, and it was richly ornamented with figures of cherubims worked upon it. It was evidently of the same nature and appearance as the inner linen curtains which constituted the ceiling. The veil was supported by four gold-covered acacia wood pillars and held by golden hooks so that it might hang in the tabernacle to separate the Holy of Holies from the Holy Place. The four supporting pillars of the inner veil rested upon sockets of silver.

In dividing off the Holy of Holies, this veil represented the body of Jesus. "Having therefore, brethren, boldness to enter into the holiest by the blood of Jesus, By a new and living way, which he hath consecrated for us, through the veil, that is to say, his flesh"

(Heb. 10:19, 20). It was through Christ's death that His righteousness was, as it were, released so that it might be imputed to others. The believer, clothed in the righteousness of Christ made available to him because He died, may now with boldness and confidence enter the Lord's presence. The temple, of course, duplicated the system of veils of the tabernacle. According to tradition, the inner veil in Herod's temple, that stood in Christ's time, was four inches thick. It was this veil that was rent at the moment of Christ's death.

The outer veil, which hung at the front of the tabernacle, was also made of finely spun linen in colors of blue, purple, and scarlet, but it was ornamented with embroidery rather than an interwoven design. It was supported on five pillars and held by golden hooks. These pillars were of acacia wood overlaid with gold and set in sockets of brass. Since brass (actually copper) speaks of judgment, it is significant that "when the priest crossed the threshhold of the tabernacle he saw copper for the last time." Judgment is behind him at the brazen altar. The pillars, in being constructed of wood overlaid with gold, speak of the humanity and deity of Christ and convey the lesson that the way to the deeper things of God is through the person of Christ. The gate, or veil, itself, by its white linen base would represent the righteousness of Christ. It would represent Christ's heavenly origin by the blue embroidery, Christ's kingship by the purple, and Christ's role of Savior by the scarlet. Whereas the outer gate of the tabernacle courtyard introduced the sinner to the ground of salvation, the outer veil of the tabernacle proper introduced the believer to the sphere of worship and a deeper insight and relationship to the things of God.

The Brazen Altar (27:1-8, 38:1-7)

The brazen altar was made of acacia wood covered with plates of brass, and it was placed in the courtyard between the door of the court and the outer veil of the tabernacle. It was of sufficient size (at least four and one-half feet high) to contain all the other furniture and vessels of the tabernacle. The description of it is somewhat vague, but it appears to have been a hollow box[8] with a grate midway between

---

[8] Some scholars think that the altar was filled with earth. (cf. 20:24).

top and bottom. The corners of the grate protruded through the sides so as to form rings through which staves were inserted when the altar was carried. At each corner there was a horn which served as a place to anchor cords which evidently were necessary to secure some of the larger heaps of kindling and offerings. When Israel was in the Land, the brazen altar became a place of refuge for those fleeing the avenger. (cf. 1 Kings 2:28). The altar was accounted especially sacred and on seven occasions in Scripture, the procedure of sanctifying the altar is mentioned. No other vessel was so treated. The sacred fire sent by God to the altar was to be maintained perpetually and never allowed to go out.

The acacia wood in the altar speaks of the incorruptible humanity of Christ. The brass covering (brass is the symbol of judgment) typifies Christ's suffering judgment unto death in order that He might be an acceptable sacrifice in God's sight. The Israelite learned that only on the basis of a consumed sacrifice--however unpleasant to the eye blood and flaming fire might be--could he be accepted by God. The fact that the altar was foursquare speaks of the universal outreach of the Gospel and also of the four-fold view of redemption: it is a propitiation, substitution, reconciliation, and ransom. Just as there were no steps to the altar, so man cannot climb to salvation.

The Court and the Gateway (27:9-19, 38:9-20)

The court of the tabernacle was enclosed by a fence of linen hangings supported by some sixty pillars set in sockets of brass. The material from which the pillars were made is not described (it was probably acacia wood) but it is recorded that they were ornamented at the top with a silver band or fillet which had been provided by the redemption money. Typically the brass at the bottom of the pillar and silver at the top would depict the believer's position between the cross and the crown. A chapiter is simply an ornamental top to a post. A fillet is a rod upon which a curtain is hung. The hangings of plain white linen were seven and one half feet high (38:18), so that they effectively concealed the court from curious outsiders. The linen hangings represent practical righteousness, and since they appeared the same within and without, they conveyed the truth that there is a single standard of holiness before God and before men. In hanging upon the pillars

set in the sockets of brass, it is evident that the rightousness implied by the curtains would be that which was dependent upon sin's having been judged.

The gate was a hanging of finely spun woven linen, embroidered with blue and scarlet. The pattern of the embroidery is not recorded, but it would not likely echo the embroidery of the inner veil, for cherubim speak of the unapproachability of God. The gate was suspended upon four pillars (which are sometimes identified with the four Gospels), and was thirty feet wide and seven and one half feet high. It was drawn either upward or to one side when the priest wished access to the court. Its color made it the more conspicuous so that no one who sought it sincerely could miss it. The wideness of the gate emphasizes the extent or breadth of God's love. Griffith Thomas contrasts the gate of the courtyard with the outer veil of the tabernacle. The gate was: "as broad as the love of God," whereas the outer veil, being one-half the width, was "as narrow as the truth of God." The fact that there was only one gate to the tabernacle emphasizes the exclusiveness of the Gospel. The court was a restricted area, open only to the priests and tabernacle workers. The place of gathering was not within the court but outside the gate. In late centuries the Romans coined the term "pro-forum" to describe the area "before the temple" but not actually in the courtyard. Our word "profane" as a synonym for "secular" has this origin.

The Oil for the Lamp (27:20, 21)

The fuel for the lamp was to be pure olive oil which had been beaten rather than pressed from the olives. Beaten oil is said to be of finer quality and of whiter color than pressed oil. Olive oil, being a vegetable oil, signifies illumination and dedication, in contrast with animal oil which signifies sacrifice and sanctification. Because the fuel was continually replenished, the lamp burned continuously. Likewise, believers must continually permit the inflow of the Holy Spirit in order that they may enjoy divine illumination and steadfastly radiate their faith.

The Altar of Incense (30:1-10, 37:25-28)

The altar of incense was made of acacia wood overlaid with gold and it had carrying rings just as the other articles of tabernacle furniture. Its top was square, and there was a rim or crown of gold about it and also horns on the corners in duplication of the brazen altar. At all times incense was kept burning upon this altar, and once a year the blood of atonement was sprinkled upon it. The perpetual sacrifice upon this altar speaks of the fragrant merits of Christ which are ever rendered to God. Though the altar never saw actual blood sacrifice, the worshippers only gained access to it on the basis of such previous sacrifice.

The continually ascending fragrance of incense from this altar is also a type of the redeemed believer's happy communion with the Father made possible by the sacrifice of Christ. Prayer, adoration, and thanksgiving may all be represented by incense offered up to God. Likewise the ascending incense represents our Lord's intercession on the believer's behalf. It is unfortunate that, typically speaking, many believers today never progress as far as the altar of incense. Thus they fail to enjoy the full blessing of the realization of the crowned High Priest in the heavenlies who ever lives to make intercession for the saints.

The Laver (30:18, 38:8)

The laver was the last vessel to be made and it is unique in that Scripture describes neither the measurements nor its physical appearance other than that it was to be made of brass. Its purpose was to contain water to be used by the priests to wash themselves during their service in the tabernacle. Scripture expressly mentions the foot of the laver and that it too should be made of brass (30:18), but there is some dispute whether the foot was the pedestal upon which the vessel stood, or a smaller basin into which water from the main vessel was poured. The majority of commentators seem to feel that the foot was simply the pedestal, and yet eminent authorities such as Keil and Delitzsch declare concerning the foot: "By this we are not to ur 'arstand the pedestal of the caldron, but something separate from the basin, which was no doubt used for drawing off as much water as was required for washing the officiating priests."[9] The metal for the con-

struction of the laver came from the polished brass looking glasses of the ladies of Israel, and no doubt represented a sacrifice of considerable significance. Archaeological finds in Egypt that have been identified with the period of the Exodus include many bronze mirrors and samples are on display in most large museums.

The laver provided a type of cleansing which served to maintain fitness for spiritual ministry. Washing with water represented a practical cleansing from the defilement of the world and it was an emblem of that true inward purity which must characterize the one who is to make atonement for the sins of the people. For the priest to proceed in his ceremonial work without washing his hands and feet would depict typically a Christian believer's continuing to serve with unjudged sin. Just as the altar was the foundation of life, so the laver was the foundation of holiness. The laver in type cleansed from the guilt of sin. In the life of the believer the role of the laver has been replaced by the Bible. "Wherewithal shall a young man cleanse his way? by taking heed thereto according to thy word" (Psa. 119:9; cf. Tit. 3:5). The fact that there was no specific size given for the laver speaks of the limitless nature of divine cleansing and reveals that there are no limitations to the holiness which becomes the believer.

The Anointing Oil and the Incense (30:22-38, 37:29)

God gave specific recipes, for both the holy anointing oil and the incense which were to be used in the tabernacle. The oil was to serve in the consecration of the furniture and of the priests; the incense was used for the perpetual offering upon the golden altar. The details of the treatment of the ingredients in order to make an ointment are not given; however, it is likely that some sort of boiling or grinding process was used. God specified that neither the oil nor the incense was to be duplicated in any manner of secular service. The stacte was a gum from the myrrh tree, onycha was a Red Sea shellfish, galbanum was a resinous gum used to give body to other fragrances, and frankincense was the fragrant gum of a tree.

Throughout the Bible, anointing oil is the emblem of sanctifying grace; while incense is the emblem of prayer and praise. Both of these are worthy elements in the service of

_____

[9]Keil and Delitzsch, op. cit., (Vol. II), p. 213.

worship and in the fellowship of believers. The Psalmist speaks of the dwelling together of the brethren in unity as metaphorically equivalent to the fragrance of the anointing oil saturating the garments of the High Priest. (Psa. 133:1-3). In the anointing oil and the incense, the spices and perfumes that previously had been for the pleasure of men now were adopted as a means of securing divine approval. The loveliest and the best that man was able to contrive was devoted to His service and His worship.

7. The Garments of the Priest (Ch. 28)

The bulk of this chapter is concerned with a description of the high priest's ceremonial robes known as the garments of glory and beauty. In style and color, the robes of the priests were rich in typical significance for they depicted both the wondrous beauties of Christ the High Priest and also the privileges and duties of all who are the priests of God, whether the appointed ones of the Old Testament or all believers of the New. In his garments of glory and beauty, Aaron became typically that which Jesus Christ was intrinsically in all the purity and holiness of His being.

The Ephod (28:6-14, 39:2-7)

Although in general, an ephod was a shawl or wrap, for the High Priest it was a particular outer garment in the style of a tunic or pinafore. It was made of linen in blue, purple, and scarlet and there were golden threads woven into it. It was made in two pieces joined together at the shoulders with golden clasps. Each clasp was set with an engraved onyx stone. The front and back of the ephod were made to be as one garment by a sash or girdle which was tied about the priest's waist. This was also of blue, purple, and scarlet linen intertwined with golden threads. In the language of Scripture for a priest to be girded with his sash was for him to be fully arrayed in his garments and prepared and ready to serve. According to Josephus, the engraved onyx stones on the shoulders were designed so that the names of the six eldest sons were engraved on the stone on the right shoulder, and those of the six youngest sons on the stone on the left shoulder. The ephod as a whole, with its different colors and materials, typifies Christ in His high priestly ministry. As it were, He bears His people upon His shoulders, the seat of power. The conspicuous purple of the robe which speaks of

Figure 11 -- The Garments of the Priests

royalty and rulership, is the outcome of the mingling of red and blue even as heaven's Savior shed His blood and thereby reigns on the basis of His redemptive work.

The Breastplate (28:15-29, 39:8-21)

The breastplate was actually a piece of elaborately finished cloth of the same material as the ephod. It was a strip twice as long as it was wide, but folded back on itself so as to form a square bag into which the urim and thummim were placed. The breastplate was held in place by golden chains attached to the onyx shoulder clasps and also by blue lace ribbons which attached the breastplate to the ephod. Evidently, there was a small golden ring attached to each corner of the breastplate to which in turn the golden chains and ribbons were connected. The stones upon the breastplate represented the twelve tribes of Israel, and they were borne before the Lord continually as a memorial. Inasmuch as the twelve stones were in one breastplate they speak of the oneness of the people of God; while their position upon Aaron's breast speaks of God's affection for His chosen ones.

Urim and Thummim (28:30, cf. Num. 27:21, 1 Sam. 28:6)

It is usually considered that the urim and thummim were two precious stones which in some way served to reveal the will of God to His people. Since Scripture explicitly states that the urim and thummim were placed in the breastplate, it would seem that they were separate from the twelve stones mounted on the outside. The name urim means "light," while thummim means "perfection;" and these meanings have led some to speculate that perhaps the stones flashed in a particular way to indicate "yes" or "no." Keil and Delitzsch say, "We can draw no other conclusion than that the urim and thummim are to be regarded as a certain medium, given by the Lord to His people, through which, whenever the congregation required divine illumination to guide its actions, that illumination was guaranteed."[10] When God was displeased with His people in later history, He refused to permit the urim and thummim to function as a means of guidance. Apparently in a day when man lacked most of the revelation of the Word of God, he required some other source of information of divine will.

The Robe of the Ephod (28:31-35, 39:22-26)

The robe of the ephod was a plain blue sleeveless garment worn directly beneath the ephod and probably extending some inches below it. Apparently there was a row of pomegranates embroidered upon the hem (see 39:24) interspaced with tinkling golden bells which sounded as the priest moved. The robe was the first outer garment donned by the priest, and it probably partly served as an undershirt. The bells represent joyfulness and the revelation and proclamation of the Word of God. The pomegranates are symbols of the Word and testimony of God as sweet, pleasant spiritual food. Also, inasmuch as natural pomegranates are

full of seeds, the fruit represents fruitfulness and abundance in His service.

The Mitre and Crown (28:36-38, 39:30, 31)

The mitre was made of fine white linen, and was bound about the head in coils like a turban or tiara. On the front of the mitre on Aaron's forehead, attached by a blue lace ribbon, there was the golden plate engraved HOLINESS TO THE LORD. By being marked, the High Priest typified the true inner holiness on the ground of which, alone, Israel could be accepted before God. The conspicuous position of the golden plate upon Aaron's forehead gave special meaning and character to all of his garments and to his office. In committing himself thus to holiness, Aaron could be assured that he qualified for divine acceptance both for himself and for the people of Israel.

The Ordinary Garments of the Priest (28:39-43, 39:27-29)

The ordinary garments of the priests (and the basic garments over which the garments of glory and beauty were worn) consisted of the embroidered coat, a girdle or sash, breeches, and a linen hat. These vestments were all made of fine linen and the girdle was attractively decorated in colors of blue, purple, and scarlet. The broidered coat was probably very similar to an ankle-length dressing robe with generous sleeves. As duly ordained priests, though in plain dress and of secondary status, Aaron's sons speak of today's believers; while Aaron, the High Priest, in his garments of glory and beauty, speaks of Christ our great High Priest. An interesting tradition declares that the old garments of the priests were unraveled and made into wicks for the lamps of the tabernacle and temple.

8. The Consecration of the Priests (Ch. 29)

Israel's priesthood was vested in the family of Aaron of the tribe of Levi, and the office was hereditary so that only by birth could one gain entrance. The first priests were: Aaron, Nadab, Abihu, Eleazar, and Ithamar. Today, all believers are priests, for the spiritual new birth includes appointment to the privilege. The New Testament further gives authority for the believer to consider Christ his High Priest. "Wherefore, holy brethren, partakers of the heavenly calling, consider the apostle and high priest of our profession, Christ Jesus" (Heb. 3:1).

---

[10]Keil and Delitzsch, op. cit. (Vol. II), p.199.

The Lord ordained specific ceremonies and sacrifices which required seven days to complete in order to consecrate a priest. The ceremony involved the offering of a bullock and two rams together with unleavened bread, and a drink offering of wine. There is specific mention of the anointing of Aaron with oil, and the fact that each of the priests participated in laying hands upon the sacrifice in order to show his identity with it. Also, each priest-elect partook of a portion of the sacrifice in a ceremonial feast. The priests-elect were carefully washed with water (which spoke of personal cleansing or sanctification), and they were also sprinkled with blood (which spoke of legal cleansing or justification).

9. The Atonement Money (Ch. 30)

All male worshippers were required to make a payment of one-half shekel (about 33¢) which served as atonement money. The amount was fixed regardless of an individual's status or circumstances in life. The atonement money was the only compulsory donation used in the service of the tabernacle, and the total collected would have been 301, 775 shekels. It is noted that on the basis of 3, 000 shekels to the talent, this amount would have equaled a hundred talents with 1, 775 shekels left over. Since there is sound basis for concluding that the number of sockets required for the tabernacle structure totaled exactly one hundred, the offering would have provided just one-talent for each socket. The additional shekels would have made possible the many hooks and catches that were used in assembling the tabernacle coverings.

This chapter also describes: the altar of incense and the laver, and the method of compounding the incense and anointing oil. These matters have previously been discussed.

10. The Craftsman. The Sabbath (Ch. 31)

The chief craftsman responsible for the building of the tabernacle was to be Bezaleel; while his assistant was to be Aholiab. Bezaleel was of the tribe of Judah, and Aholiab was of the tribe of Dan. Concerning Bezaleel, the Lord declared: ". . . I have filled him with the spirit of God, in wisdom, and in understanding, and in knowledge, and in all manner of workmanship" (v. 3).

The provision of the Sabbath is once more described, and the Israelites are specif-

ically charged to observe it. The penalty for those who would violate the Sabbath and during that time engage in secular work, was to be death. There is no particular mention of worship on the Jewish Sabbath; it was more especially a time of physical rest rather than a time of worship. An interesting contrast between the Old Testament Sabbath and the Christian Lord's Day may be found in Mackintosh and his ideas may be set forth as follows:[11]

SABBATH	LORD'S DAY
The seventh day	The first
Test of Israel's condition	Proof of Church's acceptance
Pertaining to old creation	Pertaining to new creation
Bodily rest for Jew	Spiritual rest for Christian
Work on this day led to death	No work is a poor proof of life
Jew commanded to abide in tent	Christian led by Spirit to go forth

In the Old Testament times the Sabbath remained a unique institution that emphasized to the Jew the need of remaining true to God. Faithful observance of the Sabbath made him a special individual on earth and to a considerable measure assured his loyalty to God. The New Testament neither establishes the Sabbath as binding upon Christians, nor does it reject the Sabbath idea as totally eliminated from the Christian life. Certainly there is Scriptural precedent and actual admonition to depart from ordinary secular labor on the Lord's day and invest the time in worship of the risen Christ. Jesus Himself on earth treated the Sabbath without regard to the Pharisaic rules, but He scrupulously observed the spirit and manner which God originally intended. It is to be noted, of course, that the transition of the Sabbath to the Lord's Day came about in the apostolic era and with apostolic approval. (cf. Acts 20:7, 1 Cor. 16:2. Rev. 1:10).

The mention, in verse 18, that the two tables of stone were written with the finger of God is a picturesque statement of the manner in which the Law was provided. Evidently the tables were of limited size, for Moses was able

[11]C. H. Mackintosh, Notes on the Book of Exodus. New York: Loizeaux Brothers, 1945, pps. 354, 355.

to carry them, and they are mentioned as being conveniently stored in the ark.

11. Israel's Sin and Rebellion (Ch. 32)

When Moses had been in the Mount for forty days and nights, the people became impatient at the delay, and they gathered about Aaron and requested that he would assume leadership. This act constituted the fourth wilderness murmuring. Aaron gave in to their pleading, and allowing his weakness to complement the impatience of the people, proceeded to construct the golden calf. Some have sought to excuse the violation of the second commandment by Aaron on the ground that he meant the calf to be a representation of Jehovah. There is no basis for such a claim however, and there can be no justification for introducing Jehovah into idolatrous worship. Blaikie comments:

> The worship of the bull was notoriously common in Egypt, especially Memphis, where . . . the Aphis or black bull, was worshipped with the utmost splendor; . . . The bull was a representation of Osiris, and was supposed to embody certain divine qualities-- such as strength and endurance--that were deemed worthy of homage. The golden calf, on this principle, was probably meant to represent certain divine qualities which had been exhibited in the deliverance of Israel; . . .12

The fact that the "feast of the Lord" promoted by Aaron on this occasion degenerated into a time of wild licentiousness and flagrant immorality was evidence that Aaron's methods in supposed spiritual leadership were grossly in error. When God informed Moses of the course of events and declared his intention to destroy utterly such a disobedient people, Moses responded by an elegant petition to God to spare them. Though God, at the outset pleaded, "Let me alone" in the face of Moses' prayers, eventually "The Lord repented of the evil which he thought to do unto his people." This episode wherein God's servant argues in prayer with his Lord and sets forth reasons why it must not be that God should annihilate the people is largely unique in Scripture. With God thus intreated, Moses returned to the camp carry-

ing with him the two tables of stone. As he came down the Mount he met the waiting Joshua, and the two discussed the rising crescendo of sound that greeted them as they approached the camp.

By the time that Moses actually returned to the camp, the people had broken the first three commandments which were written upon the tables of the Law which their leader carried. Upon viewing the wicked festivities, Moses' shock and anger aroused him to cast down the tables of Law and shatter them literally, just as they had already been broken spiritually. He proceeded to order the grinding up of the golden calf and he made the people add the grindings to their drinking water. After severely reprimanding Aaron, Moses grimly called for volunteers, and when the Levites responded, he sent them through the camp to destroy the wicked in their sin. Some three thousand of the worst of the idolaters were thus destroyed. Evidently, the condemnation of guilty conscience was such that the sinful ones did not resist.

In a prolonged season of prayer and supplication, Moses fervently interceded on behalf of the erring Israelites. He was so burdened and covetous for the souls of his people that he even requested that God should blot his name out of the Book of Life, rather than put aside the nation of Israel. Moses' words on this occasion constitute a classic instance of the broken sentence. "Yet now, if thou wilt forgive their sin--; and if not, blot me I pray thee, out of thy book which thou hast written" (Ex. 32:32). Such a prayer won a ready response with God, and once more Moses was commissioned to lead the people into the land of promise. Nevertheless, God insisted that those individually responsible for sin should be judged forthrightly. Comments Mackintosh, "This is God in government, not God in the Gospel. Here He speaks of blotting out the sinner; in the Gospel He is seen blotting out sin."13

12. Moses' Continued Intercession (Ch. 33)

Though God had agreed to spare the people, the fact of flagrant sin in the camp led

---

12William G. Blaikie, A Manual of Bible History. London: T. Nelson and Sons, 1890, p. 133.

13C. H. Mackintosh, Notes on the Book of Exodus. New York: Loizeaux Brothers, 1945, p. 363.

Him to declare Himself separated from such people. He would no longer dwell in their midst, but through His angel He would guide them into the Promised Land and grant them a residence there. Such tidings moved the people to mourn and to strip themselves of their ornaments, and to devote themselves to worship at the tabernacle that Moses had provided. The outcome of this new devotion on the part of the people, together with Moses' continued fervent prayer, led the Lord eventually, (v. 17) to agree to return to fellowship with the people.

The tabernacle, mentioned at this place, was not the official tabernacle that later was to be built, but probably a mere tent that for the time being served as a worship center. It is usually thought that it was the official tent of the leader, Moses. In being outside the camp, it showed that the people were estranged from God. On this occasion, Moses' spiritual longing led him to petition the Lord for a vision of Himself. It is characteristic of the most devout men of God to be those who manifest the greatest longing for a yet clearer vision of the divine glory. Although a divine God could not be physically visible. He agreed to grant a representation of Himself in a manner that Moses might perceive Him. Some versions render the words "back parts" in v. 23 as "after glow."

13. Restored Fellowship with God (Ch. 34)

To complete the restoration of fellowship with God, it was necessary for Moses once again to dwell in the Mount for forty days, and once again receive the tables of Law. However, this time Moses was required to prepare his own stone tables and carry them with him into the presence of the Lord for the inscription of the Laws. Comment Keil and Delitzsch at this juncture, "As Moses had restored the covenant through his energetic intercession, he should also provide the materials for the renewal of the covenant record, and bring them to God, for Him to complete and confirm the record by writing the covenant words upon the tables."[14]

God reiterated to Moses vital instructions for the happiness and prosperity of the people when they settled in the land. Par-

ticularly emphasized was the truth that the Israelites were to make no covenant with the pagan natives, but rather to destroy them. Repeatedly, God pointed out that an effort of peaceful co-existence with the people of Canaan would result in Israel's inevitable downfall through idolatry. Moses was reminded of the necessity of keeping the Feast of Unleavened Bread and the Passover, of the dedication of the firstborn, of the keeping of the Sabbath, of the keeping of the various feasts of the Lord, and of the necessity of three pilgrimages a year by all males.

Moses' experience with the Lord on the Mount on this occasion, resulted in a transformation to the degree that this man of God returned to his people with his face so shining that it was necessary for him to wear a veil upon it. This veil was thus a conspicuous sign that Moses was the anointed servant of God. St. Paul comments on this event and points out, that in spite of the abiding glory of God and the necessity of a veil for Moses, this man of God later died. (See 2 Cor. 3:7). Hence the glory of the Law was transient and not abiding as the glory of the Gospel.

14. The Tabernacle Constructed (Chs. 35-39)

The content of these chapters has already been considered in the section dealing with the tabernacle and its furnishings. Much of this material simply reviews the Lord's instructions, and describes the people's efforts to fulfill God's plan. The people gave so freely for the project of the building of tabernacle that they eventually had to be restrained in their giving (36:6). The gifts of the people included: gold, silver, jewels, spun linen, goats hair, spices and oils. Only on this occasion, does Scripture record an instance when God's people gave too much. Evidently a tangible building project encouraged the people to a whole hearted participation that probably engendered also a new measure of personal dedication and interest.

Moses was, of course, a competent leader and a fascinated spectator in the building of the tabernacle. It is recorded, "And Moses did look upon all the work and behold they had done it as the Lord had commanded, even so had they done it and Moses blessed them" (39:43). The tabernacle was so well built that it served Israel more than 500 years and during all that

---

[14]Keil and Delitzsch, op. cit. (Vol. II), p. 240.

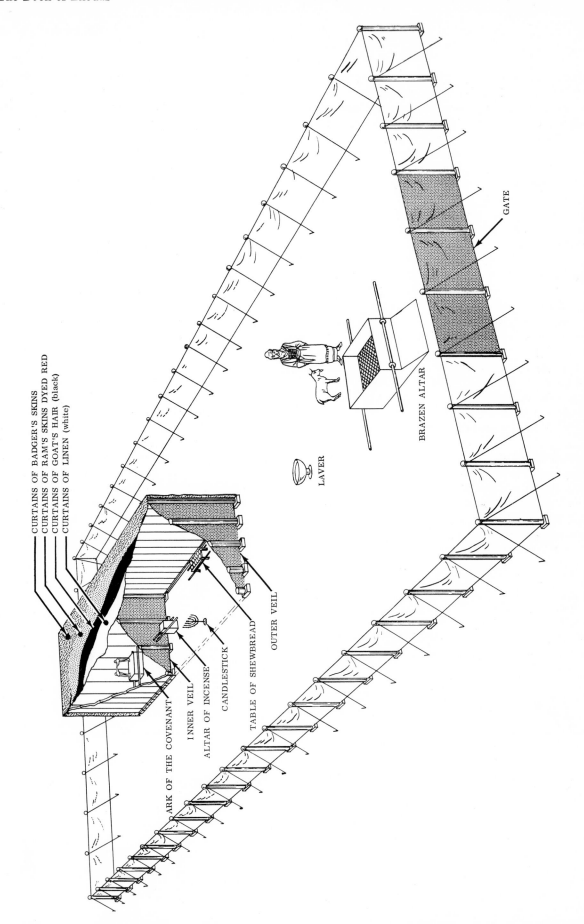

CURTAINS OF BADGER'S SKINS
CURTAINS OF RAM'S SKINS DYED RED
CURTAINS OF GOAT'S HAIR (black)
CURTAINS OF LINEN (white)

GATE

BRAZEN ALTAR

LAVER

ARK OF THE COVENANT

INNER VEIL

ALTAR OF INCENSE

CANDLESTICK

TABLE OF SHEWBREAD

OUTER VEIL

Figure 12 -- An Interpretation of the Structure and Appearance of the Tabernacle in the Wilderness

time it constituted the center of God's dwelling upon earth. A tabernacle in the wilderness constituted a unique revelation of God, making clear to the people His purpose to dwell with men on earth. Men of spiritual discernment may have learned a lesson that even as God tabernacled in a tent in Old Testament times, so He would tabernacle in a physical human body in the Gospel era. "And the Word was made flesh, and tabernacled among us (and we beheld his Shekinah) . . ." (Jno.1:14, literal translation).

The accompanying diagram represents a possible interpretation of the basic appearance of the tabernacle structure and the placement of the furniture. Since Scripture does not precisely report details in these matters, there are differences among authorities. Spink, for instance, argues that the altar would be before the door of the tent rather than just inside the gate of the court. He cites Exodus 40:29, "And he put the altar of burnt offering by the door of the tabernacle of the tent of the congregation, ..." He suggests that for the sake of utility it would be necessary that the laver be located close by it. The number of posts comprising the tent about the court is a matter of uncertainty. Some authorities feel that more would be needed than the diagram shows. The arrangement shown assumes that the corner posts were in some way doubled and therefore it counts them twice. An alternate interpretation is simply to increase by one the number of posts in each side.

15. The Tabernacle Erected (Ch. 40)

The tabernacle was erected on New Year's Day (the first day of Nisan [or Abib]), just two weeks less than a year from the night of the exodus. The structure had required upwards of six months to build, and had used materials estimated by one authority to have been valued at least at $ 1,186,457.22.

The furnishings and building were arranged according to the divine instructions, and both furniture and priests were consecrated so that the priestly ministry might begin. The glory of the Lord descended in so marvelous a manifestation that even Moses had to withdraw. The Jewish writers in the Targums and Talmud used the term "Shekinah" meaning "that which dwells" (or abides) to describe this divine glory. Thus although it is not explicitly a Biblical term, the word "Shekinah" is frequently used with this association. The outpoured evidence of the divine presence henceforth became the cloud by day and the pillar of fire by night that guided the Israelites in their wilderness journeyings. (cf. Neh. 9:19).

FOUR: The Book of Leviticus

Leviticus differs from the other books of the Pentateuch in being almost entirely a book of laws rather than an account of historical incidents. It constitutes a very concise and detailed unfolding of the requirements of God for a people who were to worship Him. Inasmuch as the tabernacle had now been erected, it was necessary that the people be instructed in the correct manner in which to approach God. They were to understand not only the principles of sacrifice and tabernacle ritual, but also correct dietary principles, treatment of disease, observance of feasts and set times, and sundry other matters wherein God's people must live in a godly manner.

In restricting itself largely to legislative or legal matters, the book of Leviticus does not particularly represent any given period of time. The only dated material is a brief section in chapters eight, nine and ten and some incidental episodes (e.g. 24:10-23). The organization of the book is topical rather than chronological. Nevertheless, it is customary to consider that in the giving and recording of the laws, and in the intoducing of them to the people, the book represents one month of historical time. It was given, of course, during the period that the Israelites were encamped at Mt. Sinai and undoubtedly the Levitical Laws followed closely in time the original ten commandments of Exodus 20.

The Name of the Book

The name "Leviticus" was first attached to the book in the Septuagint version, and it came down to the present through the Latin Vulgate. The name means "that which pertains to the Levites." This name actually applies but loosely, for the book has practically nothing to say to the Levites; though it does have a good deal of information and instruction for the priests. The Jews, in the Talmud, have called the book "The Law of the Priests" and "The Book of the Law of the Offerings," and certain commentators have referred to it as "The Priests' Guide Book." However, the name ordinarily given the book by the Jews is the Hebrew "Veyikra"

for this is the phrase with which the book begins and which we translate "And [He] called."

The Message of the Book

Whereas Deuteronomy is a book intended to guide the people, Leviticus is particularly intended to guide the priests. Thus, it places very special stress upon personal and ceremonial holiness, for this was a specific priestly obligation. The word 'holy' and its derivatives occur in the book some 131 times, while the word 'clean' and its derivatives occur some 186 times. The heavenly origin of the book is made clear through the frequent occurrence (some fifty-six times) of the expression "the Lord spake unto Moses." The theme of the book is expressed: "Ye shall be holy, for I am holy" (11:44). The book clearly sets forth the fact that the people, the priest, the tabernacle, the vessels, the offerings, and the priests' garments were all to be maintained in holiness. Probably no other portion of the Old Testament more emphatically and pointedly sets forth the lofty moral standards entailed in the very nature and essence of a holy and righteous God.

In setting forth the obligation to holiness, the book of Leviticus likewise indicates the divinely provided means for mankind to attain such holiness. It is made clear that the way to God is by and through sacrifice and the shedding of blood. Growth in godliness entails a deliberate separation from that which is unholy and unclean. The principle is plainly enunciated: "It is the blood that maketh atonement for the soul" (17:11). The doctrine of atonement through the shed blood of a vicarious sacrifice is a central truth of the Bible, and an essential basis for even a rudimentary insight into the nature of God and His plan for mankind. The Christian Church must characteristically emphasize both the blood atonement and the subsequent life of holiness based upon that atonement.

Leviticus and the New Testament

There are some 40 references to Leviticus in the New Testament, and in the incident of the healing of the leper there is record of Christ's setting His seal of approval upon the book (Mt. 8:4). Leviticus particularly relates to the New Testament book of Hebrews, and this latter is an inspired commentary upon the 'priestly guide book.' Some comparisons are as follows:

LEVITICUS	HEBREWS
God spoke through sacrifices, vestments, institutions, and direct utterances	"God, . . . hath in these last days spoken unto us by his Son" (1:1, 2)
The mediator and conveyor of the divine system was Moses, a servant of God (Heb. 3:5)	The Mediator and Conveyor of the divine system was Christ, the Son of God (Heb. 3:6)
A high priest who never completed his work	A High Priest who rests in His finished work (Heb. 4:14)
A high priest who was subject to death	A High Priest who is eternal, having conquered death (Heb. 5:6, 7:17)
A human high priest must sacrifice for himself	Christ, the God-man, authors our eternal salvation (Heb. 5:9)
The repeated ordinances accorded and complied with the old covenant	His finished work inaugurated and confirmed the new covenant (Heb. 8:8)
An inadequate and imperfect sanctuary wherein persistent repetition of animal sacrifices was demanded	An eternal heavenly sanctuary with an all-prevailing, once-for-all sacrifice (Heb. 9:11)
Worship was in meekness, uncertainty and fear	Worship is in boldness and confidence (Heb. 10:19-25)
Devotion culminated in burdensome works	Devotion culminated in miracle-working faith (Heb. 11:1-40)

In the light of what the Bible scholar is taught in the book of Hebrews, it is evident that Leviticus presents the Gospel and Person of Christ in types, figures, shadows, and emblems. Whereas Leviticus describes the approach to God under Law, Hebrews describes the approach under grace.

Types in the Offerings

When the typical implications of the various sacrificial materials are made clear, the book of Leviticus finds ready application in New Testament Christianity. Although some specific events and ordinances may imply special typical teachings, in general what is true in one place is true throughout. Thus, a generally reliable dictionary of types in Leviticus may be constructed:

Baked cakes: in being baked, they speak of degrees of suffering endured by Christ

Birds: portray Christ in His heavenly nature

Bullock: a type of the patient laborer of Jehovah; hence speak of Christ's fulfilling the will of the Father in a life of patient service

Fine flour: sinless humanity of Christ as that which is bruised and ground; type of the incarnate Christ in His work of atonement

Fire: emblem of the righteousness and holiness of God

Frankincense: Christ's life was a sweet savor, speaks of the fragrant perfection of Christ

Goat: as a sacrificial animal represents Christ who came in the likeness of sinful flesh as a substitute for sinners

Honey: mere human sweetness and perfection of character, devoid of divine impartation

Laying on of hands: an identification of the offerer with the offering

Leaven: sinfulness of character in aspects such as wickedness and falsehood

Male: particularly identifies with Christ in His active obedience

North side (of altar): side of judgment

Oil: the work of the Holy Spirit in anointing

Salt: that which opposes leaven (sin), and that which preserves

Sheep: this animal, in its attribute of meak obedience, speaks of the self-surrender of Christ, holy, harmless, undefiled, separate from sinners

Wood: as fuel upon the altar covered by the sacrifice it represents sin

ANALYSIS AND EXPOSITION

I. THE FIVE OFFERINGS (Chs. 1-7)

For the Israelite worshipper, the way to God was by means of one or more of the prescribed five offerings. Although each is distinctively set forth in the book of Leviticus, it is evident that at some points there was a certain overlapping between the offerings, and that in many instances more than one would be offered at the same time. Generally accepted facts regarding the offerings may be set forth in chart form. (which will be found on the page following).

The Burnt Offering

The burnt sacrifice was considered an ascending offering in the sense that in being entirely consumed by fire it ascended as incense or perfume unto God. Thus, not only was the sacrificial death of Christ depicted, but also His resurrection and ascension. An interesting historical comment on the burnt offering notes: "And Hezekiah commanded to offer the burnt offering upon the altar. And when the burnt offering began, the song of the Lord began also" (2 Chron. 29:27). It is evident that joy in worship is inevitably associated with devout consecration.

The Meal Offering

Since the meal offering was bloodless, it appears normally to have been observed only in conjunction with other offerings. If the experience of Cain in Genesis was meant to be a model, then it might be concluded that the meal offering was not acceptable when offered alone. The Hebrew word for meal offering could be rendered "gift" offering and it may be considered to have fulfilled this special function.

Peace Offering

Peace offerings were associated with such occasions as: harvest thanksgiving (Lev. 7:11, 12), fulfilling a vow (Lev. 7:16), or simply seeking fellowship (Lev. 7:16). In the case of this offering, as well as in the trespass offering, it is noted that all the fat is to be burned as well as what is called the "rump." The probable reference is to the fatty tail of the eastern broad-tailed sheep. This portion of the animal was considered a particular delicacy, so that to surrender it to God in sacrifice was a mark of whole-hearted piety. The wave and heave offerings spoken of apparently involved the presentation to God of portions of the sacrifice by the physical gestures implied by these names. A part of the sacrifice was thus lifted up and displayed before God in dedication and thanksgiving. Leviticus prescribed that the heave shoulder be the right shoulder and it should be given to the priest (7:32). Archaeological investigations at Lachish have made the discovery of a rubbish heap in connection with an altar of sacrifice, with the great majority of bones being from the right foreleg.

Sin and Trespass Offering

At what point to distinguish between a sin and a trespass is a matter of some uncertainty, and marked differences of opinions exist. However, the majority probably would agree with the distinction made by Spink: "The Sin Offering has to do with our evil nature which is the root from which proceed acts done against God and man; the Trespass Offering, on the other hand, is for sins knowingly committed, as well as for some done in ignorance."[1] Thus, "sin" is a falling short or missing of the mark of God's standard of righteousness; a trespass" is a passing over or a going beyond that which God permits.

A sin is abstract and involves the person of the sinner; a trespass is specific and involves the action of the sinner. A sin violates that which God is by nature, whereas a trespass violates that which God decrees in His government and authority. A sin meant that the sinner was deficient and helpless before God; a trespass meant that the sinner owed God compensation and was obligated to be cleansed of defilement.

The amount of evidence contained in the opening chapters of Leviticus probably discourages too rigorous a distinction between sin and trespass. It was not characteristic of ancient times to demand precise distinctions that are expected today. Furthermore, from the human standpoint, it is probably not possible to

---

[1]James F. Spink, Types and Shadows of Christ in the Tabernacle. New York: Loizeaux Brothers, 1946, p. 153.

Offering & Reference	What Offered	Procedure	Types and Remarks
BURNT Lev. 1 6:1-13 Num. 28: 3-15 Deut. 33: 8-10 Psa. 40 Eph. 5:2 Heb. 10:7	Choice of: bullock lamb kid turtle- doves pigeons ram male only	Presented at door-- hand laid on head-- killed--blood sprinkled--carcass cut in pieces--laid on altar and all burned Hide given to the priests	Sweet savor offering (1:17) typical of Christ's entire obedience to the Father. Given wholly to Him-- spread out unreservedly in entire consecration Typical also of our entire dedication to God All was for God and He took unqualified delight in such an offering; the offerer, by personally killing and flaying (skinning) the sacrifice, provisionally iden- tified himself with the offering Various offerings reveal degrees of faith--even a very small measure availed Distinctive feature: Wholly consumed
MEAL Lev. 2 6:14-23 Num. 28:5 15:4 Psa. 16 Jno. 6:33 Heb. 7:26	fine flour oil frankin- cense salt green ears of corn	Handful of flour and oil and all frankin- cense burnt. Priest received remainder Offering either: a. baked in oven b. baked in pan c. baked in skillet (caldron)	Sweet savor offering (2:9) signifying dedication of one's life to God. Typical of Christ's perfect hu- manity anointed with the Holy Spirit. He perfectly fulfilled His ordained work This offering speaks more of Person of Christ rather than of Calvary The meal offering normally accompanied the peace offering Distinctive feature: Bloodless
PEACE Lev. 3 7:11-34 Lev. 17: 1-9 Lev. 19: 5-8 Psa. 85	Choice of: bullock lamb goat either male or female	Presented--hands laid on head-- killed--blood sprinkled Fat burned Wave breast and heave shoulder Offerer ate remainder in the sanctuary	Sweet savor offering (3:16) depicting Christ's mak- ing peace between God and man This offering furnished a table so that God and man could fellowship together; it was not an atoning sac- rifice, but a joyous celebration of peace; an offering not to achieve peace but because of peace This offering teaches that the means of entrance into communion and fellowship with God is by sacrifice Distinctive feature: Offerer feasted
SIN Lev. 4 5:1-13 6:24-30 Psa. 22 2 Cor. 5: 21	Choice of: bullock kid turtle- dove pigeons fine flour	Presented--hands on head--killed--blood sprinkled--burned outside the camp Offering depended up- on one's status: e. g. ruler, priest, etc.	Atonement for man's sinful nature; sin expiated by a substituted life; blood emphasized. This was the first offering in the approach to God Typical of Christ who died without the camp, denied the presence of God because He became sin The person of the offerer was of importance--the grade of offering depended upon the degree of re- sponsibility of the offerer but could be male or female Distinctive feature: Expiation for sin
TRES- PASS Lev. 5:14 6:7 7:1-7 Psa. 69	ram plus restitution money	Procedure as Burnt Offering, but fat only burned at altar. Re- mainder burned eith- er without the camp or eaten by priest on day of atonement Restitution was prin- ciple plus 1/5 given injured one or priest	Atonement for man's grievance of the government of God. Speaks of particular transgression and spe- cial acts of sin. Shortcoming or defilement is of concern rather than offerer's person Typical of Christ's work in satisfying God's demands of justice and righteousness. Atonement made the foundation of restitution Neither the trespass nor the sin offering was a sweet savor offering. Sin is not sweet to God Distinctive feature: Emphasized reparation and res- titution for sin

distinguish in all cases between inherent depravity or sin and unrighteous acts or trespasses. These distinctions would be less confusing to the Israelite simply because specific trespasses were listed for him, and he knew the nature of the defilement and remedy for each case. Where sin involved condemnation, the trespass led to confession and compensation. Trespass included: a Nazarite touching a corpse (Num. 6:12), appropriating something consecrated to the Lord (Lev. 5:15), or swearing falsely (Lev. 6:2).

The Offerings in General

One vital distinction in the Old Testament provision of the offerings is that the offerings were never considered according to the primitive pagan idea as food for the gods. In all cases it was a matter of performing an expiation or a sacrifice that made atonement for wrongs done and that bridged the gulf between sinful man and a holy God. "Oblation, " the alternate name for sacrifice literally means "approach. " God clearly taught the Israelites that the sacrifices were His divinely ordained channels of communion between man and God.

The Frequency of the Offerings

The Burnt Offering was made at least twice daily, evening and morning, at the expense of the state (Ex. 29:38-43; Lev. 6:8-13). It was also made by private individuals on such occasions as: consecration of priests (Ex. 29: 15), purification of women (Lev. 12:6-8), cleansing of lepers (Lev. 14:10), removal of ceremonial uncleanness (Lev. 15:15), and the conclusion of a Nazarite vow (Num. 6:10, 14). There is some uncertainty concerning the exercise of the Peace Offering. In the light of Leviticus 17:1-6, it may be inferred that this offering was made whenever a meat animal was butchered, since most of the carcass was returned to the offerer. However, many commentators hold that the offering was made only by those who wished to express special piety or otherwise show their esteem for God. The Meal Offering seems to have accompanied the Burnt Offering (Num. 29:2, 3), and therefore it would be observed with equal frequency. The Sin Offering could be brought by an individual who became conscious of his shortcomings before God, and it was specifically observed for all the people once a year on the day of atonement. The Trespass Offering, along with the

restitution money, was brought by one who realized that he had committed an obvious wrong and who wished to be restored both to God and to man.

The Validity of Flour as an Offering

Since Scripture stresses: ". . . without shedding of blood is no remission" (Heb. 9:22), the possibility of flour as a Sin Offering (5:11) occasions some question. In this connection, Hodgkin has this to say, "In the fine flour, bruised, ground to powder, offered by fire, we see the bruising of Jesus day by day from those to whom He was ministering, for whom He daily gave Himself when He endured such contradiction of sinners. " Bodie comments: "It proves that a soul may trust Jesus as the holy Man that died, and be saved; and yet be woefully ignorant regarding that which constitutes atonement. " In a very similar vein, Wright says, "God does not accept men on the basis of their apprehensions of the atoning work of Christ. Their apprehensions may be very meager and poverty stricken and may be deeply deficient, but God looks to see if He can discern faith and whether it be Christ that the offerer brings. " It may be that God's leniency to the poor in this matter is described in Acts 17:30 as the "times of this ignorance God winked at. " In this day, the principle stands inviolate that faith in the atoning death of Christ is required for salvation and God accepts neither substitute nor that which is inadequate, for there is "none other name under heaven given among men whereby we must be saved" (Acts 4:12). Whatever may have been the imperfections of Old Testament worship, certainly there is no ground for variation or substitution in the New Testament Gospel.

The Sins for Which Sacrifices Availed

In general, the Law of Moses provided no escape for willful sins. The Levitical offerings provided for restoration to God in the case of ignorant negligence and frailty, provided the offender duly repented. Presumptuous and deliberate sins were not included in the Levitical provisions and in many instances immediate death was meted out to those who thus behaved. Sampey explains the purposes of the offerings and their role in providing forgiveness thus:

. . . the Levitical system provides atonement only for sins of ignorance and weakness, but not for sins done with a high hand. For sins committed unwitingly (through error) the sin-offering provided atonement. . . . The trespass-offering likewise made atonement only for sins done in ignorance or through weakness. . . . For many sins there was nothing left but a complete severance from Israel, either by death or expulsion from the congregation (Lev. 17:10; 18:29; 20:1-16, 27). The sacrificial system in the Pentateuch made no provision for atonement and forgiveness for such terrible sins. The blood of bulls and goats could not cover such sins. [2]

The sacrificial system of the Old Testament was by no means intended to be a way of purchasing indulgence. While there were those who were forgiven grievous crimes (i. e. David's adultery and commitment of virtual murder) in general, the willful sinner could expect only condemnation and destruction. There is a sense wherein the law of God operated not unlike civil law in today's society. Men who are caught in crime are inexorably punished according to the legal prescription. Severe crimes involve an ultimate punishment--in many instances a sentence of death. Lesser crimes may involve only the payment of a fine and a moderate inconvenience. Some crimes are counted hope-

---

[2] James R. Sampey, The Heart of the Old Testament. Nashville: Broadman Press, 1922, p. 83.

less and forever bar the offender from further association in society; others involve a greater or lesser payment of what is known as "one's debt to society."

II. THE LEVITICAL PRIESTHOOD (Chs. 8-10)

1. The Consecration of Aaron and His Sons (Ch. 8)

In its prior development in Israel the priesthood had descended from (1) the family head (e. g. Noah), (2) the firstborn (Ex. 13), (3) Levites (Num. 3:13); now it was to be committed to the family of Aaron. Although God ordained that Aaron's descendants were priests by birth, the nature of the priestly office made it necessary that they be consecrated before entering the priestly ministry. The literal meaning of the word "consecrate" used in this chapter is "have their hand filled." The thought is that by specific divine appointment these men particularly chosen by God were now to have placed in their hands their commission as servants of the Lord. In the conduct of the ceremony the priests extended their empty hands and the official as God's representative filled their hands with parts of the offering of the ram of consecration. At the conclusion, all that they so acquired was waved as a wave offering before the Lord.

The initial consecration of the priests was conducted by Moses before the door of the tabernacle. The four sons of Aaron: Nadab, Abihu, Eleazar and Ithamar were the candidates. The act of consecration included ceremonial washing, being clothed in priestly garments, being anointed with oil, sprinkled with blood and purified by sin and burnt offerings. Because consecration presupposes redemption, the sin offering was a necessary part. It was made clear that the priesthood was founded upon sacrifice and that even for themselves the priests had to offer sacrifices. The members

Goats were acceptable sacrifices in at least three of the Levitical offerings, and to this day they are common animals in the Near East. Pictured are characteristic Jordanian goats, with long black hair from which is woven the black fabric used today to make Bedouin tents. This flock was at ed-Deir, Petra, which is a mountain region immediately above the north end of the Petra basin.

of the priests were individually consecrated to convey the lesson that the ear was set apart to hear the voice of God, the hand to render service and the foot to maintain the daily walk of holiness. The ceremony of consecration was repeated daily for seven days with a concluding feast signifying their being fed at Jehovah's table. Aaron constitutes a type of Christ while the sons, dependent upon the high priest but priests themselves nevertheless, are a type of Christian believers.

2. The Priests Begin Their Ministry (Ch. 9)

As soon as the priests were duly consecrated, they began ministering. For themselves they offered sin and burnt offerings, and for the people they offered sin, burnt, meal, and peace offerings. This was a joyous occasion when Aaron publicly invoked blessing upon the nation, and the glory of the Lord appeared, and the divine fire fell. That the fire consumed the offerings was proof it had been accepted. Though the tabernacle had previously been used and sacrifices offered, this occasion appears to have been the divine confirmation of tabernacle worship and the beginning of the divinely given perpetual fire that consumed the daily offerings.

The inauguration of an official priestly ministry meant a significant change in the religious and social patterns of life in Israel. As noted above, three previous systems of priesthood were replaced with the priesthood of the family of Aaron. It is considered that this Aaronic priesthood fulfilled the following roles: 1) represent the nation before God, 2) keep the reality of God before the people, and 3) represent God to the nation and make known His will and attitudes. Notwithstanding, the Aaronic priesthood was limited in its authority and rights, and there were those things that the priests could not do: 1) offer a way of forgiveness for deliberate sin, 2) actually acquit and justify a wrong doer, and 3) bring the people into the direct presence of God.

3. The False Worship of Nadab and Abihu (Ch. 10)

Nadab and Abihu indicated gross willfulness and a flagrant disregard of the spirit and precepts of Levitical worship in their use of strange fire. The expression "strange fire" apparently indicates that they used fire that did not come from the brazen altar. Someone has commented: "it is easier to kindle a fire than to pay the price to appropriate God's fire." The immediate stroke of divine judgment was impressive evidence of the Lord's hatred of a worship not according to His divine pattern. God rejects both worship and service that has no other basis than carnality and human self will. Because of the command of God to refrain from strong drink (vvs. 8, 9), it is thought that the reason for the willful act of the sons was that they were intoxicated. At all events, God was so angry with the offenders that He did not even permit the family to mourn their death. God took particular note of the deed of Nadab and Abihu, and five times in the Pentateuch there are references to it.

Nadab and Abihu were replaced by Eleazar and Ithamar, but even these two sons, on that very day, committed a violation of the divine pattern of worship. Contrary to their instructions, they burned all of the sin offering and reserved none to be eaten. It is suggested by Kellogg that Aaron's defense of his sons might be rendered: "Could it be the will of God that a house in which was found the guilt of such a sin should yet partake of the most holy things of God in the sanctuary?" Thus it may have been that Aaron and his sons were simply too distressed to be able to eat the sin-offering. Moses was induced to overlook the incident by the earnest plea of Aaron, and apparently God likewise was forgiving.

III. LAWS OF PURIFICATION (Chs. 11-15)

1. Pure Food Laws (Ch. 11)

Even in the time of Noah, God's people had distinguished clean animals from unclean, but only in Moses' day did this distinction come to be set down in permanent laws. The Law required that for an animal to be clean it must have cloven feet and chew the cud, for a fish to be clean it must have fins and scales, and for a bird to be clean it must not be carnivorous, carrion, or predaceous in habit. It is interesting to note that Scripture names the clean beasts, but the unclean birds--the smaller number being named in each case. The Israelites also were permitted to eat certain insects, but the Law designated that it would be those that leap rather than run. God laid down scrupulous dietary laws upon Israel that He might impress the people that they were truly His chosen and separated ones. Bodie remarks, "Every meal the Israelite ate was preaching the atonement of Calvary, though he were not aware of the fact." The requirements of the clean and unclean are not obligatory upon Christians (cf. 1 Tim. 4:1-5), but the majority are worth observing for health's sake. In general, it may be concluded that Jewish diet and sanitary practices are likely to provide better health than non-Jewish dietary practices. However, on spiritual grounds, Christians are free to eat any bird, animal or reptile that they may happen to desire.

The statement in verse 6 that a hare chews the cud has been the object of scorn by Bible critics. Actually, there is no certainty that the animal intended was specifically a hare, for the original indicates an animal whose identity today is unknown. The translators assumed that the Hebrew word "arnebeth" was a hare, but of this there is no sure evidence.

2. Childbirth Laws (Ch. 12)

The ceremonial cleansing required at the birth of a child was to take place in forty days in the case of a male child, or in eighty days in the case of a female child. An explanation of this difference is found in 1 Tim. 2:14: "And Adam was not deceived, but the woman being deceived was in the transgression." Thus, the double period of cleansing was prescribed because woman was the channel through whom sin came into the world. The mother of our Lord carefully observed the provisions of this law. (cf. Luke 2:22-24).

3. The Identification of Leprosy (Ch. 13)

At least four types of leprosy are described in this chapter (vvs. 2, 4, 26, 31) as well as other leprous or cancerous phenomena in man or in his clothing. All types of leprosy were contagious and they required quarantine or segregation, at least in most of their stages. The prevalence of leprosy in the camp of Israel may have been the result of the hardships of the Egyptian bondage. The person suspected of leprosy was taken to the priest, and if the symptoms were definite, immediately pronounced unclean. If the symptoms were uncertain, the patient was shut up for seven days and at the end of that time, once more examined and either released or declared unclean. The unclean person was required to remain in permanent isola-

tion that thereby the spread of the disease might be halted.

Leprosy is strikingly a type of sin in its following characteristics: 1) loathsome, 2) progress slow but certain, 3) involved banishment, 4) far-reaching effects, 5) generally incurable by known human means, and 6) leaves its victims without hope. Leprosy especially typifies sin in a Christian congregation: havoc is caused both within and without, discipline is necessary, and judgment must be delayed until after a probationary period. Just as in the case of leprosy, so in the case of sin among God's people, quarantine is a worthy practice. " . . . Therefore put away from among yourselves that wicked person" (1 Cor. 5:13).

The rather odd case of the leper who is covered from head to foot with the plague (vvs. 12, 13) and yet is pronounced clean, has been variously explained. Wright suggests that a leper wholly covered could be pronounced clean because the prescription is for ceremonial and not physical cleansing, and:

. . . this provision is intoduced into the ordinance purely for the purpose of analogy. Sin has tainted the whole nature and whilst, in the sense in which we use language, man is not utterly depraved, yet he is hopelessly so. And it is when man acknowledges that he is unholy in every part and confesses his true state, that God is able to pronounce him clean.[3]

4. The Cleansing of the Leper (Ch. 14)

Scripture here describes the spiritual restoration of a leper who in some manner had physically recovered from his disease. Scripture does not describe a method of cure but only a religious ceremony that constitutes his declaration of healing. One who had been delivered from the defilement of leprosy needed a spiritual cleansing just as, typically, the penitent sinner must be divinely cleansed. The ceremony required two birds, one of which was sacrificed and the other released. Thus was portrayed the cleansing by Christ's shed

[3]Walter C. Wright, The Sacrificial System of the Old Testament. Cleveland: Union Gospel Press, 1942, p.121.

blood on the one hand, and His provision for the release of the sinner from his bondage on the other. The washings and shaving which the restored leper underwent spoke of the development of a holy life; the anointing of his members with blood spoke of his practising consecration. The former leper was restored to the people on the first day, and to the Lord on the eighth day. At that time, he made a trespass, sin, burnt, and meal offering. In these sacrifices the substitution of birds for larger animals was permitted if the candidate was poor. A noteworthy fact about the initial sacrifice of the birds was that it was not at the altar, the usual place of sacrifice, but outside the camp. Also, this ceremony permitted a lamb to be substituted for the customary provision for the trespass offering.

The cleansing of the leper involved a series of typical teachings of significance to the New Testament believer. The two birds in contrasting life and death speak of death and resurrection. The cedar wood speaks of the dignity of Jesus Christ; the hyssop indicates His humility. The scarlet cloth, of course, would speak of Christ's shed blood and His sacrifice on Calvary. The earthen vessel represents Christ's humanity; the running water, His anointing by the Holy Spirit. The washing of clothing signifies the laying aside of that which is unbecoming. Shaving represents the renunciation of that which is the expression of the natural man; shaving the head speaks of the renunciation of natural reason, shaving the eyebrows speaks of renunciation of the powers of observation. Wright comments on the outcome of the ceremony:

> . . . the cleansed leper had a threefold assurance of being accepted. First, he had assurance by the sprinkled blood. Second he had assurance by the word of the priest who pronounced him clean. Third, he had assurance by the live bird let loose. [4]

The procedure in the case of a leprous house was to apply in the future when the Israelites settled in Palestine. The leprous house evidently involved some sort of a mural salt or mildew. Under certain conditions, a house built without adequate footings will show dampness or salt encrustations on the walls through capillary action from below, particularly if the underground water is impure. A house so located is better destroyed just as Scripture prescribed, for it is detrimental to the occupants. Some scholars see in this account of the leprous house a figure of the house of Israel in the eyes of the Lord.

5. Concerning Issues (Ch. 15)

It is a striking testimony to the divine origin of Scripture that there is a record, thousands of years before man's understanding of the transmission of bacteria and germ life, of a divine provision for the quarantining of those with infectious diseases. In any nation or age, public health would undoubtedly be encouraged by paying heed to the Law of Moses. However, it should be recognized that this chapter deals not only with abnormal physical conditions, but with some that are wholly normal. Hence, in addition to the practical values of quarantine for the diseased, this portion is of value in graphically expressing the hopeless defilement of the human race and the need of all men for divine cleansing. Bodie comments concerning these matters:

> The Israelite could not spend a day, prepare a meal, enjoy a social time with family or friend, go on a hunting trip, or attend to his daily business avocations without being constantly reminded that he was in covenant relationship with a holy God and must obey Him. [5]

The Significance of Uncleanness

The book of Leviticus describes three degrees of uncleanness, and makes specific prescriptions for its removal in each case. 1) There was uncleanness that defiled merely until evening. (e.g. touching a dead animal) This uncleanness was removed by bathing and washing the clothes. 2) There was uncleanness that defiled for seven days. (e.g. touching a human corpse) This uncleanness was removed by a ceremony that involved the water or separation, or in some cases, the making of a simple offering. 3) There was uncleanness that defiled indefinitely. (e.g. leprosy) Cleansing depended

[4]Fred H. Wright, Devotional Studies of Old Testament Types. Chicago: Moody Press, 1956, p. 97.

[5]Mary M. Bodie, Lessons in Leviticus. Kansas City: Grace and Glory, 1928, p. 49.

upon removal of the cause of the uncleanness, followed by a lengthy and elaborate ceremony.

The state of being unclean or ceremoniously defiled meant a temporary cutting off of the individual's citizenship among God's people. During that period, both social and religious privileges were suspended; however, this suspension would not necessarily mean that the unclean person would become an object of divine judgment. God's grace is such, that even an unclean man would have the privilege of identifying himself by faith with the atoning sacrifices that were constantly being conducted in the temple. Hence, he might secure divine pardon, even though he could not participate outwardly in the acts of worship.

IV. THE GREAT DAY OF ATONEMENT (Ch. 16)

Kellog describes this chapter as: "the most consummate flower of the Messianic symbolism." By the divine provision of the great Day of Atonement, God set forth the truths of propitiation and substitution as being essential divine relationships between God and his people. He prescribed that this day should come on the tenth day of the seventh month of the Jewish Sacred Calendar and thus be observed in the early fall of each year. The word "atonement" means to cover up, to appease or to cover the face. The concept is conveyed that although sin was not settled, it was covered up until Messiah would come. This day constituted a time when the propitiatory offering covered up the violated Law; only on this day of the year was the blood of an offering taken into the immediate presence of God. In general, the Day of Atonement was a time of mourning, fasting and abstinence from all secular pursuits. It was the only day in which God specifically prescribed fasting, although later tradition added many other days of fasting.

The high priest regularly presided at these ceremonies. He was at first garbed in ordinary priestly garments, but at the conclusion he donned the garments of glory and beauty. Before the actual atonement for the people was made, the priest made an offering for himself. The atonement for the people was a sacrifice of two goats, one of which was slain and the other driven into the wilderness and known as the scapegoat. The word translated "scapegoat" is "Azazel," and this

name suggests an identification with Satan, perhaps in the sense that through the sacrifice of Christ, Satan's power is forever loosed and destroyed. The ceremonies of the Day of Atonement called for Aaron to enter into the Holy of Holies carrying the blood of sacrifice and to sprinkle blood both before and upon the mercy seat. The ratio of once upon the mercy seat and seven times before it seems to speak of the contrast between propitiating God, and obtaining access to Him. Scripture indicates that this annual offering on the Day of Atonement was for the sins that the people had committed in ignorance. All other sins were to be atoned for as soon as the guilty one became aware of his sin. "But into the second went the high priest alone once every year, not without blood, which he offered for himself, and for the errors [sins of ignorance] of the people" (Heb. 9:7).

V. THE LAWS OF HOLINESS (Ch. 17-22)

1. The Place of Sacrifice. The Sanctity of the Blood (Ch. 17)

Leviticus makes clear that God sought to emphasize the difference between the people of Israel and their heathen neighbors. Inasmuch as the latter usually poured out the blood of a slain beast as a drink offering to their god, Jehovah required that the killing of an animal relate significantly to Him. Although some commentators (e.g. Griffith Thomas) consider that this section pertains only to religious sacrifices, it is generally agreed that God imposed those requirements in every instance in which an animal was slain. Thus, to slay a beast for food was at the same time to participate in a sacrifice to God and bring that animal as a peace offering to the Lord. Bodie comments: "God ordained for Israel that their every meal was in connection with the altar. It was a feast upon an offering." God desired that the Israelites, in seeing the blood of a slain beast, recognize that only through blood was there atonement. Men were not to eat blood, for blood is life, and all life is to be dedicated to God.

If the above view concerning divine worship in all cases that an animal was slain is correct, then it would appear that this statute was repealed following the years of wilderness wandering. The divine announcement of the change is found in Deuteronomy 12:15 "Notwithstanding thou mayest kill and eat flesh in all thy gates. . . ." After settlement in the land, the requirement of bringing all animals to be slain to the door of the tabernacle would no longer have been feasible. The "sacrifices unto devils" spoken of in v. 7 is a reference to a form of Egyptian idolatry, whereby devils (literally "he goats" or "hairy ones") were actual objects of worship. It is typical of idolatrous religions to feature devil worship and to practise immoral acts in the name of worship.

2. Unholy Relationships (Ch. 18)

Inasmuch as God created male and female, it may be said: "Sex is God's idea," but this claim in no way alters the fact that God is unalterably opposed to all manner of lewdness and extramarital sex activity. Human society is founded upon the family unit involving the physical relationship of husband and wife. God jealously and scrupulously prohibited any practice or provision that would in any way substitute for the husband-wife relationship. God provided that the aspect of marriage constituted in physical attraction between husband and wife should vitally supplement the spiritual and emotional attraction between the partners, and at no level did He permit the marriage bond to be weakened, or marriage partners to be encouraged in independence. An additional reason for not permitting consanguinity was simply that the intermarriage of near relatives with similar genetic characteristics would lead to the excessive exaggeration of certain traits and thereby to abnormal offspring.

God desired that in every expression of the bodily appetites His people maintain purity and virtue. The people of Israel were to live in sharp contrast with the pagan inhabitants of the land. Acts of incest and perversion that characterized pagan society were wholly prohibited for the people of God. Israel was soon to encounter the sexual depravity of the Canaanite pagan religions with their emphasis upon ritual prostitution. The worship of Molech was forbidden (v. 21), not only because such worship was idolatrous and denied worship of Jehovah, but also because it involved the sacrifice of living children by fire in acknowledgment of Molech. The law prescribed that the penalty for disobedience to any of these divine restrictions was to consist of judgment and deportation from the land. "Ye commit not any one of these abominable customs, which were committed before you" (18:30).

3. Personal Duties (Ch. 19)

This chapter, which is sometimes described as the Old Testament counterpart of the Sermon on the Mount, contains miscellaneous instructions and regulations for the daily life of God's people. It sets forth legislation pertaining to such subjects as: worship, the poor, the physically handicapped, gossip, grudges, mixtures and hybrids, marriage relationships, agricultural practices, personal adornment, the Sabbath, fortune tellers, the aged, and the conduct of business. God prescribed reverence, kindness, and fairness in each situation. Quite obviously the survival of the fittest is not a holy doctrine. The words "thou shalt love thy neighbor as thyself" in v. 18 constitute the so-called "Royal Law." It is cited seven times in the New Testament. From this chapter it is evident that the Lord is opposed to mixed fellowships, mixed teaching and mixed conduct.

4. Warning Against Other Special Sins (Ch. 20)

Here, once more, there are prohibitions against Molech worship, fortune telling, adultery, and kindred perversions. Likewise, there are exhortations to respect one's elders and to practise holy living. The death penalty is repeatedly prescribed for violation of these express commands of God. The mode of execution authorized by God was to be stoning, and inasmuch as the victim is usually stunned early in the process, this method is probably as humane as any. God's purpose in these manifold provisions for Israel is once more stated in v. 26: "Ye shall be holy unto me; for I the Lord am holy, and have severed you from other people, that you should be mine."

5. Regulations for the Priests (Chs. 21-22)

In their official duties, the priests were identified with their offerings, and hence, just as the offering had to be perfect, so also the priest. Absolute cleanliness within and without was to characterize them always. Some specific regulations enumerated in these chapters include: 1) They were not to mourn for the dead, except in the case of the death of close relatives. 2) They must be exemplary in their marriage and family relationships. 3) They must be physically normal. 4) They must manifest due reverence and honor to holy things and see that all others did likewise. 5) They must see that only the best of creatures were brought for the offerings and that no cruelty be permitted.

VI. THE LAWS CONCERNING FEASTS (CHS. 23, 24)

1. The Sabbath and the Annual Feasts (Ch. 23)

The word "feast" found in our Bibles is a translation of two different Hebrew words, one meaning "appointed time" or "season" and the other meaning "festival." Thus, of the seven great religious feasts that Israel observed annually, only three were feasts in fact: Unleavened Bread, Pentecost, and Tabernacles. The other four were simply appointed times. Only in the case of the Day of Atonement was fasting prescribed, but the others also were likely to minimize any celebration by feasting. In the Levitical system the special annual days were not occasions to mark great men but rather to mark great events with God.   Three times yearly: at Pentecost, Passover, and Tabernacles all male Israelites were to make a pilgrimage to the center of worship. The term "convocation" means "assembly" or "gathering." It was not until the institution of the synagogue (after 586 B.C.) that the Israelites began the custom of meeting together on the Sabbath.

The order of the feasts is usually considered to portray past and future events in the divine calendar. The first four feasts, coming in the spring of the year, speak of Christ's first advent and the events of that time, including the Pentecostal inauguration of the Church. The interval speaks of this present era of grace. The last three feasts, held in the fall, speak of the rapture of the Church, the gathering together of Israel, and Israel's restoration to God in the millennial era. It is unquestionably a fact that God gave the Israelites their special days and prescribed their significance and some details of their manner of observation. However, this is not to say that the claims of archaeologists that identify these feasts with Israel's pagan neighbors are necessarily wholly in error. It well may have been that there were pagan counterparts of the festivals of Jehovah that were observed by pagan nations as agricultural celebrations. However, in Israel's case the whole significance and emphasis was given a divine focus and a legitimate spiritual significance. In the same manner, today's Christian observance of such special days as Christmas and Easter is seen to have links with the pagan past of the Western world.

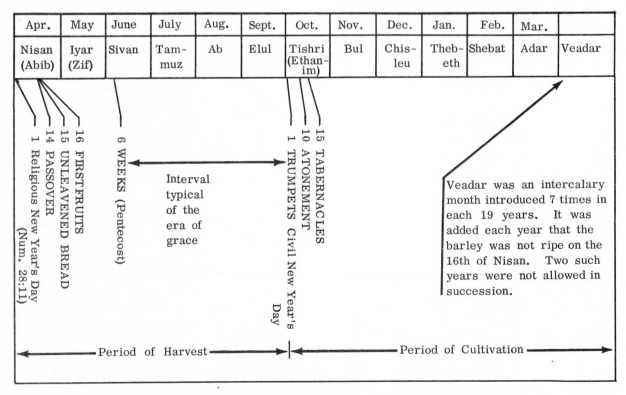

Figure 13 -- Israel's Sacred Calendar During the Old Testament Era

Modern Jewish Religious Feasts and their
Biblical Backgrounds

Passover and Unleavened Bread

In modern Jewish observance, the Passover (Pesach) and the Feast of Unleavened
Bread (Matsoth) are brought together into one.
An orthodox Jewish family prepares carefully
for the occasion, and if possible, all members
of the family come home. The house is thoroughly cleaned and an effort made to find and
dispose of all traces of leavened bread. On
the night of the Passover, there is a joyful family dinner and worship service known as the
Seder. Though there are regional differences
in the customs at this time, the elements of:
wine, three unleavened cakes, a lamb shank,
a roasted egg, salt water, horseradish, pars-
ley, and Charoseth (a mixture of apples and
nuts), commonly comprise the meal and the
symbols for the religious service. In compli-
ance with the Bible command that children be
informed concerning these events (Ex.12:26),
children are customarily given an important
role in observing the Passover. The Seder
home service closes with the singing of Psalms
and sometimes with the pathetic prayer: "O
God, send us the Messiah, this was the night
we expected Him: We faint, yet we hope. Perhaps He will come next year, surely next year."

Trumpets

Modern Jews observe the Feast of
Trumpets as Rosh Hashonah or the New Year
and this tends to take precedence over the Passover as the beginning of their calendar. Thus
they have departed from the Biblical prescription of Rosh Hashonah (beginning of months)
mentioned in Exodus 12:2, which identifies the
name with the Passover. Scholars hold that
the Rosh Hashonah observed in the fall (usually
September) came into being through the influence of the Babylonian captivity. The seventh
month was the first month of the agricultural
year of the Babylonians. In modern practice
the Jews recognize this day as one in which
every Jew is called upon to take spiritual inven-
tory of his own life and to reorder his way in
keeping with God's will. It is considered as a
kind of judgment day in which God decides the
fate of every Jew for the year to come. The
synagogue service involves the ceremonial
blowing of the ram's horn or Shofar to announce
the occasion of the chosen time to become re-

conciled to one's fellow man and to God and
also for the purpose of confusing Satan. A
custom in some areas is the casting of bread
crumbs upon a river or lake as a symbol of
God's casting sins into the depth of the sea
(Mic. 7:19).

Atonement

On the day before Atonement, or Yom
Kippur, every Orthodox Jew procures for himself either a chicken or a goose. Where possible, the father of the family secures a roost-
er for the male members of his family, and
a hen for the females. He then recites a
prayer in which he declares that the birds are
the atonement and sacrifice for their sins.
Clearly the idea of such an informal sacrifice
is contrary to the Bible pattern: "Whatsoever
man . . . that offereth . . . a sacrifice, and
bringeth it not unto the door of the tabernacle
of the congregation, to offer it unto the Lord:
even that man shall be cut off . . ." (Lev. 17:
8, 9). Nevertheless, the sincere Jew is likely to make this season the occasion of devout
worship and attendance at the synagogue. Services begin the preceding evening with a traditional service of impressively beautiful litur-
gies. The holy day itself is spent in the synagogue in prayer and fasting, and not even water
is permitted to break the fast. The day ends
only when the first evening star appears, and
frequently the closing prayer is uttered: "Next
year may we be in Jerusalem."

Tabernacles

This feast commences four days after
the day of Atonement, and in all, lasts nine
days. The additional two days are concerned
with rejoicing for the gift of the Law. In part,
at least, the Feast serves as an occasion to
render thanksgiving to God for a bountiful harvest. During the seven days of Tabernacles,
the people eat their meals in especially constructed booths, and the pious attend the synagogue daily. One element of the service at
these times is a procession of worshippers
marching about the reading desk, carrying
palms and citrons, and reciting prayers. As
the worshippers return to their places they
strike the back of the pew in front of them with
the palm branch. This ritual is thought to be
a vestigal survival of tabernacle and temple
worship, and to represent the smiting stroke
upon the sacrificial animal with which the

Feast	Procedure	Types	Remarks
PASSOVER Lev. 23:5 Num. 28:16 Deut. 16:1	1) Lamb slain, roasted 2) Lamb eaten by family 3) Burnt and sin offerings	Speaks of Christ's redemptive work and the sinner's union with Christ thus provided	A memorial feast commemorating the deliverance from Egypt's bondage
UNLEAV- ENED BREAD Ex. 23:15 Lev. 15:6	1) Unleavened bread eaten 7 days 2) Barley sheaf waved on 2 days 3) Daily burnt offerings 4) On 1st and 7th offerings holy assembly	Speaks of the believer's new life through the cleansing out of the leaven of sinful nature	This bread constituted part of the Passover Feast. Barley was a farmer's first spring harvest
FIRST FRUITS Ex. 23:16 Lev. 23:10 Num. 29:26	1) Barley sheaf waved 2) Burnt, meal, drink offerings 3) None to be eaten before this dedication	Since Christ rose on this day, His resurrection is prefigured	An expression of gratitude for harvest. Sin offering unnecessary
WEEKS (Pentecost or Harvest) Ex. 34:22 Lev. 23:15 Deut. 16:9	1) Wheat loaves waved 2) Burnt, meal, drink, sin offerings 3) People rested	A type of Jerusalem converts--firstfruits of Calvary. The 2 loaves indicate both Jews and Gentiles	Constituted the end of the barley harvest and the presentation of the firstfruits of the wheat harvest. In N.T. times the Spirit given on this day
TRUMPETS Lev. 23:24 Num. 29:1	1) Trumpets sound work ceases 2) Burnt and meal offerings made	Speaks of God's ending His present silence with the rapture of saints and the regathering of Israel	Historically this feast was considered to commemorate Sinai. Ram's horn trumpets called "Shofar"
ATONE- MENT Lev. 16:3 Lev. 23:27 Num. 29:7	1) People fast & rest 2) Burnt and meal offerings 3) Slain goat & scapegoat 4) Blood within veil	Speaks of Israel's present mourning but future joy when their High Priest emerges from His prolonged present sojourn. Her conversion is implied	A day of fast when Israel's sins for another year were covered. Israel's greatest day of the year
TABER- NACLES (Ingathering) Ex. 23:16 Lev. 23:34 Num. 29:12 Deut. 16:13	1) For seven days people dwell in booths of tree boughs 2) Daily burnt & meal offerings 3) An assembly on the eighth day	Speaks of the millennial restoration of Israel and the recollection of long years of exile.	Memorial of tent life in wilderness. On this day Jesus stood and cried aloud (Jno. 7:37). Commemorated ingathering of vine and tree fruits at end of year

"Speak unto the children of Israel, and say unto them, Concerning the feasts of the Lord, which ye shall proclaim to be holy convocations, even these are my feasts" (Leviticus 23:2).

Figure 14 -- Feasts and Set Times in the Old Testament Era

offerer had identified by the laying on of hands. The Jew is thus related to his Scriptures: ". . . and the Lord hath laid on him the iniquity of us all" (Isa. 53:6). The justification for the palm waving is also found in Scripture: "And ye shall take unto you on the first day the fruit of the goodly tree, branches of palm trees, . . . and ye shall rejoice before the Lord your God seven days" (Lev. 2:40).

Pentecost

This feast observed fifty days after the Passover is known as the Feast of Weeks or Shevouth. Since devout Jews believe that this day marks the anniversary of the occasion when God gave the Law they carefully review the sacred Torah (i.e. the Pentateuch), if necessary remaining up all night in order to do so.

Hanukkah

Although not strictly a Biblical feast, Hanukkah, or the Feast of Lights, is rooted in events prior to the time of Christ. However, it is mentioned in the New Testament and there called the Feast of Dedication (Jno. 10:22). It commemorates the victory of the Jews over Antiochus Epiphanes in the time of the Maccabees, and reenacts the miracle whereby a single day's supply of oil in the temple lasted for eight days. Thus the festivities include the lighting of one candle each day for eight days, daily prayer in the synagogue, and the reading of the Hallel Psalms (Psa. 113-118), together with other hymns of thanksgiving. Hanukkah begins on the thirteenth of Kislev and continues for eight days so that it roughly corresponds to the Christian's Christmas. Modern Jews have added the practice of the exchange of gifts at this time.

2. Priestly Duties. The Sin of Blasphemy (Ch. 24)

This chapter is concerned with three main topics: 1) The continually burning lamp is a noteworthy type of the Christian. The lamp of beaten gold signifies the crucified Christ upon whom the New Testament message depends. The pure olive oil speaks of the indwelling Holy Spirit Who empowers the believer for a continual and consistent Christian testimony. 2) As previously noted (Ex. 25:30), the shewbread consisted of little flat cakes.

They were arranged on the table in two rows of six, and were renewed each seven days. Only Aaron and his sons were authorized to eat the bread that was removed. The eating of the shewbread speaks to the believer of spiritually partaking of Christ, the Bread of Life. 3) The crime of the man who lost his temper as a result of a petty scuffle was that he used the name of deity and holy things irreverently and improperly in venting his wrath upon his adversary. For this sin of blasphemy he suffered stoning. This incident served as a pattern for all of Israel's later dealings with blasphemers.

VII. LAWS CONCERNING THE LAND
   (Chs. 25-27)

1. The Sabbatic Year and the Year of Jubilee (Ch. 25)

The Sabbatic year was to be observed when the people were settled in the Land. Every seventh year was to be counted a Sabbath, and in that time the land was entirely to rest. The people, except the very poor, were forbidden to gather even that which grew of itself, but the Lord promised ample provision through an increased harvest each sixth year. Also, during the seventh year, the people were free to hunt, feed their flocks, repair their buildings, and engage in commerce. The people failed to observe this provision for the Sabbatic year, and the Babylonian captivity was one of the consequences. (See 2 Chron. 36: 20, 21).

God designated that every fiftieth year was to be counted a "Year of Jubilee." The name "Jubilee" appears to be an adaptation of the Hebrew word for trumpet, and it was evidently attached to the year because this is the way in which it was announced. As this year was launched, all civil, property and personal rights and possessions were automatically to revert to their original owners. Prisoners were to be released and lost estates were to be restored. The provisions for the year of Jubilee thus prevented the accumulation of wealth by a Jew, and taught the fact of God's ownership of Palestine. God maintained prior right to the land, and had determined that it might never be sold. In all business dealings at all times, the Israelite would have to bear in mind the fact that within a given time another year of Jubilee would be announced

and no contracts would extend beyond that period. Inasmuch as this year followed the forty-
ninth, itself a Sabbatic year, only the special
intervention of God made it possible for the
people to be sustained without a harvest.

Today in modern Palestine, some Jews
have made an effort to observe the old Sabbatic year. In 1951, for instance, since
there was no real sentiment to observe the law
the rabbis technically "sold" the entire territory of Israel to an obliging Arab. At the
end of the year they bought it back. Only a
few hundred people were not satisfied by this
device, but these latter faithfully left their
fields fallow and then duly celebrated the close
of the period with the first ceremony of Hakhel
since 42 A.D. in the time of King Agrippa.

2. The Blessing and the Curse (Ch. 26)

The Lord took occasion once more to
remind the Israelites that they would be blessed for obedience and cursed for disobedience.
If they were obedient they were to enjoy such
blessings as: rain, a fruitful land, peace, deliverance from wild beasts, and victory over
their enemies. If they were disobedient they
would suffer: disease, famine, defeat by
enemies, inroads from wild beasts, dispersion, and the desolation of the land.

Historically, of course, Israel fell
beneath the curse. One has commented: "The
tragedies of Israel's history constitute her
people's monuments of Jehovah's inflexible
truth and justice." The exercise of God's
government toward Israel in this era has historically led them into suffering; the exercise of God's grace to His people during the

millennium will lead them into happiness.

3. Concerning Vows (Ch. 27)

The Lord prescribed that whatever or
whoever was given to Him in a moment of religious devotion, was thenceforth to remain His
and could be recovered by the original owner
only by due payment. There was no compulsion about taking a vow, but strict compulsion
about keeping it once it was made. However,
as Evans points out: "No man was allowed to
impoverish his family by vowing all that he had.
Simply saying 'Corban' (it is a gift, cf. Mark
7:11, 12) did not relieve a man from responsibility for the care of his family."[6] The one exception to compulsion in keeping a vow was in
the case of the man who vowed more than he
had. In this case God chose to exercise a
certain sentimentality. Mackintosh observes
in commenting upon v. 8:

> . . . if it be a question of a man's un-
> dertaking to meet the claims of righteous-
> ness, then he must meet them; but if, . . .
> a man feels himself wholly unable to meet
> these claims, he has only to fall back upon
> grace, which will take him up just as
> he is.[7]

To recover a devoted person, it was
necessary to pay into the tabernacle treasury
a sum equal to the value of the person to the
Lord's service. A clean beast could not be
recovered, but the unclean could be redeemed
by a payment of its value, plus one-fifth more.
A house and field, likewise, could be redeemed
only by payment of its value, plus one fifth.
Neither firstlings nor tithes could be dedicated
to the Lord, for they were already His.

[6]Williams Evans, The Books of the Pentateuch. New York: Fleming H. Revell Co.,
1916, p. 226.

[7]C. H. Mackintosh, Notes on the Book
of Leviticus. New York: Loizeaux Brothers,
1945, p. 379.

FIVE: The Book of Numbers

Those who prepared the Septuagint gave to this fourth book of the Pentateuch the name Arithmoi. The Latin Vulgate, in turn, rendered this name Numeri, and English translators adopted the name Numbers as a variant of the Latin. The Hebrew name for the book is the word Bemidhbar meaning "in the wilderness." The name Numbers was given to indicate that the book contains an account of two censuses or numberings of the Israelites. (See Chs. 1 and 26).

The Nature of the Book

The book describes Israel's history for almost the entire forty years in the wilderness, and thereby, as a historical narrative constitutes a marked contrast from Leviticus. Mackintosh says: "In Leviticus we are almost entirely occupied with the worship and service of the sanctuary; but no sooner have we opened the book of Numbers than we read of men of war, of armies, of standards, of camps and trumpets sounding alarm."[1] In content, Numbers is almost equally divided between history and legislation. However, the legal pronouncements are given in a historical context--laws were enacted when the affairs of the people made a new decision necessary. In general, the arrangement is chronological, though the occasional incident is reported out of context in order to provide a smoother literary composition. Christians find many valuable lessons in the book of Numbers, not so much by precept as by negative example. Though God does not intend believers to wander in a wilderness, should they find themselves there, they may observe that those standards of submission to God and obedience to His will that Numbers teaches, constitute the inevitable way of deliverance.

Key Words and Key Verse

The key words of Numbers have been suggested to be: service, sojourning, or pilgrimage. A proposed key verse is 10:29--"We

---

[1]C.H. Mackintosh, Notes on the Book of Numbers, New York: Loizeaux Brothers, 1945, p. 23

are journeying unto the place which the Lord said, I will give it you . . ." A key verse that accords with the theme of service is not available, though this theme is important in the book. One has said: "In Genesis we see man ruined, in Exodus man redeemed, in Leviticus man worshipping, and now in Numbers, man in service."

The Scope of the Book

The narrative in Numbers commences exactly one month after the tabernacle had been erected, or just a year and a month after the exodus from Egypt. (cf. Ex. 40:2, Num. 1:1). For practical purposes the book of Numbers may be considered as taking up historical events directly from the close of the book of Exodus and proceeding to report Israel's history for a period representing nearly thirty-nine years. (cf. Deut. 1:3). Of this span of years, however, only two are reported in any detail, the remaining thirty-seven are virtually passed over. It is usually considered that there is a gap of this duration between chapters 19 and 20.

Problems in Numbers

Those who look for problems in Scripture find Numbers to be a ready target, and such scholars have characterized the book as: "the most perplexing in sacred history." The usual "problems" cited include: the population totals, other statistics, chronologies, and various physical phenomena. Bible believers may answer that though there may be portions of the book, the acceptance of which calls for an exercise of faith, on the whole this work adequately responds to an open-minded, scholarly approach. The alleged problems of Numbers are no greater than those of many other portions of Scripture, and the main "problem" is not the contents of this book but the skeptical minds of the critics who prefer not to accept literal Scripture.

The diverse content of the book has been another reason for its attack by critics. It has been argued that such a variety of topics must indicate that it is a composite work with many authors and editors. However, careful study reveals that there is a vital connection between the various sections, and that there are no valid grounds for impugning the authenticity of the book or its Mosaic authorship. As Clarke explains:

In this book, which comprehends the history of between thirty-eight and thirty-nine years, we have in one word a distinct account of the several stages of Israel's journey in the wilderness, the various occurrences on the way, their trials, rebellions, punishments, deliverances, conquests, etc., with several laws and ordinances not mentioned in the preceding books, together with a repetition and explanation of some others which had been previously delivered; the whole forming a most interesting history of justice, mercy, and providence of God.[2]

ANALYSIS AND EXPOSITION

I. ISRAEL AT SINAI (Chs. 1:1 - 10:10)

1. The People Numbered (Ch. 1)

The people had been numbered only about a month previously on the occasion of the assessing of the silver for the sanctuary (Ex. 38:26); hence it is to be expected that the two totals would agree. (Some scholars consider that there were simply two accounts of the same census.) It would appear that on this occasion, the purposes of the numbering were: to determine the number of able-bodied warriors, to register all Israelites, and to determine each individual's ancestry for the genealogical tables. The reported total was 603,550 males "twenty years old and upward . . . that are able to go forth to war." It is noted that all men were regarded as soldiers unless otherwise disqualified. Actually the word number in the original meant not so much "count" as to "muster an army."

The numbering was accomplished by deputies who made a careful check of the genealogy of each individual. Those who were ignorant of their pedigree were barred from fighting the Lord's battles with the armies of Israel;

---

[2]Adam Clarke, <u>Bible Commentary</u> (Vol. I). New York: Abingdon-Cokesbury Press, ------, p. 608.

just as in this era, Christians of uncertain spiritual pedigree have no place in the Lord's army. The Levites were not numbered, for they were not considered eligible for military duty. Their task was to care for the tabernacle and be constantly by it.

2. The Organization of the Camp (Ch. 2)

The Lord's care in organizing the camp seems typical of His directions in general, for He is the God of order and not the God of confusion. Just as the Israelites were to unite about the standard of their chosen leaders, so Christians are to unite about the standard of the Lord Jesus Christ. When the nation marched, the order was to be: Judah's standard, Reuben's standard, Levites and tabernacle, Ephraim's standard, Dan's standard. Apparently this particular order put the strongest divisions at the head and rear. The prominence given to Judah both in her encampment in front of the gate and in her leadership in the order of march seems to have been, at least in part, an anticipation of the tribe's honor in bringing forth the Savior.

3. Concerning the Levites (Ch. 3)

God was moved by His sovereignty and grace to choose as His servants the tribe of Levi in place of the firstborn of all the tribes. Though the Levites had at one time been in obscurity and virtual rejection (cf. Gen. 49:5-7), they now took a place of preeminence. Of course, they had recently revealed themselves to be "on the Lord's side" in the golden calf episode (Ex. 32:25-29). The Levites were appointed to do service in the tabernacle in outward matters; while the priests (actually a special group within the tribe) performed the ceremonial tabernacle worship exercises. In the numbering of the Levites, all were included from a month old and upwards with the totals in the three family divisions: Gershon 7,500, Kohath 8,600, and Merari 6,200. The grand total was 22,300, though v. 39 declares the total was an even 22,000. This discrepancy is explained as: a round number, a textual error (Moffat says the total of the Kohathites should read 8,300), or because 300 were firstborn and not eligible for exchange.

The Lord appointed that there was to be an exchange of one Levite for one firstborn and that the surplus of non-Levite firstborn be redeemed for five shekels. In the Levite families, the cattle were devoted, since the firstborn had already been given to the Lord and were not eligible to be dedicated twice. The proportion of non-Levite firstborn was 22,273 out of 605,550 or one out of each twenty-seven men. Various theories have been offered to explain this very low figure. 1) the total on this occasion may have included only those males under twenty who had not been counted in the recent census; 2) the oldest child may have been counted as firstborn only if he were a boy; 3) only one firstborn per house-hold was counted. If both father and son were firstborn, only the father would be counted, and 4) only one firstborn for each family or clan was counted rather than for each household.

4. The Work of the Levites (Ch. 4)

All male Levites over one month were included in the numbering, but only those between the ages of thirty and fifty were accepted for service. The Old Testament explicitly sets forth the qualifications for God's servants a total of six times. On these grounds 8,580 Levites were considered fit and 13,720 unfit. The Levites assisted the priests and divided their duties by families. The Kohathites, honored most, were appointed to care for the tabernacle furnishings; the Gershonites, next honored, cared for the hangings and curtains; the Merarites, least honored, cared for the heavier and least important parts of the tabernacle. An interesting exception to the division of work in the assignment of heavy items to the Merarites was their appointment also to care for the pins that attached the various hangings. This chapter teaches that: no service is too small to be indifferent to God, each worker must fulfill his appointed task, and non-workers are likely to outnumber workers in any given group of believers. It is to be noted that in the case of the Merarites with their heavier, grosser work, only one-third of the candidates were disqualified, in contrast with upwards of one-half of the candidates of the other tribes.

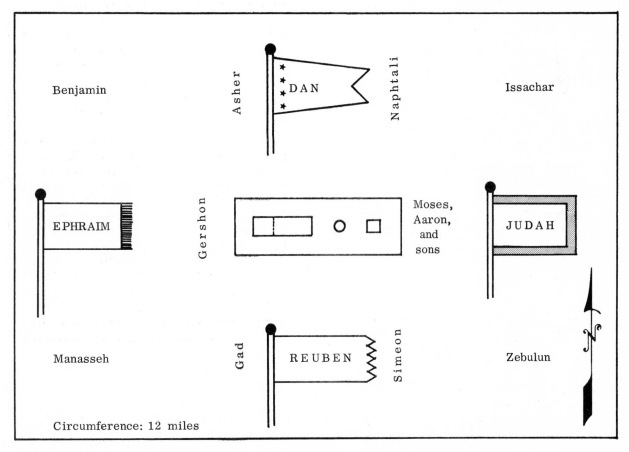

Figure 15 -- Israel's Organization During Encampments

5. Uncleanness and Jealousy (Ch. 5)

Because iniquity has no part in the camp of believers, the Lord once more emphasized that the unclean person should be put out of the camp. In the New Testament times St. Paul advised the Corinthian church, "Put away from among yourselves that wicked person" (1 Cor. 5:13). The Lord prescribed as restitution for wrong doing the standard payment of equivalent value plus one-fifth. This amount was to be paid to the one wronged or to his family, or to the priest if there was no heir. Restitution payment considered in this chapter was to be the voluntary response of conscience; the punishment of the convicted criminal was another matter.

The husband who suspected the faithfulness of his wife might bring her before the priest and require her to drink "bitter" water. The drink was comprised of water from the laver with dust sprinkled into it. If the woman died, it would be known that she was guilty; if she did not, her innocency would be established. Since it was a miracle if the woman died, this ceremony is in sharp contrast to pagan trials by ordeal which require the accused to drink poison so that survival is a miracle. One effect of the ceremony of bitter water would be that the very mechanics of such a procedure would restrain any unjust or precipitant divorce. The expression "holy water" in v. 17 does not occur elsewhere in the Bible. On this occasion the phrase could have been rendered "fresh water."

6. The Order of the Nazarites (Ch. 6)

The Nazarite (or Nazirite R. V.) was in basic concept one separated to Jehovah. The name Nazarite comes from the Hebrew "Nazir" meaning "a devoted or consecrated one." The Nazarite might be: 1) bound for life, 2) bound only for a specific time. The Bible records three lifelong Nazarites: Sampson, Samuel, and John the Baptist. In each case these individuals were consecrated as a result of the vows of their parents. Temporary consecrations to the vow of the Nazarite were usually in response to some special blessing or spiritual experience that an individual underwent. Women as well as men were eligible to be Nazarites. The Bible does not indicate that the Lord Jesus was a Nazarite (He was more than that), although artists often depict Him thus.

Rules that apply to the Nazarite included: 1) he was to refrain from all products of the grapevine, 2) his hair was to remain uncut, and 3) he was to be separated from the dead. No doubt a large measure of the significance of these regulations inhered in their typical application. To abstain from the products of the vine would imply depriving oneself of physical pleasure and social activity. Human hair is associated with the development of strength, both physical and intellectual. Dead bodies are emblems of sin and the results of the curse upon mankind. Such external regulations maintained men holy unto the Lord in the society in which they lived. The termination of a Nazarite vow involved the making of an offering and a special ceremony at the altar which included the burning of shorn hair. It was from the Nazarite that some of the prophets came (e.g. Amos 2:11, 12). New Testament examples of those taking Nazarite vows included St. Paul and Epaphroditus.

NAZARITE	CHRISTIAN
Separated	Those in Christ set apart
Denied earthly joy	Required to abstain from the world
A Nazarite by choice --not legally demanded	The believer is a willing bond-slave
Vow ended, could drink wine	Christians look forward to feasting with their Lord
Long hair a reproach and emblem of subjection	Believer bears the reproach of Christ and yields his will to His

The benediction in vvs. 24-26 is threefold and suggests the Trinity. The form is a good example of parallelism in Hebrew poetry. It is a beautiful passage and well worth memorizing.

7. The Offerings of the Princes (Ch. 7)

In an impressive demonstration of sincere devotion to the Lord, each of the princes of the tribes made a special offering. The gifts were presented one each day for 12 days. The total offerings consisted of: 6 wagons, 12 oxen, 12 silver chargers (a dish like a serving platter), 12 silver bowls, 12 golden spoons, 12 bullocks, 72 each of rams, lambs, goats, and 24 additional oxen. The animals constituted: burnt, sin, and peace offerings. The value of the metals was about $3,000. Each of the princes of the tribes made a special identical offering.

The wagons were given to the Levites to haul the heavier parts of the tabernacle. Merari received four of the wagons, Gershon two, and Kohath none. This distribution was based upon the burdens that each family was required to carry. God was favorably impressed by these generous gifts, and He instructed Moses to accept them and put them to use. This record of giving constitutes the second longest chapter in the Bible. The same Lord who noticed the widow's mite is aware of every measure of devotion of His people toward Him.

8. The Consecration of the Levites (Ch. 8)

A brief description of the golden candlestick precedes the setting forth of the ceremony for the consecration of the Levites. These workers were to minister to the people by service rather than by sacrifice as in the case of the priests. However, they were just as genuinely commisioned and consecrated by God for this special religious service. The consecration of the Levites involved ceremonial cleansing and the making of: sin, burnt and meal offerings. The pure water and the sharp razor speak of the cleansing and the cutting off which must always characterize God's servants. The consecration of the Levites especially stressed washing and sacrifices, rather than anointing and investiture as in the case of the priests. The Levitical candidates offered themselves spiritually to God, and through the laying on of hands by appropriate representatives, all of the people were identified with them.

The age of service for the Levites is here given as twenty-five to fifty, whereas in 4:3 it is stated that they were to begin service at age thirty. It may have been that the first five years was a training period, and hence this apparent discrepancy. It has been suggested that those over age fifty who were still to minister but "do no service" may have been set apart as the teachers of the probationers.

9. Regulations Concerning the Passover (Ch. 9)

The incidents concerning the Passover that are here reported occurred at the time of the erection of the tabernacle, just a year after the exodus from Egypt. At that time, God provided that those who found it necessary to miss the observance of the Passover at the regular time might observe it as a special occasion one month later. Thus the grace of God provided for all, but if anyone deliberately ignored the Passover, he would be cut off from the people. It should be noted, however, that it is inferred that the neglect of circumcision during the years of wandering required the suspension of the Passover ordinance during that time (See Josh. 5:10 et al).

The cloud and the fire guided the people night and day, and required that they be ready to encamp or depart at any moment. Though God guides the Christian in a manner less spectacular, He guides him nonetheless truly.

10. The Trumpets of Silver (Ch. 10:1-10)

God prescribed that two trumpets (or clarions) should be made, each from a single piece of silver. These instruments were formed as straight tubes flared at the mouth. Their code of usage included: 1 blast--assemble congregation, 1 blast of one trumpet--assemble princes, and 2 alarms (probably a sort of fanfare with with several sharp notes)--camp to move. In general, the trumpets served to rally troops (see 2 Chron. 13:13-16), and to gather the people on the occasion of making proclamations. In their achievement of expressing the will of God to the people, the trumpets are a type of Scripture in its ministry to the New Testament believer. Some scholars consider that the Jubilee trumpet of Lev. 25:9 was a different and special instrument from the standard trumpets of silver, but there does not seem to be ground for insisting upon such a distinction.

II. FROM SINAI TO KADESH (Chs. 10:11 - 19:22)

1. Israel's Departure from Sinai (Ch. 10:11-36)

The departure from Sinai at this juncture brought an end to the stay of fully eleven months and six days. (cf. Ex. 12:18, 19:1). The people proceeded northward, encouraged by Moses' rallying prayer: "Rise up, Lord, and let thine enemies be scattered; and let them that hate thee flee before thee" (v.35). It has been suggested that the change in the order of march from that prescribed in chapter two was permitted by God for the sake of expediency in erecting the tabernacle.

Moses evidently invited Hobab to accompany the people in order that the desert dweller might guide and instruct the people in the matter of achieving a comfortable existence while they travelled in the wilderness. It may be assumed that Hobab was the brother-in-law of Moses, since Raguel is said to be Moses' father-in-law. Thus Raguel is identified with Reuel or Jethro. However, it should be noted that for the Hebrews "father-in-law" is a general term that signifies little more than the status of being related by marriage. Although Scripture does not report whether Hobab accepted the invitation, it is later recorded (Jud. 1:16, 4:11) that his people, the Midianites, were with the Israelites as they settled in the land. Thus, it may be concluded that at least there was a close association between the two nations, and concerning Hobab most scholars agree with Maclear who says: "There seems little doubt that Hobab consented to accompany the people, and to be to them instead of eyes amidst the dangers of the inhospitable desert."[3]

2. At Taberah and Kibroth-hattaavah (Ch. 11)

The name "Taberah" means "burning" or "conflagration." Evidently the complainers lagged behind so that they were consumed by the fire which fell on the outermost parts of the camp. This occasion marked Israel's fifth murmuring under Moses' leadership.

At Kibroth-hattaavah, no doubt under the delusion of an inexact memory, the Israelites began lusting for the diet that they had enjoyed in Egypt. The foods they missed included: fish, cucumbers, melons, leeks, onions, and garlic. These are considered to have been the common foods of Egypt's lower classes. Their

craving for these items contrasts with what might have been a grateful anticipation of the foods of Canaan: wheat, barley, vines, fig trees, pomegranates, olives, and honey. The complaining of the people drove Moses to the Lord and led him to pray plaintively and to some measure to exaggerate his own responsibility. ". . . have I begotten them, that thou shouldest say unto me, Carry them in thy bosom, as a nursing father beareth the sucking child, . . .?" (11:12). Such discouragement led Moses to entreat the Lord to kill him "out of hand" (i.e. at once). God's response was the appointment of the 70 elders and their enduement with a portion of the Spirit that had been upon Moses. This transfer empowered the elders for their tasks and lightened Moses' burdens. However, it has been said that though Moses was spared great labor, he thereby forfeited dignity and reward. Comments Scofield, "There was no more power than before--only more machinery."

The flock of quails has been estimated to have extended for 20 miles (i.e. a day's journey in each direction), and the 2 cubits evidently refers to the height at which the birds flew. That illness should befall those who gorged themselves upon meat after months of deprivation is understandable enough. The name Kibroth-hattaavah means "graves of lust" and it appropriately serves to indicate the fate of the greedy.

Joshua, who previously had been mentioned on the occasion of the battle against Amalek and as the special companion of Moses on Mt. Sinai, now figures in the story of Eldad and Medad. Scripture seems to indicate (v. 26) that these two men belonged to the seventy elders. However, whereas the other members restricted the manifestation of their spiritual gifts to the tabernacle, these men took their gift of prophecy out among the people. Thus, they made themselves to appear especially anointed leaders who directly ministered to the people, and in such light they might have posed a threat to the leadership of Moses. It was Moses' diagnosis that Joshua's concern was rooted in envy (v. 29), and in contrast to Joshua, Israel's leader chose wholeheartedly to endorse this spiritual manifestation and to declare he wished it were the general pattern among God's people. There is no evidence that the spiritual prowess of Eldad and Medad became a schismatic power in Israel, and thus Moses' generosity of spirit was vindicated.

---

[3]G. F. Maclear, A Class Book of Old Testament History. Grand Rapids: Wm. B. Eerdmans Publishing Company, 1952, p. 169.

3. The Rebellion of Miriam and Aaron (Ch. 12)

The bitter criticisms which Miriam and Aaron uttered against Moses were evidently motivated primarily by jealousy. They objected to: 1) Moses' wife, and 2) his monopoly of divine revelation. Although it is possible to consider that Miriam's and Aaron's objections were against some unnamed negro woman that Moses had married, it is usually considered that Zipporah was the object of their criticism. Ethiopia of Moses' day was not only a country of Africa but it may possibly be identified with a territory of the Kenites from which Zipporah came. Although Moses had been married to Zipporah for several years, only recently had she joined her husband in his new role of leader. Hence, Miriam and Aaron may have met her only a short time before.

God's testimony exonerating his man is duly recorded: "Now the man Moses was very meek, above all the men which were upon the face of the earth" (12:3). Although Moses himself recorded these words, he was simply reporting the divine testimony as an abjective fact. Centuries later, St. Paul also found it necessary to testify of himself in similar manner "Serving the Lord with all humility of mind, . . ." (Acts 20:19). The Lord sternly rebuked Moses' critics and provided that Miriam's leprosy was healed only as Moses prayed for her. In addition, Miriam remained subject to seven days of exile to provide for her ceremonial cleansing. It may be concluded that these events, which took place at Hazeroth, left Miriam and Aaron much enlightened and wiser.

4. Events at Kadesh (Ch. 13)

When the people arrived at the oasis, Kadesh, (also called Kadesh-barnea [Num. 32:8]; En-mishpat [Gen. 14:7]; and identified with Meribah [Deut. 32:51]), they sent out spies to reconnoitre the land and decide on the advisability of immediate attempts to conquer it. While the sending forth of the spies is not usually considered a justifiable action, it is described in Scripture in the following ways: at the people's request, with Moses' pleasure, and by the Lord's approval (See Deut. 1:22, 23). The words in this chapter: "Send thou men, . . ." (13:2), may be rendered "Send for thyself men" and they convey the impression that God wished Himself to be disassociated from the project.

The twelve spies were leaders in their respective tribes and they included: Joshua (Oshea) and Caleb as representatives of the tribes of Ephraim and Judah. Although the tribe of Joseph had been divided into Ephraim and Manasseh the total number of representatives remained twelve; there were none from Levi since the Levites were to possess no land. In their forty-day travels throughout the entire length of the land, the spies were to determine: the fertility of the soil, the military strength of the cities, the wealth of the people, and the extent of the natural forces. Since they made their foray in the fall of the year, they were to bring back some of the typical harvest products of the land.

The spies returned with a huge cluster of grapes and some pomegranates and figs, and to a man they were impressed that the land indeed flowed with milk and honey. However, the ten spies were overwhelmed by the strength of the inhabitants so that they brought an "evil report" (literally: slanderous report) that was calculated to deter even the bravest from an attempt at conquest. Only Caleb, with Joshua as a silent supporter, spoke forth in favor of immediate possession of the land. As Evans says: "The ten spies saw God through circumstances; the two saw circumstances through God." It is characteristic of unbelief that it never proceeds beyond difficulties.

5. Israel's Unbelief. Moses' Intercession (Ch. 14)

At the report of the spies, the whole congregation murmured against Moses and Aaron and declared that they would have been better off to have died in Egypt. This occasion marked Israel's seventh murmuring, and in Heb. 3:8 it is called "the provocation." The people even went so far as to elect a new captain to lead them back to Egypt (see Neh. 9:17), and they planned to stone Joshua and Caleb. Only the appearance of the glory of the Lord restrained the people in their rebellious actions.

Moses prayed fervently about the matter and pointed out that in order to vindicate His own Name, the Lord was obliged to spare the people and bring them through safely. God responded by offering to pardon the people, but He decreed that the existing generation should be deprived of the privilege of entering the land. Only Caleb and Joshua were named as exempt from this pronouncement. (cf. vvs. 24, 30). The existing generation who were to perish in the wilderness included all who were twenty years old and upward. God proceeded to visit the ten faithless spies with instant death.

The following day, the people realized their folly, and thus hastily attacked the inhabitants of the land in an effort to achieve conquest. Griffith Thomas comments: "From unbelief they went to presumption, and so from mourning and murmuring they swung over to rashness." Moses warned them that they would fail, but in their headstrong blindness they proceeded nonetheless. The outcome was sorry defeat and flight before the hordes of the Amalekites and Canaanites, just as Moses had predicted.

6. Various Laws. The Sabbath Breaker
   (Ch. 15)

This chapter repeats instructions previously given concerning the offerings. It is evident that man was to offer to God the same food that he enjoyed at his own table. The drink-offering is declared to be a fourth part of a hin of wine. The hin was a liquid measure which was a little less than one and one-half gallons. The stoning of the man who gathered sticks on the Sabbath is an example of presumptuous sin which was punishable by death. The episode indicates the true nature of the Law and the degree of its severity. The ribbon of blue that the people were to wear upon the border of their garments spoke of their high and heavenly calling. The wearing of such a blue ribbon is still practised among some Jews today, though usually it is attached to undergarments. Also, the practice by Jewish males of wearing a tallith or prayer shawl when in the synagogue is related to this Scripture. A tallith consists of an oblong cloth decorated with a fringe of tassels at the ends and of such proportions as to drape attractively over the shoulders.

7. The Rebellion of Korah (Ch. 16)

Apparently intense jealousy was the motive that led to the rebellion of Korah, Dathan, Abiram, and On, and their 250 followers. The revolt was not only against the leadership of Moses but against the priesthood of Aaron. It constituted the most serious of all of Moses' career of leadership. Korah, who appears as the ringleader, was a Levite and of the honored family of Kohath. The other three rebels were all of the tribe of Reuben. Among other charges, the group accused Moses of attempting to blind the people by false promises. (cf. "wilt thou put out the eyes of these men?" [v. 14]).

The outcome of the clamorous demands of the group was, once more, the direct intervention of the Lord. The rebels and Moses were each commanded to offer incense that the Lord might demonstrate the person of His choice. At the appointed time, the rebellious company stood defiantly awaiting the acceptance of their incense and steadfastly resisting Moses. In accord with Moses' prayer that the Lord "make a new thing," God caused the earth to open and swallow alive the leaders, together with the families of Dathan and Abiram. However, as Numbers 26:11 plainly declares, "the children of Korah died not." As a climax to this terrifying demonstration, fire came forth and consumed 250 of the chief supporters of the rebels.

Though the people were temporarily impressed by this demonstration of God's will and power, by the morrow they had forgotten it and they again became critical and resistant declaring that Moses and Aaron had killed the people of the Lord. It was only the prayers of Moses and the intercession of Aaron that spared the entire camp from destruction. This occasion was unique in that incense served as an offering to make atonement for wrong doing. Some 14,700 perished in God's disciplinary plague before Aaron was able to make his atoning offering.

8. The Priesthood of Aaron Confirmed (Ch. 17)

God chose to provide the Israelites with a visible lesson to impress them once and for all of His choice of the leading tribe and of the priesthood of Aaron. At the Lord's instruction, each of the tribes took a rod and placed it in the Holy of Holies in the tabernacle. On the morrow, Aaron's rod not only had budded, but also it bore blossoms and ripe almonds as fruit. God thus vindicated the priesthood of Aaron and set forth His over-all endorsement of the tribe of Levi. This springing to life of Aaron's rod has been compared to the resurrection of Jesus Christ, for each event vindicated the plan of God in its respective sphere.

In the camp Israel, the reaction to this divine demonstration was a period of profound spiritual depression.

9. The Priests' Duties and Their Method of Support (Ch. 18)

God provided that the priests were to preside at the sacred altar; while the Levites were to attend to all other duties involved in tabernacle worship. Elsewhere, it is made clear that the priest was associated with legal administration (Deut. 17:9, 17, 19), and it was his responsibility to teach the Law (Deut. 24:8). The Levites were to be supported by the tithes of the people; the priests were to receive the tithes of the Levites, plus free will offerings, and specified portions of the sacrifices that were brought to the tabernacle. Although this system ought to have provided adequately for the religious leaders, in later history the combination of spiritual apathy on the part of the people, and carnal greed on the part of the religious leaders, made their support become an oppressive burden.

10. The Water of Purification (Ch. 19)

This ceremony was known as the "Ordinance of the Red Heifer" and it was a means of providing cleansing for those who had been defiled through contact with a dead body in warfare or through touching a defiled vessel. The water that was to be used in this ceremonial cleansing was to be especially prepared: to "running water" was to be added the ashes of a sacrificed heifer, the carcass of which had been wholly burned. The sacrifice was to be a heifer (speaking of vitality and abounding life), it was to be red (rare in Palestine and consequently costly, also typical of sin in the sense of Isa. 1:18), and was to be slain in the presence of the priest by "one" (i.e. anyone). In general, Scripture prescribed the offering of male animals in all instances when actual sin was concerned and a female animal in the case of passive defilement.

The water of separation was sprinkled on the unclean on the third and seventh days to effect ceremonial cleansing; hence it is a type of the provision for the believer's daily cleansing apart from the initial step of having his sins forgiven. The provision of the red heifer is mentioned in Heb. 9:13 "For if the blood of bulls and of goats, and the ashes of an heifer

sprinkling the unclean, sanctifieth . . ." It is a curious fact that anyone that touched this purifying water was himself temporarily rendered unclean. (cf. v. 21). The red heifer is a type of Christ in the following characteristics: without spot or blemish, known no yoke, slain outside the camp, and constituting the means of purification. Some have seen a connenction between the red heifer and the name "Adam" which literally means "red earth." Thus, it is inferred that God's intention in this ordinance is to depict Christ only in His role as the son of Adam or the one made incarnate.

The ashes of the red heifer which were to be the basis of the water of purification were to be carefully tended. "And a man that is clean shall gather up the ashes of the heifer, and lay them up without the camp in a clean place, and it shall be kept for the congregation of the children of Israel for a water of separation" (19:9). Being thus available for the outcast, the ashes were convenient to achieve cleansing. Since cleansing could be achieved only when the ashes were added to the water, the provision speaks typically of the need for the Holy Spirit to implement and validate the virtue of Christ's sacrifice in a specific believer's life.

Most commentators consider that the gap of thirty-seven years comes at this juncture in the book. However, from the standpoint of the narrative, the gap could come any time after chapter 14. Out of a total of nearly forty years in the wilderness, the record of only a little more than two years is actually preserved. Other ancient historical records have been found to be similarly characterized; all catastrophes and misfortunes are wholly obliterated on the ground that that which is cursed simply does not exist.

III. FROM KADESH TO MOAB (Chs. 20-36)

1. At Kadesh in the Fortieth Year. Moses' Sin. (Ch. 20)

With the exception of the scant material in chapter 33, Scripture passes over the events in Israel's history between the time of the defeat of the nondescript army at Kadesh (ch. 14) and the arrival of the new generation at Kadesh in the fortieth year. This chapter takes up the story at that point. The death and burial of Miriam in the first month of the fortieth year is reported as the first event during this sojourn at Kadesh. With the wilderness journey now completed, what apparently is the last appearance of the guiding pillar of cloud and fire is now reported (20:6).

It was at Kadesh at this time that Moses displeased God, and incurred His pronouncement of penalty. In spite of all the experience of the wilderness, the people still yielded to a spirit of murmuring when they found neither water nor fruit at Kadesh. Moses took the matter to God and there he was patiently reassured and instructed to provide for the people's need of water.

The exact nature of the sin of Moses is not specifically noted, for Scripture simply states: "Because ye believed me not, to sanctify me in the eyes of the children of Israel, therefore ye shall not bring this congregation into the land which I have given them" (v. 12). It has been suggested that Moses failed to "sanctify God" in the following aspects: he lost his temper (see Psa. 106:32, 33), he spoke to the people rather than to the rock, he took credit to himself, he doubted God's willingness to provide, he seems to have had faith in the rod rather than in God, he used the wrong rod, he smote the rock twice, and he insisted upon smiting the rock when he had been instructed only to speak to it.

Although neither the nature of Moses' wrong, nor the punishment that God prescribed, were especially severe, the sin of Moses sadly mars an otherwise exemplary record. After eighty years of preparation, this man of God had emerged with exceptional qualifications of character and of spirit. He would not have been expected to fail even in minor matters. Comments Sampey:

When God puts men before the world as His representatives, He holds them to a strict account. Unbelief in a great leader of God's people brings reproach upon God Himself. If even Moses, after a long career of singular faithfulness, finally failed through human weakness, who may presume upon his past achievements? "Let him that thinketh he standeth take heed lest he fall."[4]

----

[4]James R. Sampey, The Heart of the Old Testament. Nashville: Broadman Press, 1922, p. 72.

Subsequent events at Kadesh included Israel's polite request to Edom for the privilege of passing through her land. The people promised to remain on the king's high way and to refrain from any trespassing beyond it. Edom's "king's high way" has been a road for some four thousand years and the same route is still in use today. In Roman times, it was expertly paved and and divided into two lanes. In Israel's time the King stubbornly refused even this permission and thus he subjected his people to later punishment.

Israel left Kadesh and journeyed far south to skirt Edom, and thus the nation was at Mount Hor when Aaron died. The high priest was 123 years old at the time of his death. Israel mourned thirty days for Aaron, and then installed Eleazar, his son, as his successor. The divine concern and provision on the occasion of the death of Aaron indicated God's respect for the office of the priesthood.

2. The Fiery Serpents. Later Conquests
   (Ch. 21)

The incident involving Arad the Canaanite undoubtedly resulted in a new confidence in the ranks of Israel. The king apparently attacked a company of the people and took some of them prisoners. The situation led the people to vow to God the utter destruction of these Canaanites if He would give them victory. God intervened accordingly, and Scripture records "they utterly destroyed them and their cities" (v. 3). The Canaanitish king, Arad, evidently gave his name to a geographical site also. (cf. Josh. 12:14; 1 Chron. 8:15). It is significant that the victory that Israel won over these Canaanites at this time was at a site almost identical to that of Israel's ignominious rout some thirty-eight years previously when the Canaanites defeated the presumptuous Israelitish armies. (cf. ch. 14:40-48).

In the journey from Mount Hor by way of the Red Sea, the people once more began to murmur because of the scarcity of water and the monotonous diet. God's response was to send fiery serpents among them, so that many were bitten and in danger of speedy death. The Lord's provision for the healing of the afflicted was a brazen serpent on a pole, that those who looked might live. This uplifted serpent was the only Old Testament type personally acknowledged by Jesus as speaking of

The almond tree is widely known throughout the Near East, and thus the flourishing of Aaron's rod concerned a familiar type of growth. This tree, photographed at Dothan in North Jordan, is an unusually large and mature specimen. Today, almond nuts in Palestine are used primarily to produce oil.

His crucifixion. (cf. John 3:14). The symbol was preserved in Israel until the time of Hezekiah, but at that time it was destroyed because the people began to worship it (2 Ki. 18:4). Evidently the fiery serpents taught the Israelites an abiding lesson, for this occasion marks the last recorded murmuring of the travellers.

The people continued their journeys until they arrived at Pisgah (v. 20). Encamping there, they began their conquests east of Jordan. In conquering Sihon, king of the Amorites, they possessed the land from Arnon to Jabbok. The conquest of Og, king of Bashan, gave them territory from Jabbok northward to Edrei. Archaeologists report a vast underground city at Edrei, and evidently Israel's conquest there was a noteworthy military achievement.

3. The Journey of Balaam (Ch. 22)

When Balak, king of Moab, saw the military might of Israel, he became alarmed. In an effort to protect himself he called for the services of the prophet Balaam that he might pronounce a curse upon the people. Evidently Balaam had a wide reputation in the ancient world, but whether or not he was actually a prophet of God is not known. He may have worshipped the true God just as Melchisedek, but more likely he was a heathen soothsayer to whom and through whom God spoke. Finegan comments: "Balaam who figures in the story at this point . . . seems to have been a typical Babylonian diviner, and has been shown from parallels in Mesopotamian ritual to have proceeded with what was at the time quite an approved ceremony of divinations." The possibility that Balaam was a heathen soothsayer or diviner is strengthened in view of his conduct and his ultimate fate.

Balaam was quite ready to hire himself to Balak, but he was restrained in his plans by a divine warning. However, when Balak sent a second corps of messengers and additional promises of reward, Balaam somehow managed to cajole the Lord into allowing him to go to Moab, though not to curse Israel. It was during this journey that the well known incident of the talking ass occurred. By this means, the Lord gave Balaam additional warnings of his perverse course and the necessity of speaking only the divine message.

4. The First and Second Prophecies of Balaam (Ch. 23)

It is noted that Balaam's choice for his altar sites was "the high places of Baal" (22: 41) in accord with the theory that the objects to be cursed must be visible. At three such sites Balaam erected a total of twenty-one altars and offered a bullock and a ram upon each. Thus, the prophet dramatically demonstrated his desire to conform outwardly in the rites of worship, and in addition he may have considered the offering as a bribe to impress God to change His will. The irony of the entire incident was that in spite of Balak's purpose for Balaam's ministry and Balaam's personal wishes in the matter, the prophet was unable to pronounce the curse that Balak wished to hear. The themes of Balaam's first two prophecies may be stated: 1) Israel was to enjoy unlimited expansion, and 2) righteous Israel was to prosper mightily. God's immutability is clearly stated in v.19: "God is not a man, that he should lie; neither the son of man, that he should repent: hath he said, and shall he not do it? or hath he spoken, and shall he not make good?" The "unicorn" mentioned in v.22 is simply a translator's effort to indicate that the animal named is unknown.

5. The Third and Fourth Prophecies of Balaam (Ch.24)

The themes of Balaam's third and fourth prophecies may be stated: 3) the enthusiastic praise of Israel, and 4) Israel's coming Messiah and King. Balaam's Messianic prediction is in v.17: ". . . there shall come a Star out of Jacob, and a Sceptre shall rise out of Israel." In spite of Balak's extreme displeasure, Balaam was unable to pronounce a curse upon Israel, for God clearly overruled so that Balaam could utter only what God gave him to say. The prophet discovered that God chose to bless the people, and that it was impossible for him to turn God from the people. The word "advertise" (v.14) means to "advise" or "inform." Although it is stated that at the conclusion of these events Balaam "returned to his place," (v.25) other evidence makes it clear that he actually remained in Moab and did not again return to Mesopotamia.

The New Testament roundly condemns Balaam and successively denounces: his doctrine, his error, and his way. (cf. Rev.2:14, Jude 11, 2 Pet.2:15). Balaam became the object of divine condemnation because of his subsequent behavior following his four prophecies. When the coveteous prophet found he was unable to turn God from the people, he sought still to earn Balak's reward by seeking to turn the people from God. It was the evil counsel of Balaam that led the Israelites into their sin with the daughters of Moab. (cf.ch. 25). Balaam's guilt in this episode is declared in 31:16 "Behold these [i.e. the Midianite women] caused the children of Israel, through the counsel of Balaam, to commit trespass against the Lord . . . ." Balaam's doctrine was the teaching of a way of evil, his error was the impression that God could be

induced to curse the people, and his way was that of the hireling who sells God's gifts for money. In 2 Peter 2:16 his way is characterized as "madness."

6. Israel's Sin Through the Doctrine of Balaam (Ch.25)

In acting upon Balaam's evil advice, the women of Moab evidently joined with those of Midian in urging upon the Israelites the practice of the rites of worship to Chemosh. This particular system of idolatry involved adulterous fertility rites, and judged by God's standards, was an exceedingly perverted and vicious religion. Moses, at God's instructions, sought to cope with matters by dispatching elders through the camp to behead the adulterers on the spot. It is reported that 24,000 died (v.9), and in 1 Corinthians 10:8, it is stated that all but 1,000 of these died in a single day. Because Phinehas, the son of Eleazar, so forthrightly executed the divine sentence on this occasion, he was promised an everlasting priesthood. The deed of Phinehas in immediately exercising the stroke of judgment is the only act in the Old Testament to which is ascribed the virtue of atoning for sin. God testified of him: "Phinehas, son of Eleazar, the son of Aaron the priest, hath turned my wrath away from the children of Israel, . . ." (v.11).

7. The Second Numbering (Ch.26)

The total of the second numbering is given in verse 51 as 601,730. This numbering was about thirty-eight years after the first, and the total was 1,820 fewer. (cf.1:46). Two verses of significance in this chapter report: "But among these there was not a man of them whom Moses and Aaron the priest numbered, when they numbered the children of Israel in the wilderness of Sinai. For the Lord had said of them, They shall surely die in the wilderness. And there was not left a man of them, save Caleb the son of Jephunneh, and Joshua the son of Nun" (vvs.64, 65).

8. The Daughters of Zelophehad. Moses' Forthcoming Death (Ch.27)

The daughters of Zelophehad were the only heirs of the family, but until the question of the right of females to hold property was settled, their inheritance was withheld. As an outcome of this situation, the Lord decreed that henceforth daughters should be permitted to receive the family inheritance if there were no male heirs.

God spoke to Moses informing him of his forthcoming death, and instructed him in his final acts in order to view the promised land. Although some scholars hold that the different names are of no significance, others consider that the Biblical narrative is best interpreted if it is understood that Mount Abarim that Moses was to climb was the name for the mountain chain; Nebo was the name of the individual mountain; and Pisgah was the name of the peak. With Moses' departure pending, God arranged that Joshua be installed, ready to take office and carry on His work. In view of the fact that Joshua was a man indwelt by God's Spirit, he was the divine choice as Moses' successor. Joshua inherited a great task, but a somewhat reduced authority than Moses, inasmuch as he was to be inferior to the priesthood rather than above it as in Moses' case. In a

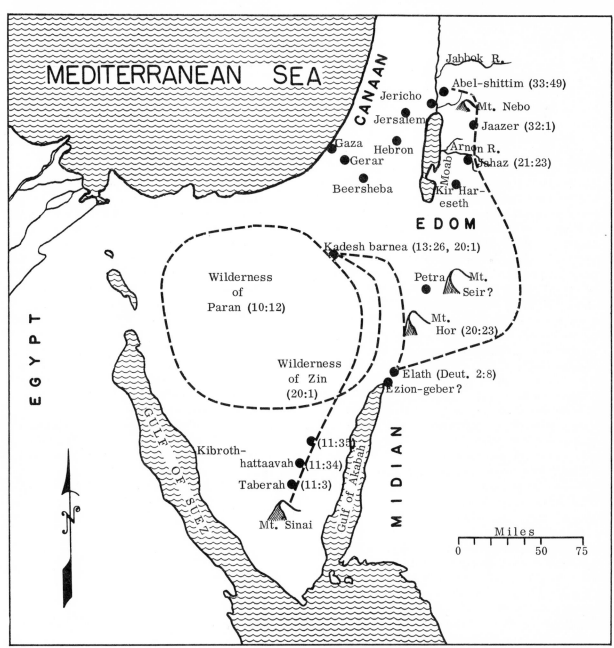

Figure 16 -- Israel's Wanderings Recorded in Numbers

ceremony involving the laying on of hands, Moses symbolically transferred authority to Joshua and charged him with his new duties.

9.   Offerings and Set Times (Chs. 28, 29)

These chapters review and enlarge upon the provisions for the Levitical offerings. One new requirement, introduced here for the first time, concerned the additional special offerings that were to be offered on the Sabbath. On that occasion it was to be doubled (v. 9). These chapters speak of "the continual burnt-offering" (v. 10), and thus set forth a relationship with God that is intended to prevail consistently at all times. The data on the monthly Sabbath of the new moon when a number of additional special offerings should be made (28: 11) is also presented here for the first time.

10.   Concerning Vows (Ch. 30)

The making of vows appears to have been fairly common among the Israelites, normally as a means to express a particular measure of piety and devotion. It was required that vows be publicly and formally made, and their non-performance was pronounced a sin. However, only mature, independent persons were judged capable of making a vow; minors and dependents (including wives and daughters in their father's home) were required to have the consent of the head of the household before the vow became binding. It is interesting to note that the male head of the household might give his consent merely by silence, and that in the area of vows the authority of the family head took precedence over that of the outside priest administrator. In common usage a vow constituted a pledge to perform an act; while a bond constituted a pledge to abstain from the specified actions. The expression "to afflict the soul" (v. 13) is probably a reference to fasting or a similar type of self-denial.

11.   War Against the Midianites (Ch. 31)

The events of this chapter are an aftermath of the episode when the Moabites and Midianites led Israel into sin and idolatry at Baal-peor (ch. 25). This was a holy war, and except for the delivery of his farewell sermons (recorded in Deuteronomy), its conduct was the last official act of Moses. The death of Balaam that is reported here speaks eloquently of the fate of those who attempt to defy God.

Israel was overwhelmingly victorious and they virtually annihilated the Midianites except for the female children. Their justification in thus destroying a nation was based upon the fact that the Midianites, as a nation, had acted deliberately to entice and seduce the Israelites to lead them away from God. It should be realized that the destruction of a nation pertains only to judgment in this life. Each individual citizen would continue to anticipate judgment on his own merits in the divine presence. This victory of Israel resulted in the collection of much spoil and the destruction of several hostile kings and of the scheming Balaam. The spoils were divided, with the soldiers and the people sharing equally. The priests received one five hundredth of the portion of the soldiers; the Levites received one fiftieth of the portion of the people.

12.   The Tribes of Reuben, Gad, and Half-Manasseh (Ch. 32)

Since all of Transjordania was now the possession of Israel, it was not surprising that the two and one-half tribes should ask to be granted this portion for their permanent home. In receiving it, they acknowledged the efforts of the other tribes, and that it was their duty to assist in conquering the territory west of Jordan. Moses stressed their obligation in this regard and declared that if they did not help their brethren: "Behold, ye have sinned against the Lord: and be sure your sin will find you out" (v. 23). The two and one half tribes seemed to have overlooked the fact that although the land east of Jordan was desirable, it was strategically without natural defences and was necessarily isolated from the rest of the tribes by virtue of the Jordan River and Valley.

13.   Encampments in the Wilderness (Ch. 33)

Although stopping places are recorded in this chapter and twenty-four of them are the same as named in Exodus, only about a dozen

---

This strange coiled serpent monument is located far out in the western fringe of the Petra basin. Beside it is a conventional shrine or high place. The monument is notably significant in the light of Israel's experience with the fiery serpents in this same general area. The monument is carved from the basic sandstone of the area and the serpent head is now wholly eroded away. The coiled portion of the carving is about six feet high.

can be identified today. This rather barren catalog is almost the total information that Scripture provides concerning the long years of wilderness wandering between the two visits to Kadesh.

14. Instructions Concerning the Boundaries
    of the Land (Ch. 34)

Since Israel had not yet possessed the land, this chapter looks to the future when the nation would take up official residence in Palestine. Detailed studies of the geography of Israel's homeland are usually related to the historical period when the nation had achieved occupancy. It should be noted however, that the boundaries of Canaan were of direct concern to God, and He prescribed their location in detail. Also, the Lord designated the committee of men who were to be responsible for superintending the divisions and settlement.

15. The Cities of Refuge (Ch. 35, cf. Deut. 4:
    41-43, Deut. 19:1-13, Josh. 20:1-9)

The Lord commanded that the Levites should be given a possession of 48 cities and their suburbs. Six of these cities were especially designated "cities of refuge" and they were to be appointed as a place of safety from the avenger of blood for the one who was guilty of manslaughter. These cities did not provide refuge for the deliberate murderer, but they did assure that those who accidentally caused death should be spared destruction at the hands of angry relatives. Also, if the nature of the deeds of the accused were in dispute, the cities provided a place of safety until such time as a fair trial could be held. The flight to the city of refuge was typical of the flight of the sinner to Jesus Christ: the refuge was for those who sinned unawares, the avenger might overtake and slay those who did not flee, and one's security depended upon abiding.

16. The Marriage of the Daughters of
    Zelophehad (Ch. 36)

These young ladies, who previously had secured the right to hold property, now sought advice concerning the ownership of their property in the event that they should marry. The Lord ruled that women who possessed property should marry only within their tribe. Thus, inasmuch as the title to the property would be transferred to the new husband, the tribal grant would stand perpetuated without loss or confusion. The ladies forthwith conformed to this regulation by proceeding to marry their paternal cousins.

Six: The Book of Deuteronomy

The Hebrew name for this book, Devarim, meaning "words," is derived from the opening phrase "these are the words." The English name "Deuteronomy" is derived from the rendering of 17:18 in the Septuagint. In our version this passage reads: ". . . a copy of this law . . . " but in the Greek the phrase is: "to deuteronomion touton" (i.e. this second law) and hence the translators adopted the key word of this phrase as the title of the entire book. Standing alone, the name deuteronomion simply means "second law." Commentators frequently object to this name, and particularly to that point of view which counts the book of no more interest and value than the name implies. Mackintosh makes a typical comment: "What a poor idea must the man entertain of inspiration who could imagine for a moment that the fifth book of Moses is a barren repetition of what is found in Exodus, Leviticus, and Numbers."

The Nature of the Book

Deuteronomy is primarily a book of oratory, for it consists of a series of addresses or sermons by Moses, plus brief transitional sections reporting historical events. The messages were delivered by Moses to the massed throngs of Israel gathered on the Plains of Moab, and they preceded Moses' death by only a few days. Manley describes the style of the book: "The book of Deuteronomy is written in easy flowing Hebrew prose of great charm and beauty with rolling undulating sentences of long range and majestic sweep. It is essentially oratorical and hortatory, as befits its subject."[1] Moses found great value in rehearsing to the people the account of the great experiences of the past, for as Mackintosh notes, he found them: "a mighty moral lever wherewith to move the heart of Israel." The fact that Moses' sermons contain so much historical matter constitutes an interesting and valuable cross reference and review of the historical events of the previous

---

[1]G. T. Manley, The Book of the Law, Grand Rapids: Wm. B. Eerdmans Publishing Co., 1957, p. 24.

books of Scripture. Occasionally, Moses' words clarify or provide additional insight into an incident mentioned in the previous books.

The introductory verses (1:1-5) give the setting for these sermons. Israel is described as being on "this side Jordan in the wilderness" (i.e. on the east of Jordan). Forty years and eleven months had passed since the memorable night of the exodus from Egypt, and all who had been adults at that time, with the exception of Joshua and Caleb, were now dead or about to die. It was necessary and fitting that the new generation should receive from the lips of the departing Moses a rehearsal of the Law and an accurate statement of God's past dealings with the nation. The hearers are declared to be "all Israel" (1:1), for it was God's intention that the entire population should sit under this farewell ministry of Moses. A nation whose parents had undergone the experiences of Exodus and Numbers were now to be impressed with the moral and spiritual lessons that such experiences involved.

The reference to the Red Sea in 1:1 is better read simply "sea" or "deep valley." The depression marked by the Gulf of Akabah, the Dead Sea, and the Jordan Valley is what is implied.

The Theme and Key Word of the Book

By reference to the past experiences of the nation, Moses sought to show God's ways of dealing with mankind and His expectations of and for them. The abiding conclusion was that God expected obedience. Hence, in Deuteronomy, obedience constitutes both a theme and a key word. A motive for obedience was to be the goodness of God, and the standard was to be His Word. A typical key verse declares: ". . . what doth the Lord thy God require of thee, but to fear the Lord thy God, to walk in his ways, and to love him, and to serve the Lord thy God with all thy heart and with all thy soul . . ." (10:12). (cf. 5:29, 11:26-28, 28:1). In commenting upon this theme,

Barrows says:

As the book of Genesis constitutes a
suitable introduction to the Pentateuch,
without which its very existence, as a part
of the divine plan, would be unintelligible,
so does the book of Deuteronomy bring it
to a sublime close. From the goodness
and faithfulness of God, for his special
favor bestowed upon Israel, for the excellence of his service, from the glorious rewards of obedience and the terrible penal-
ties of disobedience, it draws motives for
a deep and evangelical obedience--an obedience of the spirit and not of the letter
only.[2]

It is interesting to note that the words
"Jehovah our [or your, or thy] God" are
found 300 times in Deuteronomy and less than
50 times elsewhere in the Pentateuch. The
expression "which I am commanding you [or
thee]" is found 30 times in Deuteronomy and
only once elsewhere. Other significant word
usages include the word "land" used over one
hundred times and the word "possess" used
nearly seventy times.

Deuteronomy and the New Testament

It may be inferred that this book was a
special favorite of our Lord during His days on
earth, for it was the only book from which He
quoted in His conflict with Satan. In His re-
plies to the tempter He used: 6:13, 6:16, and
10:20 (cf. Mt. 4:1-11 and Lk. 4:1-13). Jesus
called the declaration of the unity of God to be
found in this book (6:4, 5) the "first and
great commandment." St. Paul preached
upon texts from Deuteronomy (Rom. 10:6-9;
cf. Deut. 20:12-14), and cited the book in his
writings. (Gal. 2:10, 13; cf. Deut. 27:26,
21:23). It is said that in all the New Testament there are 53 direct quotations from Deuteronomy and 38 references to events or facts
in the book.

ANALYSIS AND EXPOSITION

Following the brief statement of introduction and the unfolding of the setting (1:1-5),

_____

[2]E. P. Barrows, Companion to the
Bible. New York: American Tract Society,
-----, p. 239.

Moses began the first of his sermons. These
may be considered topically, although there is
no particular agreement among commentators
concerning the division of the sermons. Traditionally the tendency has been to restrict the
number of divisions and show only three major
sermons in the entire book. Since the central
sermon in this division extends over twenty-one
chapters, convenience and symmetry indicate
that it might be further divided. However, it
should be recognized that probably any division
of the book is simply a personal appraisal for
the convenience of students.

I. ISRAEL'S GLORIOUS HERITAGE (1:6-4:40)

1. From Horeb to Kadesh (1:6-19)

Moses begins his sermon by implying
that the people must depart from mere legal
formality and begin their spiritual journey to
a better land. The fact that God declared "Ye
have dwelt long enough in this mount:" is peculiar to Deuteronomy, for Numbers declares
only that the cloud began to move. In comparing the population of Israel to the stars of
heaven (v. 10), Moses was evidently engaging
in metaphor. There are said to be only 3,010
stars visible to the unaided eye, and Israel's
population was certainly vastly greater than
that. The story of the original appointment of
the deputies is found in Exodus 18:24-26.

2. Events at Kadesh (1:20-46)

Moses' account on this occasion makes
it clear that the sending forth of the spies was
specifically at the request of the people. (cf.
Num. 13:1-3). Only in this book do we learn of
Moses' unique encouragement of the people when
they hesitated in the command to possess the
land (vv. 29-31). The words of verse 30 constitute a promise to all believers "the Lord
your God which goeth before you, he shall fight
for you, . . ." Moses reports that in the wilderness "the Lord thy God bare thee, as a
man doth bare his son in all the way ye went,
. . ." (v. 31). God had said of Himself: "I
bare you on eagles' wings, . . ." (Ex. 19:4).
The figure of a father carrying his weary child
was an Old Testament counterpart that prepared
the way for the Christian concept of the loving
heavenly father. Although the people "wept before the Lord" (v. 45) following their defeat at
Kadesh, these were not the true tears of repentance, and thus God withheld forgiveness.

3. The Wanderings and Conquest (2:1-23)

At this juncture (2:1), by the use of the pronoun "we," Moses specifically identified himself with the erring Israelites. The "many days" that Moses mentioned were actually 38 years. It was a merciful act on Moses' part to pass over the sorrow and hardship of the wilderness period. He made it clear that the sparing of Edom, Moab, and Ammon was in obedience to the divine command. They were not to attack Edom because the Edomites were descendants of Esau; Moab and Ammon were to be spared because of their relation to Lot. (cf. Gen. 19:37, 38).

4. Conquest and Settlement of the Eastern Tableland (2:24-3:22)

No doubt Moses' review of the victories and conquests of the nation was meant to provide reassurance and confidence in the face of forthcoming battles to possess the land itself. He reiterates the fact that each of the resident nations in the eastern tableland area had successively resisted Israel, as reported in the book of Numbers, but he notes that the people had been able to secure some food and water both from the children of Esau (or Edomites) and the Moabites (2:29). It may be assumed that although the kings of these regions adopted an official policy of non-cooperation as set forth in Numbers, there were certain citizens on the borders of the lands who adopted their own policy of combined friendliness and business enterprise. The fate of Sihon whereby "the Lord thy God hardened his spirit" (v. 30), was not unlike that of Pharaoh during the contests in Egypt. Moses especially reviewed the victory of the nation over formidable Bashan with its sixty cities and its king Og with his nine cubit bedstead (13 1/2 feet). He implied that if the nation could subdue even the great Og at a time when physical prowess so overwhelmingly displayed itself in hand-to-hand combat, then they need fear nothing in the future.

5. Moses' Own Fate (3:23-29)

Even the divine prohibition upon Moses' entrance to the land could serve as an impressive warning to the people to teach others to avoid such pitfalls. At the same time, Moses explained that though divine government shut him out of the land, divine grace took him to the top of Pisgah. God is holy and just on the one hand, but He is tender and gracious on the other.

6. Concluding Applications (4:1-40)

With this brief historical sketch, Moses sought to make application to the present. He declared: "Now therefore hearken, O Israel; unto the statutes and unto the judgments, which I teach you, . . ." (4:1). The Israelites had been greatly blessed: they had witnessed both the Law and the acts of God, and by virtue of such privileges could be expected to be obedient to the will of the Lord. Privilege is always accompanied by responsibility, and the Israelites could expect to be punished if they disobeyed God. The tender, loving God is also "a consuming fire" (4:24). Moses emphasized that even under the Law, religion was a personal matter. In the passage 4:33-38, there are at least ten second-person, personal pronouns (thou, thee, you). Thus ended the first sermon.

Transition: Further Narrative and Setting (4:41-49)

This brief section recounts Moses' establishment of the cities of refuge and declares that succeeding sermons are to present: "the law which Moses set before the children of Israel" (v. 44), as well as: "the testimonies, and the statutes, and the judgments (v. 45). Traditionally, the Jews considered that a statute was a precept imposed by God, the reason for the observance of which was withheld from man. The prohibition upon swine's flesh was considered a typical statute.

II. PRECEPTS AND PRINCIPLES FOR JEHOVAH'S PEOPLE (5:1 - 11:32)

1. Introduction and Setting (5:1-5)

Moses began his discourse by pointing out that what was to follow merited that the people should: hear, learn, keep and do. Each of these words is characteristic of Deuteronomy and they occur in the book with the following frequency: hear--30 times, learn--7 times, keep--39 times, and do--100 times.

2. The Ten Commandments (5:6-33)

This statement of the ten commandments is almost identical with that of Exodus 20, except

that the observance of the Sabbath is linked
with the commemoration of emancipation from
toil and servitude in Egypt (v.15). This addition was Moses' prerogative, since he was
both quoting and expounding the Law. The differences between this statement of the Law and
that of Exodus 20 are the differences between
the document that is intended for all men and
one which is intended particularly for Israel.
As it were, this portion sets forth the Ten Commandments in suitable form for the Israelites.
In this passage, Moses proceeded to describe
the events associated with the giving of the
Law with graphic vividness.

3. The Keeping of the Law (6:1-25)

Moses emphasized that inasmuch as the
people had the Law, they were to observe it
carefully and rigidly and to teach their children
to do likewise. The outcome of obedience to
the Law was to be divine blessing and prosperity in the land.

The words of 6:4 have been adopted by
the Jews as an epitome of their entire distinct
religious doctrine. The statement is known as
the Shema because this is the Jewish word for
"hear," the first word of the verse. Comments
Mackintosh of this verse: "It was their national
bulwark, and that which was to mark them off
from all nations of the earth. They were called
to confess this glorious truth in the face of an
idolatrous world, and its gods many, and lords
many."3 It may be pointed out that even though
this is a clear statement of monotheism, it
does not rule out a triune deity. The word
"God" is Elohim which actually is plural, and
the word "one" is echod in the Hebrew. Echod
means a compound unity as contrasted with
yochid which means a single one.

The Lord Jesus made the words "thou
shalt love the Lord thy God with all thine heart,
and with all thine soul, and with all thine might"
(6:5) the first and greatest commandment. He
joined with it a portion from Leviticus 19:18:
"thou shalt love thy neighbor as thyself." It
has been said that Judaism was the only religion of ancient nations that demanded that its
followers love their God. In this tradition, a

3C.H. Mackintosh, Notes on the Book
of Deuteronomy. (Vol. I) New York: Loizeaux
Brothers, 1945, p.377.

Christian's love for his God in this present day
is, or ought to be, distinctive among all other
religious motives and systems.

The reference to the placing of Scriptures on the doorposts (6:9), and the later reference to divorce proceedings (24:1), implies
that writing was generally practised by the Hebrews at this time. The thought of 6:13 is repeated in 10:20 (with an added clause) "Thou
shalt fear the Lord thy God; him shalt thou
serve, . . ." It was this verse that Jesus quoted
to Satan. (cf. Mt.4:10). He also used 6:16 "Ye
shall not tempt the Lord your God, . . ." (cf.
Mt.4:7). The prohibition in Deuteronomy was
intended to prevent presumptuous demands for
God to prove His power. Massah was an alternate name for Rephidim or Meribah. (cf. Ex.
17:1-7).

4. Life and Prospects in the New Land
    (7:1-8:20)

It was the will of God that Israel's conquest of the land result in the total destruction of
the usurping Gentile nations there. The degree
of depravity of these nations gave God no other
alternative. The people of Canaan, as national
groups, had developed a system of "worship"
that actually consisted of degrading acts of sexual immorality. They practised the sacrifice by
fire of their living children and their general
moral life was grossly corrupt. God in His
sovereignty had chosen Israel to be His people
in this land, and even though the Israelites in
some cases lacked personal merit, they were
His choice to populate Canaan. Moses declared,
"The Lord did not set his love upon you, nor
choose you, because ye were more in number
than any people; . . . But because the Lord
loved you, . . ." (7:7,8). Even the weapons
that God promised the people (hornets) to aid
in the conquest of the land were unique and no
doubt strikingly effective (7:20).

The purpose of the wilderness wanderings was concisely expressed: " . . . the Lord
thy God led thee these forty years in the wilderness, to humble thee, and to prove thee, to
know what was in thine heart, whether thou
wouldest keep his commandments, or no" (8:2).
Moses declared that even God's provision of the
manna was for the purpose of teaching the people that "man doth not live by bread only, but
by every word that proceedeth out of the mouth
of the Lord . . ." (8:3). These words were

later quoted by Jesus in His reply to Satan. Moses' advice in 8:10 constitutes the basis of the custom of pious Jews who recite prayers of thanksgiving following their meals. Moses promised the people an abundant and prosperous land if only they would maintain godly obedience. Israel would enjoy: brooks of water, fountains, wheat, barley, vines, fig trees, pomegranates, olive oil, honey, bread, iron, brass (i.e. copper). In modern times archaeologist Nelson Glueck discovered, in a region about twenty miles south of the Dead Sea, an area that was obviously the ruins of an ancient copper mine. The ore was sufficiently abundant that veins of mineral literally protruded above the surface.

5. Jehovah's Requirements of the People (9:1-11:9)

Moses faithfully pointed out to the people the shame of their past conduct and the fact that the nation had no claim to any real righteousness. He plainly declared that the past provided nothing wherein to boast: "Not for thy righteousness, or for the uprightness of thine heart, dost thou go to possess their land: but for the wickedness of these nations . . ." (9:5). And again, "Ye have been rebellious against the Lord from the day that I knew you" (9:24).

The information of 10:6, 7 is a parenthesis which does not fit chronologically with the context. God's requirements are stated in 10:12, 13--fear God, walk in His ways, love Him, serve Him, and keep His commandments. These commandments apply to redeemed Christians just as much as to Old Testament saints. God's bestowment of plagues upon Egypt is described by Moses as "his miracles and his acts, which he did in the midst of Egypt . . ." (11:3). For those who reject the Person and power of God, His works may constitute destruction and annihilation rather than blessing and life.

6. Conclusion--Abundant Future Blessings (11:10-32)

The repeated portrayal of abundant blessings for an obedient nation surely ought to have been an incentive to the people to conform to God's will. When Israel possessed the land west of Jordan, the people enacted the pronouncement of blessing and cursing at Ebal and Mount Gerizim, just as the Lord here commanded. (See Josh. 8:30-35). Hence, the advice and influence of this Mosaic sermon remained, long after the messenger himself was at home with the Lord. The report of life in Egypt (11:10) conveys the impression of wearisome toil. The Israelites probably understood: "wateredst it with thy foot" as a description of the process of irrigating with a foot propelled water wheel elevating water out of the Nile. The word "champaign" (11:30) refers to the general territory of the Arabah or plain in the Southern region. It is generally agreed that the expression "plains of Moreh" should be "oaks of Moreh."

III. THE DIVINE CODE OF POLITICS AND RELIGION (12:1 - 27:19)

This section seems to represent a new sermon by Moses constituting "statutes and judgments" (v. 1); though some scholars (e.g. Erdman) consider that chapters 12 through 26 are the second part of the preceding sermon.

1. Laws of Worship (12:2 - 13:18)

Moses revealed that it was God's wish that Israel ruthlessly destroy all that savored of idolatry. As long as the trappings of false worship remained, it seemed an easy matter for the people to be coaxed into adopting the heathen systems. For God to countenance idolatry would be for Him to deny Himself. As Erdman points out: "One must remember that Israel was a theocracy. God was the acknowledged King. To seduce one from absolute devotion to Him was an act of high treason, to be punished as such."[4]

Moses declared that when the people were settled in the land, God would choose out a place as a center of worship. It was not until five hundred years later, under David, that God actually chose the city of Jerusalem. (cf. 2 Sam. 5:7). In this discourse, Moses emphasized that public worship should be in one place but he did not preclude private worship elsewhere. He declared that it was God's order that animals slain ceremonially could be slain

---

[4]Charles R. Erdman, The Book of Deuteronomy. Westwood: Fleming H. Revell Company, 1953, p. 49.

only at the one central worship center, though
non-ceremonial slayings could take place any-
where as the need for food arose. (cf. 12:15).
In this day, the principles of Christian worship
require only that man worship "in spirit and
in truth" (Jno. 4:24) rather than in some particular place. In concluding his section on foods,
Moses emphasized that it would be as serious
to add to his words as to subtract from them
(12:32). The Word of God and the words of
God's servants frequently have been subject to
alteration in emphasis and meaning by this
subtle means.

Three agencies that are capable of
leading believers into idolatry are discussed
by Moses: false prophets (13:1-5), one's family (13:6-11), and one's neighbors (13:12-18).
He declared that miracles were no criterion of
a prophet's authenticity or credibility; rather
it was his doctrine that counted. The people
were to resist all agencies that sought to turn
them from God, regardless of how inviting or
influential they might be.

2. The Required Separation of the People (14:1-16:17)

God intended that His people behave
and appear differently from their heathen neighbors. Thus, whereas the heathen frequently
marked their bodies in order to propitiate their
gods, the Lord decreed that His people were to
participate in no such practice. Their diet was
to be strictly regulated according to the previous Levitical ordinances. The pygarg included
among the clean beasts (v. 5) is thought to have
been a species of antelope. The glede was evidently a scavanger type bird perhaps a buzzard.
The Lord carefully specified the tithes were to
be paid upon all their increase.

The Sabbatic year is here called by
Moses the "year of release" (15:1). Whereas
previously, in Leviticus, the year had been
described as an occasion for the rest of the
land and the freeing of slaves, Moses here
emphasizes that release from debts was to be
part of the year's provisions. This was not a
matter of entire remission of the debt, but
rather the postponement of it until the end of
the Sabbatical year. A postponement was necessary because the land would not be under
cultivation and productive during this year.
Foreigners who would not observe the Sabbatic
year were not allowed the privileges of the
postponement of their debt (15:3).

Moses instructed the people to be generous and charitable: "If there be among you
a poor man of one of thy brethren within any
of thy gates in thy land which the Lord thy God
giveth thee, thou shalt not harden thine heart,
nor shut thine hand from thy poor brother"
(15:7). He reviewed for the people the provision of the perforated ear lobe as the sign of a
voluntary bond slave. This custom had been
appointed previously in Exodus 21:6. Moses
stressed that the people were to be scrupulous
in their observance of the sacred festivals and
the thrice annual pilgrimage of all males to the
place of worship. His intructions here are necessarily brief but they are intended for the
general populace and are not meant to be characterized by technical details in the matter of
instructions of the priests in Leviticus chapter
twenty-three.

3. Civil and Religious Leaders (16:18-18:25)

Moses proceeded to explain the divine
plan of civil and religious administration of the
nation that should be implemented when they
settled in the land. Since the government was
to be God's channel to convey His instruction
to the people, its nature was of vital concern to
God. The rulership was to be primarily by divinely appointed judges and officers. Idolatry
was to be looked upon as treason and practices
that in any way even hinted at a false religion
were to be shunned. Since groves of trees were
particularly associated with the worship of Ash-
taroth, they were prohibited (16:21). The penalty for deliberate idolatry was to be stoning
(17:2-15).

At this point, Moses declared that the
authority of the judges and officers of the land
be subordinate to that of the priests and Levites.
Thus, cases of appeal would be referred from
the civil authorities to these religious leaders
who would conduct, as it were a higher court
of appeal. Typical cases that could be expected
to be referred to the priestly court would be
those between blood and blood, that is those
involving manslaughter or murder, those between plea and plea, which would be serious
cases of property disputes, and those between
stroke and stroke, which would be cases involving bodily injuries. The Lord, through Moses,
clearly stressed that at such time in the future
when a monarchy was to be introduced it was

to be only under the Lord's direction. It was not to be the privilege of God's people to appoint their own ruler on the basis of mere natural discernment. Even at this point, God imposed restrictions upon the future ruler. He was to multiply to himself neither horses nor wives. In ancient times, horses were inevitably associated with warfare and they were the symbol of the military strength of the heathen nations.

It was God's provision that the Levites were to be supported by the tithes and gifts of the people. They were to receive no inheritance among the tribal grants in the land, although it is elsewhere set forth that they might have possessions in the Levitical cities. God's provision for the support of the ministering Levites assured that as long as the Lord received His portion, the Levites would receive theirs. The portions of the sacrifice given to the priests were comparatively limited (18:3), and would be considered inferior meat, but apparently the quantity made up for other deficiencies. The maw or stomach would probably make a kind of stewing meat or flank steak.

A Levite might leave his residence in a Levitical city to come to the tabernacle to serve, and if he did, he would be supported by the portions of sacrifice, just as the other Levites. He would also be partly provided for by the sale of his patrimony or heritage in the Levitical city. The case of Samuel is suggested as an application of this divine provision.

Moses once more warned against heathen customs and practices, particularly relating to communion with spirits or the consultation with the dead (i.e. necromancy). In 18:15, Moses set forth a classic Messianic prediction "the Lord thy God will raise up unto thee a Prophet from the midst of thee, of thy brethren, like unto me; unto him ye shall hearken." In primary meaning, these words seem to say simply that God in each generation will have his prophet to represent Him to men. However, this verse is taken elsewhere as specifically implying the fact of the Messiah who was to come. (cf. Acts 3:22, 7:37). Orthodox Jews regard this verse as a prophecy of the Messiah, for they argue that no one can be likened unto Moses except the Messiah.

Today, just as in ancient times, olives are an important product of the Mediterranean climate and soil. These olive trees are fairly young, and thus not as large as some. This orchard is in the hill country about twenty miles north of Jerusalem in what is known as the "Valley of Robbers." The soil in this area is a rich red in color, and it is especially well adapted both to tree crops and to grain or cereal culture.

4. Manslaughter, War, and Murder
   (19:1-21:9)

That the cities of refuge were of considerable importance in Moses' thinking is established by his frequent reference to them. The cities were not, of course, established until the people were settled in the land. The stress upon the value of a landmark was no doubt dictated by the limited facilities for surveying and map making in the time of Moses. To this day, two or three witnesses in agreement (19:15) constitute a powerful argument in a court of law. Moses taught the people that they could count upon divine help and enabling in warfare; and yet they were responsible to manifest the greatest strength they could. For the nation of Israel, military exploits were primarily the Lord's battles, and they were thereby justified. While the Lord provided a generous list of conditions for exemption from compulsory military service, such duty nevertheless devolved upon the great majority of male Israelites sooner or later in their lifetime. The course of action prescribed by Moses in the event of an unexplained death (21:1-9) is the ancient counterpart of the modern custom of holding an inquest. The expression "rough valley" means one that is uncultivated because it is a drainage channel, with a stream flowing through it. One apparent purpose of the choice of this site would be that it would provide a means of carrying away the blood of the sacrificial heifer.

5. Miscellaneous Precepts (21:10-26:15)

Moses' sermon at this point becomes intensely practical and deals with the everyday life and affairs of the people. The military man might take the fair captive to wife only after a month's delay; a flagrantly delinquent and rebellious son should be executed; the body of the hung criminal should be removed at sundown (this provision applied in the case of the body of Jesus), kindness and concern for others should characterize all dealings by an Israelite, an immoral woman should be stoned, and an innocent woman given full protection.

God's provision allowing marriage to a captive woman was a revision of the previous law "Neither shalt thou make marriages with them" (Deut. 7:3). It may be assumed either that the previous prohibition related specifically to the nations who are there named and that this regulation applied to other nations, or that God

considered the spirit of that which He desired would be accomplished by the one month waiting period. The usual method of execution by the Hebrews was stoning, and the instance of the body hung upon a tree (21:22) involves not an execution but the exhibition of one already dead. God once more reinforced the truth that His people were to be separated and that they were to avoid all unwarranted associations and unions (cf. Lev. 19:19). The word "amerce" in 22:19 means to impose a fine.

Moses declared that those who were physically abnormal, without legitimate parentage, or of Ammonite or Moabite ancestry were disqualified as worshippers. The Edomites and Egyptians were also disqualified, but less rigorously and only to the third generation. Adequate sanitation was to be practised in military camps, and the Israelites were to give refuge to an escaped slave rather than return him to his heathen master. Prostitution of all types was forbidden, as well as the imposing of usury. A vow that was made was scrupulously to be kept, although there was no obligation to make a vow. All citizens were to be free to satisfy their immediate hunger from someone's vineyard or cornfield, but they were to take only as much as they could immediately consume on the premises.

A sodomite (23:17) was a male prostitute or homosexual. Scripture also derisively calls such a person a "dog" (23:18). At this place the word "usury" simply means interest of any kind, and it is forbidden by God. However, the reference is to charitable rather than to commercial loans, so that it is not a blanket condemnation of financial transactions in the business world. The provisions in 24:1-4 did not serve to introduce divorce as a practice in Israel; rather they were intended to forbid the remarriage of a divorced couple to one another after each had taken other partners. In this chapter (twenty-four), once more Moses reported miscellaneous divine regulations that taken together spoke of consideration and thoughtfulness by the Israelites in all their dealings. In a similar spirit it is noted in 25:4 that the divine ordinances provided that even animals had rights.

The custom of the marriage of a widow to her brother-in-law described in 25:5-10 was the basis of the redemption of Ruth by Boaz. Such a union is known as levirate marriage, and it appears in Scripture as early as Genesis 38:8-11. Since in ancient times childlessness was a disgrace, this remarriage of the widow would maintain the family honor. The expression "A Syrian ready to perish was my father" (26:5), refers back to the humbling fact that Jacob was a nomadic Syrian (or Aramean), the son of an Aramean (cf. Gen. 24:10), himself a nomad shepherd in Aram, with Aramean women becoming the mothers of his children.

6. Conclusion (26:16-19)

Moses appears to be concluding this portion of his message when he says: "This day the Lord thy God hath commanded thee to do these statutes and judgments . . ." (26:16). In common with all preachers, Moses sought to impress the people that the real value of his sermons would be attained when the truths that he had asserted became the practices of the daily lives of his audience. The rules and laws of Moses' messages are not necessarily to be imposed literally today, although the spirit of them is surely to be heeded.

IV. BLESSING OR CURSE--AN OBVIOUS ALTERNATIVE (27:1-28:68)

1. Introduction (27:1-13)

In looking forward to the future when the nation would have crossed the Jordan and be ready for residence in the land, Moses prescribed that at Mt. Ebal they should erect stones or pillars with the Law of God inscribed.

Mt. Ebal and Mt. Gerizim as they appear today from a point due east. On the left is Mt. Gerizim and on the right, Mt. Ebal, with the ancient city of Shechem between them. Just this side of Shechem is Jacob's well and Joseph's tomb, and to the right on the lowest flank of Mt. Ebal, is the village of Sychar. Beyond Shechem, though not visible in this photo, is the modern city of Nablus which occupies the valley between the mountains.

These memorial pillars were to be coated with "plaister" which would likely be a coating of lime or gypsum just as modern plaster. The inscription would be in the plaster surface rather than in the harder stone. It may be inferred that the ceremony of blessings and cursings which followed was to constitute something of a dedication of these pillars of stone with their inscribed laws.

When Moses set forth the ceremony of blessing and cursing, Mt. Ebal and Mt. Gerizim were still in the hands of the Canaanites. Thus, it was some years later before the ceremony was actually observed. (cf. Josh. 8:30-35). Moses prescribed that the entire nation was to participate, and the bases of Mount Ebal and Mount Gerizim were to serve as a natural amphitheatre for the event. Five tribes were to gather on each of the mountains, with Ebal the mount of cursing, and Gerizim the mount of blessing. The Levites were to stand in the valley between. The commandments that involved cursing were either chanted or agreed to (perhaps the tribes said "amen" to show accord) by those on Mount Ebal; which the commandments that involved blessing received a similar response from the tribes on Mount Gerizim.

2. Individual Cursings (27:14-26)

The words of cursing to be pronounced by the Levites were given by Moses in precise detail. As it were, this message constituted a preview of the forthcoming ceremony, and by this advance notice the Israelites were given a period of time wherein to conform their lives to the divine requirements. Of the twelve curses in this chapter, eleven were against particular sins, and the twelve against all breaches of the Law. The range of topics covered by the curses included: idolatry, immorality, perversion, homicide, bribery, and similar sins that we consider more flagrant.

3. National Blessings (28:1-14)

The catalog of blessings that God, through Moses, indicated was to be promised the obedient nation was indeed appealingly attractive. Surely the people must have longed after all these blessings, and no doubt many made resolutions to achieve them. If Israel's actions were such that they failed to accord with the divine requirements, they certainly

had no excuse on the grounds that they were uninformed of the rewards of righteousness.

4. National Cursings (28:15-68)

Moses revealed a divinely inspired eloquence in his account of the cursings that would befall the disobedient nation. In words that are as forcefully graphic as they are plain, he revealed a future of awful horror should the people choose to provoke the wrath of God. It is one of the tragedies of history that Israel, in succeeding centuries, did turn from God and thereby incurred these predicted punishments. At the sieges of Jerusalem (see 2 Ki. 6:28 et al) some of the most horrible events in the history of blood and tears on this poor earth took place. There is no parallel among nations to the vicious and prolonged retribution visited upon Israel, for her people have been chastened above those of all nations. Though in 1948 the Jews proclaimed Palestine their national home, only a minority have been able to migrate there. Thus are Moses' words fulfilled: "And among these nations shalt thou find no ease, neither shall the sole of thy foot have rest: but the Lord shall give thee there a trembling heart, and failing of eyes, and sorrow of mind" (28:65).

V. ISRAEL'S TITLE-DEED TO CANAAN (29:1-30:20)

1. Introduction (29:1-12)

This message was comprised of the statement of the covenant by which Israel was to enter the land of Palestine. Since Israel had failed under the Sinaitic covenant, it was necessary that the nation be tendered another. Though the idea of the possession of Palestine was not new, the people had not previously been extended a formal covenant. This document is often called the Palestinian Covenant.

2. Conditions of the Covenant (29:13-30:10)

Although Moses recognized that possession of the land by Israel was unconditional, (cf. Gen. 13:15, 17:8, 48:4) he asserted at this place that Israel's habitation of the land required: Israel to be a people of God, the judgment of an individual apostate, national curse and dispersion for national sin, restoration upon repentance, and spiritual and material prosperity for a penitent people. It is implied that this is not the highest possible covenant (it involved a literal land and material blessings and thus it contrasts with the covenant of grace) and God yet held His greater blessing in reserve, but for the present He required as much obedience as the people had light (29:29). In a few verses (30:1-8), Moses succeeded in presenting a concise, but thorough history of the nation of Israel: 1) dispersion [v.1], 2) repentance [v.2], 3) restoration of the land [vv.3-5], 4) national conversion [v.6], 5) foes judged [v.7], and 6) Israel prospered [v.8].

3. Obedience to the Covenant Required (30:11-20)

Just as Moses declared that the Covenant was available to every one who would accept, so also is the Gospel to this generation. Moses called "heaven and earth to record this day" as witnesses of the fact of the Covenant and its solemn requirements. Though Israel disobeyed God and broke the Covenant, it was God's abiding wish and provision that they enjoy the blessings that He offered. The people were given the unfailing word of Almighty God, and it was theirs to choose whether or not they would take advantage of their privileges.

VI. MOSES' DEPARTING COUNSELS (31:1-33:29)

1. Setting and Introduction (31:1-9)

This final sermon was delivered on Moses' 120th birthday, just a few days before the Lord took the aged warrior to be with Himself. Moses set himself first to reassure the people, and then to charge Joshua with the tasks of leadership.

2. Counsel to the Levites and to Joshua (31:10-30)

In his final instructions to the Levites, Moses especially requested that each seven years at the Feast of the Tabernacles, the Law should be read to the assembled people. Thus, the rising generations might be informed of the Word of God, and adults might have their memories refreshed. God revealed to Moses that there would be times historically when the people would depart from the faith, and He instructed His servant to prepare a farewell song that would be one more means of impressing the people with truth. "And it shall come to

pass, when many evils and troubles are befallen them, that this song shall testify against them as a witness; for it shall not be forgotten out of the mouth of their seed" (31:21). The passage in 31:24-27 constitutes a very clear claim to the Mosaic authorship of the Pentateuch. The "words of this law in a book" would include not only the decalogue, but the Levitical commentaries also. The record of the charge to Joshua at the door of the tabernacle (31:14, 15) is the only mention of the tabernacle in the entire book of Deuteronomy. In his charge Moses exhorted his successor: "Be strong and of a good courage: for thou shalt bring the children of Israel into the land which I sware unto them: and I will be with thee" (Deut. 31:23).

God commissioned the sacred song in an attempt to impress His people with the tragic outcomes that would result if they became guilty of sin. The song is necessarily negative, and it contrasts with Moses' blessing of the following chapter. Nevertheless, Moses' song has been called the "Magna Charta of Prophecy" and it is seen as being combined with "the Song of the Lamb" and constituting the Song of the Redeemer in the Lord's presence. "And they sang the song of Moses the servant of God, and the song of the Lamb, saying, Great and Marvelous are thy works, Lord God Almighty; . . . (Rev. 15:3). In the original, Moses' song is a superb poem. Its approach is set forth in verse two which speaks of Israel's tender hopes finding quickening and refreshing after the long drought of their captivity. Moses plainly declared that they must expect punishment for their disobedience, but that God's goodness would mean eventual restoration and blessing.

In verse two the word "doctrine" means "message." Depicting God as a "Rock" (32:4) serves to reveal His unchangeableness and His provision of refuge. The expression "apple of His eye" (32:10) probably means "pupil of His eye." The "high places" of verse thirteen are simply highlands. The name "Jeshurun" (32:15) means "little righteous one" and it is a poetic name for Israel.

4. Moses' Last Blessing (Ch. 33)

Moses' blessing upon the tribes resembles that of Jacob upon his sons many centuries previously (Gen. 49). Although in his sons, Moses had talked of coming failure and apostacy, in his blessing, he speaks of a glorious

future and the favor of God. In the list of
tribes who are blessed the tribe of Simeon is
omitted, but the number is brought to thirteen
by the inclusion both of Joseph (v. 13), and of
his two sons Ephraim and Manasseh (v. 17).
It has been suggested that the Simeonites may
have been especially guilty in the licentiousness
at Baal-peor (Num. 25:14), and hence they had
lost their right to the patriarchal blessing.
There is no apparent reason for the order of
the sons in the bestowment of the blessing except possibly a certain topical sequence.
Verses of note selected from this blessing include: "Thy shoes shall be iron and brass; and
as thy days, so shall thy strength be" (v. 25);
"The eternal God is thy refuge, and underneath
are the everlasting arms:" (v. 27); and "Happy
art thou, O Israel: who is like unto thee, O
people saved by the Lord, . . . " (v. 29).

VII. MOSES' LAST DAYS. HIS DEATH AND
       BURIAL (32:48-52, Ch. 34)

When Moses had concluded his presentation, he proceeded to witness upon himself
the inflexible justice of the Law of which he had
been the mediator and exponent. In the company
of God he proceeded to the top of Pisgah and
there he was allowed to view the land that the
people were to possess. God called him home
apparently by special intervention so that:
"Moses' soul was caught away by the kiss of
God." The body of Moses was divinely cared
for and secretly buried in a sepulchre in the
land of Moab. Jude nine mentions the body of
Moses and indicates the celestial concern for
it. God preferred to keep the secret of Moses'
resting place to Himself that no idolatrous
shrine be established and that the people in
remembering Moses be directed toward heaven
rather than to an earthly site.

Although Moses wrote the remainder of
the book of Deuteronomy, this chapter recording his death and burial, evidently was written
by someone else. It is generally agreed that
Joshua was the author of this portion of Deuteronomy, that the record might be closed in order
to introduce his own work, the book of Joshua,
which follows. It is no valid argument to deny
the Mosaic authorship of Deuteronomy on the
ground that since the book contains the record
of his death, he could not have written it. Comments Joseph Free: "If in the days of Moses,
books had been provided with full title pages,
might we not read something like this: Deuter-

onomy, by Moses, the servant of the Lord, with
biographical note by Joshua, the minister of
Moses?"[5]

It has been pointed out that the highlights
of Moses' experience involved three mountains.
(1) Mt. Horeb at which he was called to lead his
people. (2) Mt. Sinai at which he was given the
law and (3) Mt. Pisgah from which he viewed
the land. A Muslim tradition identifies Moses'
viewpoint with Jebel Osha, and near the sum-
mit of this mountain, the Muslims have built a
small structure to mark the supposed site of
Moses' grave. It is gratifying to realize that
although Moses in his lifetime was not admitted
to the promised land, in the transfiguration at
the time of Christ, at least by some interpretations, he was personally there and in the presence of Christ.

Among all the heroes of Scripture, Moses
stands upon an exceptionally lofty plane. He
deliberately made his choice for God as a young
man, and thereafter for eighty years he permitted himself to be to Israel the channel of God's
operation and direction. This great man constitutes a type of Christ as follows: 1) as an infant escaped destruction at the hands of a hostile ruler, 2) underwent a training period during the "silent years," 3) forsook the splendors
that he knew in order to fulfill the plan of God,
4) meek above all men, 5) completed his work
and brought the people to the place of promise,
6) exercised a ministry of intercession, and
7) enjoyed a special communion with God that
transfigured his being.

Scripture provides a noble epitaph for
this great man of God. "And there arose not
a prophet since in Israel like unto Moses, whom
the Lord knew face to face" (34:10). Moses
served not only as a prophet but a lawgiver and
the great administrator of his nation. He distinguished himself for his meekness (Num. 12:3),
and seems to have seen himself as a mere instrument through whom the almighty God might
accomplish His work. In his personal being,
Moses may have manifested failings just as
other men, but he remains outstanding by virtue of a deep and enduring faith, and for the
notable accomplishments of his forty-year ministry.

---

[5]Joseph P. Free, Archaeology and
Bible History. Wheaton: Van Kampen Press,
1950, p. 120.

BIBLIOGRAPHY

Angus, Joseph, The Bible Handbook. Revised by Green. Grand Rapids: Zondervan Publishing House, 1952.

Allis, Oswald T., The Five Books of Moses. Philadelphia: The Presbyterian and Reformed Publishing Company, 1949.

Barrows, E.P., Companion to the Bible. New York: American Tract Society, n.d.

Beecher, Henry Ward, Bible Studies. New York: Fords, Howard, and Hulbert, 1893.

Blaikie, William G., A Manual of Bible History. London: T. Nelson and Sons, 1890.

Bodie, Mary M., The Book of Sanctification or Lessons in Leviticus. Kansas City: Grace and Glory, 1928.

Bright, John, A History of Israel. Philadelphia: The Westminister Press, 1959.

Deane, William J., Abraham, His Life and Times. New York: Fleming Revell Company, n.d.

Dods, Marcus, The Book of Genesis. Edinburgh: T. and T. Clark, n.d.

Elder, John, Prophets, Idols and Diggers. Indianapolis: Bobbs-Merrill Company, 1960.

Erdman, Charles R., The Book of Exodus. New York: Fleming H. Revell Company, 1949.

----------, The Book of Deuteronomy. New York: Fleming H. Revell Company, 1953.

Evans, William, The Books of the Pentateuch. New York: Fleming H. Revell Company, 1916.

Finegan, Jack, Light From the Ancient Past. Princeton: Princeton University Press, 1959.

Francisco, Clyde T., Introducing the Old Testament. Nashville: Broadman Press, 1950.

Free, Joseph P., Archaeology and Bible History. Wheaton: Van Kampen Press, 1950.

Gaebelin, Arno C., The Pentateuch. Vol. I of The Annotated Bible. New York: Our Hope, 1913.

Graham, James R., A Philosophy of Scripture: A Connected Commentary on the Book of Genesis. Butler: The Higley Press, 1955.

Grant, F.W., Genesis in the Light of the New Testament. New York: Loizeaux Brothers, n.d.

Griffith Thomas, William H., Through the Pentateuch Chapter by Chapter. Grand Rapids: Wm. B. Eerdmans Publishing Co., 1957.

Handrich, Theodore L., The Creation: Facts, Theories, and Faith. Chicago: Moody Press, 1953.

Hughes, Philip E., Christianity and the Problem of Origins. Philadelphia: Presbyterian and Reformed Publishing Co., 1964.

Keil, C.F. and F. Delitzsch, The Pentateuch. Vols. I and II of Biblical Commentary on the Old Testament. Edinburgh: T. and T. Clark, 1878.

Lee, Robert, The Outlined Bible. London: Pickering and Inglis Limited, n.d.

Mackintosh, Charles H., Notes on the Book of Genesis. New York: Loizeaux Brothers, 1945.

----------, Notes on the Book of Exodus. New York: Loizeaux Brothers, 1944.

----------, Notes on the Book of Leviticus. New York: Loizeaux Brothers, 1944.

----------, Notes on the Book of Numbers. New York: Loizeaux Brothers, 1944.

----------, Notes on the Book of Deuteronomy. 2 Volumes. New York: Loizeaux Brothers, 1944.

Maclear, G. F., A Class Book of Old Testament History. Grand Rapids: Wm. B. Eerdmans Publishing, 1952.

McNeile, A. H., The Book of Numbers. Cambridge: Cambridge University Press, 1911.

Manley, G. T., The New Bible Handbook. Chicago: The Inter-Varsity Christian Fellowship, 1948.

----------, The Book of the Law. Grand Rapids: Wm. B. Eerdmans Publishing Co., 1957.

Meyer, F. B., Moses, The Servant of God. Grand Rapids: Zondervan Publishing House, 1953.

Murphy, James G., Commentary on the Book of Exodus. Boston: Estes and Lauriant, 1874.

Newberry, Thomas, Types of the Levitical Offerings. _____ : Bible Study Classics, n.d.

Newell, William R., Old Testament Studies. Vol. I. Chicago: The Moody Press, 1950.

Pember, George H., Earth's Earliest Ages. New York: Fleming H. Revell Company, n.d.

Pfeiffer, Charles F., The Book of Genesis. Grand Rapids: Baker Book House, 1958.

Pont, Charles E., Tabernacle Alphabet. New York: Loizeaux Brothers, 1946.

Price, Ira M., The Monuments and the Old Testament. Philadelphia: The Judson Press, 1925.

Ramm, Bernard, The Christian View of Science and Scripture. Grand Rapids: Wm. B. Eerdmans Publishing Company, 1954.

Rehwinkel, Alfred M., The Flood. St. Louis: Concordia Publishing House, 1951.

Ridout, S., The Pentateuch. New York: Bible Truth Library, n.d.

Sampey, James R., The Heart of the Old Testament. Nashville: Broadman Press, 1922.

Simpson, A. B., Christ in the Tabernacle. Harrisburg: Christian Publications, 1896.

Smith, George A., The Book of Deuteronomy. Cambridge: Cambridge University Press, 1918.

Spink, James F., Types and Shadows of Christ in the Tabernacle. New York: Loizeaux Brothers, 1946.

Street, Harold B., The Believer-Priest in the Tabernacle Furniture. Chicago: Moody Press, 1946.

Torrey, Elizabeth C., A Guide to Bible Study. Grand Rapids: Wm. B. Eerdmans Company, 1950.

Von Rad, Gerhard, Genesis. A Commentary. Philadelphia: The Westminister Press, 1961.

Whitcomb, John R., and Henry R. Morris, The Genesis Flood. Philadelphia: The Presbyterian and Reformed Publishing Company, 1963.

Wight, Fred H., Devotional Studies of Old Testament Types. Chicago: Moody Press, 1956.

Wright, Walter C., The Sacrificial System of the Old Testament. Cleveland: Union Gospel Press, 1942.

Zimmerman, Paul A., et al., Darwin, Evolution, and Creation. St. Louis: Concordia Publishing House, 1959.

APPENDICES

APPENDIX ONE: THE AUTHORSHIP OF THE
             PENTATEUCH

By long tradition, and on the basis of internal and external evidence, it is quite generally agreed by Bible believers that Moses was the author of the Pentateuch. Although it is recognized that this claim poses some problems, it may be considered that overwhelmingly from the standpoint of Scripture and spiritual confirmation, the claim of the Mosaic authorship must be upheld. It may be pointed out, of course, that to declare that Moses wrote the Pentateuch is not to declare that he composed every word. Since written records had been preserved for at least fifteen hundred years prior to Moses, it was his right, and likely his procedure, to incorporate these as he saw fit. Moses was trained in all the "wisdom of the Egyptians" and thereby equipped to understand and use cuneiform writings of the ancient Near East as well as the hieroglyphics of Egypt. With this understanding we may proceed to the following evidences that Moses wrote the Pentateuch.

1)   Several important sections of the Pentateuch are definitely assigned to the pen of Moses, and it may thereby be inferred that the entire document is his work. Moses is said to have written: the account of Amalek's attack (Ex. 17:14), the contents of the Covenant (Ex. 24:4; Ex. 34:27), the report of the journeyings (Num. 33:2), the ceremonial law (Deut. 31:9, 24), and his song (Deut. 31:22). These passages indicate a considerable literary activity on the part of Moses.

2)   The remainder of the Old Testament indicates belief in the Mosaic authorship. Joshua, who would have known of any fraud, since he was contemporary with Moses, strictly conformed to the precepts of the Pentateuch and made frequent mention of Moses. (cf. Josh. 1:7). The writer of Judges acknowledged that the law had been recorded "by the hand of Moses" (Jud. 3:4). David charged Solomon to conform to the code of life "as it is written in the law of the Book of Moses" (1 Ki. 2:3). The book discovered in the time of Josiah is called: "a book of the law of Jehovah given by Moses

(2 Chron. 34:14). Ezra twice refers to the book of Moses (Ezra 2:2 and 6:18), and Nehemiah spent his time reading it (Neh. 8:1-8). Both Daniel (9:11, 13) and Malachi (4:4) make significant reference to Moses. In all, a total of fourteen Old Testament books refer to Moses and relate him to the written law.

3)   The New Testament pointedly credits Moses with authoring the Pentateuch. The Lord Jesus freely committed Himself to the Mosaic authorship: "Offer the gift that Moses commanded (Mt. 8:4), "For Moses said, Honor thy father and thy mother . . . " (Mk. 7:10). He testified "For had ye believed Moses, ye would have believed me: for he wrote of me. But if ye believed not his writings, how shall ye believe my words?" (Jno. 5:46, 47). When the Jews ascribed the first division of the Old Testament to Moses, Jesus freely accepted the claim. (cf. Mt. 19:7, Mk. 12:19, Lk. 20:28, Jno. 9:28). In general, the Mosaic authorship of the Pentateuch appears to have been unquestioningly accepted in Jesus' time by all contemporary scholars, and our Lord likewise endorsed this viewpoint. (cf. Mk. 10:5, Lk. 20:37, Jno. 7:19, Acts 28:23).

4)   Moses possessed the qualifications to write the Pentateuch. He had been taught the wisdom of the Egyptians (Acts 7:21), he had the necessary information, he had the time (during the 40 years), and he had ability as a writer (cf. his superb sermons in Deuteronomy). The mention of Egyptian names and references to Egyptian customs indicate that the author had knowledge of Egyptian culture as well as of the religion and culture of Israel.

5)   Ancient authorities seem universally to have ascribed authorship to Moses without question. Ecclesiasticus, an apocryphal book written about 250 B.C., declares: "He [Jehovah] made him [Moses] to hear his voice and brought him into the dark cloud, and gave him commandments before his face, even the law of life and knowledge . . ." Other ancient works including Second Maccabees and the Talmud and the writings of Philo and Josephus each mention Moses and indicate that he was the author of the Pentateuch. Both the Jewish and Christian Old

Testament canons included the Pentateuch as the "Law of Moses" and gave it an especially honored place.

APPENDIX TWO: THE GAP THEORY

The conventional arguments that are presented as evidence in favor of the Gap Theory as a means of reconciling geologic science and the Bible record are as follows:

1) Isaiah 45:18 in revised versions declares that God created the earth <u>not a waste.</u> This verse may be interpreted to teach the fact of an original perfect creation and to assume a later catastrophe that made the earth without form and void.

2) In Genesis 1:28 man is instructed to "be fruitful, and multiply, and replenish the earth." The English word "replenish" means to fill again or to stock anew. Although the Hebrew word <u>male</u> does not necessarily imply the thought of repetition, the fact remains that "replenish" is deemed a suitable translation.

3) In Job 38:7 the laying of the foundation of the earth is spoken of as a time "when the morning stars sang together and all the sons of God shouted for joy." It was unlikely that a dismal, chaotic mass would call forth such an angelic oratorio. Furthermore, the notion of a created chaos is itself a contradiction.

4) Many Hebrew scholars agree that Genesis 1:2 is best translated, "And the earth <u>became</u> an empty waste and ruin." What was perfect became ruined.

5) Ezekiel 28:13 describes an Eden of mineral, not vegetable beauty. Since Adam and Eve's Eden was made beautiful by growing things, it is felt that Ezekiel's was an Eden of a past creation. *[handwritten: Not a strong argument]* *[handwritten: Describes downfall of Satan.]*

6) Two verses that describe events to come may also be assigned an application to the past: "Behold, the Lord maketh the earth <u>empty, and maketh it a waste,</u> and turneth it upside down, and scattereth abroad the inhabitants thereof" (Isa. 24:1), "I beheld the earth, and lo, it was [i.e. became] <u>without form and void; and the</u> heavens, and they had no light" (Jer. 4:23). *[handwritten: looks to the future]*

[handwritten: Tohu w' Bohu - without form and void Used in these verse the same word]

APPENDIX THREE: THEORIES OF THE FLOOD

A. THE LOCAL FLOOD THEORY

In this view, the Flood is described as extending over the Tigris-Euphrates Valley and being world wide only in the sense that the area that it covered comprised the known inhabited world. Since the purpose of the Flood was to destroy sinful man, a local flood would have served the purpose if these were the boundaries of man's migration at that time. Throughout human history the Tigris-Euphrates Valley has been subject to floods, so that the plausibility of such a flood is by no means in question. Noah's efforts, singlehandedly to evangelize his generation prior to the Flood, are more understandable if only a limited geographical region was involved. Scripture describes two natural processes for the production of water (rain and the breaking up of the fountains of the deep) and a flood that could be thus explained would be expected to be limited to a particular geographic region.

The announcement in 1929 by archaeologist C. Leonard Woolley of the discovery of a conspicuous layer of water-laid clay at Ur gave fuel to the local flood theory. In one shaft that Woolley sank on the site of ancient Ur, almost nine feet of water-laid clay was found sandwiched between layers of regular soil deposits containing specimens of pottery and other artifacts. A similar layer of water-laid clay was found at other archaeological sites, including: Uruk, Shuruppak, and Kish. Unfortunately, the concept of a general flood was not necessarily strengthened by Woolley's findings, for as close as four miles from his first site in Ur, he found no similar clay layer. Thus, all that these findings seem to prove was that floods were neither impossible nor uncommon in the Tigris-Euphrates Valley, but it is highly doubtful if these specific findings can be related to the Flood of Noah. Most Bible scholars feel that the local flood theory requires an interpretation of Scriptures too generalized to be acceptable.

B. THE WORLDWIDE OR UNIVERSAL FLOOD THEORY

In spite of the difficulties that it might seem to engender, the theory of a universal flood appears most readily to accord with the description of Scripture. Rehwinkel notes:

It is evident beyond a doubt that Moses intended to convey the idea that the Deluge was a universal flood, that every continent, every island, and every place inhabited by man or beast was covered with water, and that the flood rose to a height sufficient to cover the loftiest mountains with fifteen cubits of water.[1]

An interesting evidence for the universal flood theory is the Siberian mammoths. These creatures, to this day, are found remarkably preserved, complete with undecayed skin, flesh, and hair. They have been found with the contents of their stomachs intact, and with every evidence of their well-being up to the moment of their death. They evidently died through being suddenly suffocated or drowned as by water or mud, and then were immediately frozen that they might be preserved through the centuries. The fact that the food found in their stomachs, as well as the evident nature of the animal, is strictly tropical in character is evidence that the sudden death of the mammoths involved an equally sudden change of climate. Events adquate to explain the mammoths might be coupled with an account of a worldwide flood in Noah's day.

The objections to the universal flood theory are mainly practical. At the present time there is by no means enough water on the earth's surface to cover simultaneously all land and mountain areas such as the Bible describes. The release of all water now stored in glaciers would raise the sea level a mere 150 feet, whereas the highest mountains tower nearly five miles above sea level. The difference in level between the ocean deeps and mountain peaks is more than nine miles, but there is only enough water on earth to cover the surface to a depth of one and one-half miles. It would appear that if the Flood were universal, it would require some such concurrent phenomena to have been: the sinking of the continents, tidal waves sweeping around the earth, the atmosphere ceasing to retain water in suspension, vast quantities of water pouring forth from subterranean chambers, or the Lord miraculously adding to the volume of the earth's water. Any, or all, of these outcomes are, of course, possible, but they each lack any specific evidence to prove them actually true.

---

[1]Alfred M. Rehwinkel, The Flood, St. Louis: Concordia, 1951, p.96.

C. THE FLOOD THEORY OF GEOLOGY

According to this theory, the Flood involved such a tremendous upheaval of the earth's surface, that it resulted in the laying down of the geologic strata and thus produced the earth's crust in its present form. In the process, animals and plants were entombed, and by this means the fossil deposits were produced. Facts that favor this theory include: the absence of erosion on the surface of some strata, the piercing of two or more strata by a single fossil, the finding of creatures buried enmasse and fossilized without evident decomposition, and the wide dispersion of fossils from their natural habitat. On the other hand, a theory that calls for events on so vast a proportion seems to involve almost devastating difficulties. The fact that exposed strata reveals successive massive plant growths, one above another, would seem to demand that the geologic strata could not be compressed into scarcely more than one year of historical time. It is further noted that not all rock formations are water laid, and that in the case of those that are, a mile or more of mud sediment is necessary in order to provide sufficient compression to form rock.

D. THE CAUSE OF THE FLOOD

Apart from the fact that the Lord simply caused a great rain, there are two commonly advocated theories to account for the Flood. One view holds that at the appropriate moment, God tilted the earth on its axis to its present 23.5° and thus threw the oceans out of their beds, and in general caused violent geological and meteorological phenomena. The emphasis, after the Flood upon the changing seasons, is thereby accounted for (8:26). It is the tilt of the earth that causes many variations in climate and the change of seasons. The mystery of the Siberian mammoths would be satisfactorily explained by this theory.

Another theory, chiefly credited to Howard W. Kellogg, is the so-called "canopy theory." This view holds that the Bible description of the separation of the waters on the earth from the waters above was an actual cleavage to achieve a suspended sea above the earth's surface, just as a glass roof would cover a greenhouse. Thus the light and heat of the sun would be distributed evenly over the whole earth. The canopy would serve to filter the sun's rays and limit their power to cause decay. It would lead to the extension of life-spans and the prevention of fermentation (thus Noah's experience of drunkenness after the flood). According to the theory, the rainbow was a new phenomenon resulting from the change in the atmosphere. The canopy arrangement would be similar to the rings of Saturn, or the shroud surrounding Jupiter. When it collapsed, a vast quantity of water was spilled upon the earth, and thus Noah's Flood would be accounted for. It is doubtful whether scholars in general are willing to admit that the existence and collapse of a canopy would produce the results that are claimed, but at least the theory does possess some appeal.

APPENDIX FOUR: HIGHER CRITICISM AND THE DOCUMENTARY HYPOTHESIS

The documentary, or Graf-Wellhausen, hypothesis was advanced a little over a hundred years ago as an alternate to the claim of the Mosaic authorship of the Pentateuch. In this theory, the Pentateuch is a composite document made up of several manuscrips that have been loosely collated together, and then accorded a superficial final editing to give a semblance of unity. Supporters of this view usually hold that Joshua was written in the same manner, and thus they refer to the "Hexateuch" or six books rather than the Pentateuch. Historically these higher critics have set themselves the task of determining which of the several authors and editors is actually responsible for any given portion of the Hexateuch (or Pentateuch). Such a system, of course, makes possible the claim that at least portions of this work were not compiled until late in Israel's history, and thus they were modified for convenience to accommodate specific historical situations.

The documentary hypothesis goes far beyond the plausible claim that Moses may have used source materials in compiling the Pentateuch. It has already been noted that evangelicals do not deny that Moses may have used some existing sources. (cf. the "book of the wars of the Lord" Num. 21:14). Since Moses did not live at the time that the events of Genesis occurred, he would necessarily be dependent upon some external source of information. It is not inconsistent with a sound concept of the nature of divine revelation to allow the use of available sources as the literary basis upon which revelation and inspiration might operate.

One of the first to develop the documentary hypothesis was the Frenchman, Jean Astruc, who proposed and published his theory in the season of 1753-54. However, he probably was influenced by the writings of the Jewish philosopher, Benedict Spinoza (1632-1677). Astruc limited his hypothesis to Genesis, and declared that in this book he had found two major sources and ten minor sources. Johann Eichhorn, who published his views in 1782 and 1787, further modified and enlarged upon the concepts of Astruc. Although these men claimed to be merely distinguishing sources of information used by Moses, Wilhelm De Wette in 1805 took over their position and modified it to constitute a definite attack upon the claim of Mosaic authorship. His system claimed that Deuteronomy was not completed until the time of King Josiah. In 1822, Friedrich Bleek proposed that Joshua should be included with the five books because he held it too was compiled from miscellaneous documents. Hermann Hupfeld in 1853, Heinrich Graf in 1865-66, and Julius Wellhausen in 1889 and 1899 successively published refinements and expansions of the theory.

In general, the documentary hypothesis claims that the authorship of the various portions of the Pentateuch may be determined on the basis of subject matter and literary style. The two names of deity "Elohim" and "Jehovah" are thought to indicate different authors. The reviews of the giving of the law, and the regulations concerning the priests, are also thought to be criterions for distinctions. The four main documents comprising the Pentateuch are considered to be: the Elohistic, dated at the eighth century, the Jehovistic, dated at the ninth century, the Deuteronomistic, dated at the seventh century, and the Priestly Code dated at about 500. The initials E, J, D, and P are used to designate the alleged authors of the portions. No letters are assigned to the editors or redactors, but it is believed that several had a hand in the final product. In later refinements of the documentary hypothesis a second Jehovist, designated J_2 was advocated by Smend in 1912, an L document by Eissfeldt in 1922, a Kenite document by Morgensterns in 1927, and an Edomite document by Pfeiffer in 1941. Within such a system of analysis, Bible study is a matter of determining who said it, when he said it, and why he said it, but there is little interest in what was said.

The documentary hypothesis is rejected

by Bible believers particularly because it is generally coupled with an explanation of the development of Judaism that may be described as evolutionary. It is considered that the four primary sources represent pages in the evolution of the worship of Yahweh (i.e. Jehovah) from a primitive nature religion to a centralized cult in Jerusalem. The documentary hypothesis apparently possessed the characteristics of a truly scientific theory, and to many scholars at least until recent times, it proved to be very appealing. Even those who professed to believe in the inspiration of the Scriptures, such as W. Robertson Smith or S.R. Driver, simultaneously accepted the documentary hypothesis theory.

The tendency to reject the documentary hypothesis has emerged from the very quarter that might have been expected to give it support. Scholarly research and Bible archaeology repeatedly have denied the basic tenets and claims of the theory. The lack of agreement concerning the boundaries of the individual sources has also shown the theory's weaknesses. Although no general view has taken its place, even its own former supporters are now describing the Wellhausen hypothesis as a "well ordered but entirely fictitious and anachronistic construction." One of the earliest critics of the documentary hypothesis was Rudolf Kittel, editor of Biblica Hebraica who published his views in 1888. He denied the validity of the hypothesis and sought to replace it by the Formgeschichte theory. Other theories have been suggested. The "strata hypothesis" is an alternate view that claims that the Pentateuch is a product of the tradition of individual generations or "social strata" in which a particular portion was developed. The supporters of this theory claim that the scholars' task is to analyze the Pentateuch by comparing the cultural and literary strata, portion by portion, in the light of their concepts of actual times and places.

APPENDIX FIVE: QUESTIONS AND PROJECTS

One: The Book of Genesis (Part I)

1. Memorize: Gen. 1:1, 2; Gen. 3:15; and the events of each of the days of the creative week.
2. Make a list of the ten natural divisions of the book of Genesis. Each may be identified by the expression "generations of."
3. Name eight great men with whose history the book of Genesis deals.

4. Investigate recent and current and secular theories of the origin of the solar system (e.g. nebula hypothesis, tidal theory, planetesimal theory). Discuss their claim to validity in the light of Bible facts.
5. In a paragraph or two discuss God's reason for creating the universe and mankind.
6. Comment upon the significance of light the first day. Why did God see fit to assign a whole day for the creation of light?
7. Comment on why God chose to create fish and fowl on the same day. Why did He create animals and man the same day?
8. Scripture says that God breathed into Adam's body "the breath of life." How may we explain the presence of life (or soul) in each newborn infant? Does God create a new life in the case of each birth?
9. Why did God permit man in Eden to be tempted?
10. How would you explain the fact that God did not send the Savior immediately after the fall when man first needed salvation?
11. What evidence can you compile that monotheism was the most ancient religious outlook of mankind?
12. Discuss Cain's motive for killing Abel. In your opinion why was Cain not put to death for the murder which he committed?
13. What is your opinion of the identity of the sons of God in Genesis 6? Why?
14. Determine the following: How long before the Flood did Lamech die? How long before the Flood did Methuselah die? For how many years were Adam and Lamech contemporaries? How long were Adam and Enoch contemporaries?
15. Compare the Biblical account of Creation and the Flood with the so-called "Babylonian Genesis." Report on your impressions.
16. Prepare a statement (in two or three paragraphs) of your own theory of the Flood.
17. Discuss the possibility of the frozen bodies of mastodons that are found in Siberia having been there since the Flood. What Flood theory is best supported by the existence of these carcasses?
18. Compile a list with a brief discussion of at least five spiritual lessons to be gleaned from the Bible story of the Flood.
19. Write a brief character sketch of Noah.
20. Relate briefly the history of Babylon from its founding by Nimrod until the present.
21. Comment on the presence of Terah and Lot

The Two Babylons

Book of Revelation (Ch. 17)

Ironside

with Abraham during his migration. Do
you think God intended Abram to retain
the company of these relatives? Did
they hamper his obedience to God?

22. Enumerate and briefly describe the occasions of the special visitations of God
to Abraham. *Chap. 12-26*

23. Prepare a simple outline map tracing the
migrations of Abraham within the boundaries of Palestine. *(when he left Ur)*

24. Consider the events of chapter 16 and write
a report showing how Abraham, Sarah,
and Hagar were each at fault.

25. Explain in what sense Christians can be
said to be Abraham's seed (Gal. 3:29).

26. Compile a dictionary of the meaning of the
names of 15 important individuals who
figure in this section of Scripture.

Two: The Book of Genesis (Part II)

1. Compare the accounts of the wives of Esau
(26:34, 28:9, 36:2, 3). How would you
identify these individuals?

2. Compile a list of incidents in Joseph's life
that illustrate the truth: "All things
work together for good to them that
love God."

3. Discuss whether Joseph was partly to
blame for his brothers' hatred of him.

4. The dreams of the butler, the baker and
Pharaoh specifically were God-given
revelations of the future. Does God
today use dreams in this manner?

5. Discuss the desirability of Joseph's marriage to the Gentile woman, Asenath.

6. Do you consider that in appropriating the
land of the people of Egypt during the
years of famine, Joseph drove too
hard a bargain? Could this have contributed to the later persecution of Israel?

7. Discuss the matter of the wives of the sons
of Jacob. What would be their racial
background ?

8. Comment on the fact that Jacob and his
sons did not return to Canaan when the
famine was past. Were they wrong in
staying in Egypt?

9. With the help of an analytical concordance,
find occasions in Genesis when in the
original the following names of God are
used: Elohim, Jehovah, El Elyon, and
El Shaddai.

10. Prepare an argument either defending or
criticizing Joseph for his treatment of

his brothers in Egypt. Do you consider
that there was ground for his hardness
and severity?

11. Were Jacob and his sons really in the will
of God in going to Egypt to make it their
home? Discuss.

12. Do you approve of Jacob's blessing on
Pharaoh? Is it right to pronounce divine
blessing on an unbeliever?

13. Report what has been determined about
Habiru (Hapiru, Apiru, Aperu). Consult
both archaeological and historical
sources.

Three: The Book of Exodus

1. Investigate Josephus' stories about the
beauty of the boy Moses and Moses'
youthful leadership of Pharaoh's armies.

2. Memorize in correct order the nine plagues
upon Egypt.

3. Trace each reference to the "rod of God" in
Exodus.

4. Using the outline of Pharaoh's four compromising offers, prepare a brief Gospel
address on the subject: "The World's
Invitation to Compromise."

5. Prepare a defence of Israel's action in bor-
rowing jewels from the Egyptians at the
time of the exodus.

6. Prepare a sketch and description of the
hyssop plant.

7. How do you account for the fact that the en-
slaved Israelites could emerge from
their bitter bondage with "flocks and
herds, even very much cattle?"(Ex. 12:38)

8. Do you consider that Pharaoh would have
been among the Egyptian victims drowned
in the Red Sea? Discuss.

9. Report what you can find concerning the
Pharaohs of Moses' time and the identity
of the Pharaoh of the oppression according to secular scholars.

10. Locate and read the poem "Miriam's Song"
by Thomas Moore. Do you feel that the
author has caught the spirit of the Bible
account? Is this interpretation Scriptur-
ally accurate?

11. Write from memory the gist of each of the
ten commandments.

12. Compile a brief history of the two tablets
of the Law. Describe their form and
appearance, including the manner in
which the laws were inscribed upon them.
You may draw a diagram if you prefer.

13. Do you think that some of God's ancient laws

now discarded could be profitably restored?

14. Study the civil laws that the Lord gave from Sinai. Give examples of those accepted in our society today. Give examples of those we do not accept.

15. Report on the Code of Hammurabi, giving details that you derive from research sources.

16. Obtain and study a Jewish phylactery and write a brief description of it, or prepare your description from a picture.

17. Compile a list of the furniture of the tabernacle and briefly describe each piece.

18. In the tabernacle structure, why did the whole outer court, including the gate, hang on pillars set in brass sockets?

19. Write a note on types of Christ in the tabernacle.

Four: The Book of Leviticus

1. Make an intensive study of one of the Levitical offerings and submit a report of your findings.

2. Explain and comment upon the expression "sweet savor."

3. What is significant in the fact that the Lord accepted the offering rather than the offerer in the case of Levitical offerings?

4. How would you account for the fact that the Ras Shamra tablets reveal the provision for pagan sacrifices among the Canaanites very similar to those prescribed by God for Israel?

5. Compare the civil laws found in the Code of Hammurabi with those prescribed by Moses.

6. Discuss the problem of unpardonable sin under the Old Testament sacrificial system.

7. Comment concerning the validity of modern economic system proposing present day property and civil adjustments each half century as in the Levitical Jubilee.

8. Gather and report further data on one of the modern holy days of Israel.

9. Find five civil or practical ordinances in Leviticus which you think it is wise and necessary to observe today, and five that it is unnecessary or impossible to observe.

Five: The Book of Numbers

1. Compare the order of march prescribed in chapter two with that actually followed in chapter ten and explain the reason for the change.

2. Comment on the invitation to Hobab in Numbers 10 to be their guide, in the light of God's provision of the ark and the pillar of cloud and fire as their special guides.

3. On the basis of data gleaned from Numbers 4, compile a table of the coverings used for each of the six furnishings of the tabernacle when they were transported. What typical significance would be associated with each of these coverings?

4. Prepare a harmony of the accounts of the journeys of Israel from the departure from Sinai to the entrance into the land. Include: Num. 33, Deut. 2:8; 10:6, 7 and other parallel passages.

5. Comment concerning the appointment of the 70 elders. Did this arrangement lead to ultimate gain or loss for Moses?

6. Trace the murmurings of Israel in the book of Numbers. *Show where and give reasons*

7. Comment on the reason why only Miriam was smitten with leprosy when she and Aaron had both murmured against Moses.

8. What ministry was left to the Levites when the nation ceased wandering?

9. A preacher entitled his message: "Balaam: The World's First Ecumenical Evangelist." What point was he attempting to make? Would you agree?

10. Name those redeemed from bondage in Egypt who were still surviving at the close of this book.

Six: The Book of Deuteronomy

1. Locate several verses in Deuteronomy that give hints on how to achieve material and spiritual success.

2. How many Gospel texts can you find in Deuteronomy? How many precious promises? How many Messianic promises?

3. Discuss briefly the contents of Deuteronomy in relation to the other books of the Pentateuch and point out what parts of this book are especially unique.

4. Write a note on the sons of the Anakims (1:28) and the Zamzummins (2:20).

5. Compile a list of verses from Deuteronomy that contain teachings on the following subjects: charity, commerce, humane acts.

6. Peter identified the Lord Jesus as the

prophet like unto Moses as prophesied
in Deuteronomy 18:15-18. Compare the
ministry of Moses and the earthly ministry of Christ.

7. Prepare a simple outline map showing the
names and locations of the six cities of
refuge that eventually were established.

8. Review each occasion in Scripture when the
twelve tribes are listed (as in Deut. 33)
and make a comparison of these listings.

9. Locate, read, and criticize the poem, "The
Burial of Moses" by Cecil Frances
Alexander.

Projects on the Pentateuch as a Whole

1. Write a term paper on a topic such as the
following: The Canaanitish Nations
Conquered by Israel, Types of Christ
in the Pentateuch, Lessons in Christian
Living in the Pentateuch, Material Culture of the Israelites, Difficulties in the
Pentateuch, Archaeological Light on the
Pentateuch, or The Gospel in the Pentateuch.

2. Prepare a documented, annotated sequence
map of the wilderness wanderings.

3. Make a thorough study and prepare a report
of the present day observance of the
Passover by orthodox Jews.

4. Prepare a genealogical table showing to
the close of the Pentateuch, the line of
Christ and other important genealogical
lines.

5. Make a study of the theology of the Pentateuch reporting on the aspects of deity
in His person and work that are revealed
in this portion of Scripture.

6. Build a model tabernacle or prepare some
detailed colored drawings of the structure.

7. Make a study and report on the flora and
fauna of the Sinaitic peninsula.

8. Review one or more books that deal with
the Pentateuch.

9. Write a fictional story or a drama based
upon the events of this portion of Scripture.

10. Prepare a biography and character analysis
of Moses.

11. Prepare your own commentary on a section
or book of the Pentateuch.

12. Prepare a dictionary of the meanings of
proper nouns in the Pentateuch.

13. Describe in general the content and nature of the Jewish Talmud and Targums.

14. Make a study of Moses' intercessory prayer
for the people and report your findings.

15. Prepare a report on dating by Carbon 14
and explain the significance of this process for students of Scripture.

Index :